GREAT
MOMENTS
IN SEX

GREAT
MOMENTS
IN SEX

Cheryl Rilly

Three Rivers Press
New York

PHOTOGRAPH CREDITS

Most of the photos that appear in this book are courtesy of arttoday's Internet site. My thanks to Michael Gariepy for permission to use the illustrations. Reach the Web site at www.arttoday.com.

United States Patent Office	Creators Syndicate	© *Playboy* magazine
G. D. Searle & Co. © 1960	King Features	Jerry Springer Show
BodyCare Products	Kobal Collection	Hooters Restaurant
Pfizer Inc.	The Coca-Cola Company	*Screw* magazine

Permission to reprint cover by *Playgirl* magazine
© 1998 Sara Lee Intimates. Wonder Bra is a registered trademark of Canadelle, Inc.

Published by Three Rivers Press, 201 East 50th Street, New York, New York 10022. Member of the Crown Publishing Group.

Random House, Inc. New York, Toronto, London, Sydney, Auckland
www.randomhouse.com

THREE RIVERS PRESS is a registered trademark of Random House, Inc.

Printed in the United States of America

Design by Susan Maksuta/Kay Schuckhart

Library of Congress Cataloging-in-Publication Data
Rilly, Cheryl.
Great moments in sex : the people, places, things, and events that helped shape humanity's favorite pastime / Cheryl Rilly. — 1st ed.
1. Sex—Miscellanea. 2. Sex customs—Miscellanea.
3. Sex—History. I. Title.
HQ25.R55   1999
306.7—dc21   98-47740

ISBN 0-609-80243-7

First Edition

To
Aretino's monkey

ACKNOWLEDGMENTS

Nothing ever gets accomplished by one person alone. So it is with this book. I'd like to thank the people who helped me with the research, particularly the Mount Clemens, Michigan, library staff and adult reference librarian Jacqueline Wisswell; the Harper Woods, Michigan, library staff; Abby Schiffman of Ortho Pharmaceuticals; the International Planned Parenthood Federation; and Shirley Beauchamp, who can always think of more than one way to do things.

I'd also like to thank my family and friends for tolerating my absences. Two wonderful women figured prominently in the writing of this book. My agent-mentor-shrink, Carole Abel, who has a knack for always saying the right thing at the right time, and my editor, P. J. Dempsey, whose professionalism and supply of jokes are never ending. Also, a special thanks to production editor Camille Smith, whose contributions to this book are gratefully appreciated.

A special note of gratitude to Joshua, whom I'll always remember. And to my sweet young niece, Jessica, who was barred from my office for the duration of writing this book: I'm finished, sweetie, you can come in now.

CONTENTS

INTRODUCTION ix

Chapter One THE TOOLS 1

Chapter Two THE HISTORY OF SEX 20

Chapter Three THE EXPERTS AND THE MANUALS 59

Chapter Four SEX SYMBOLS: THE WOMEN 77

Chapter Five SEX SYMBOLS: THE MEN 97

Chapter Six SELLING SEX, SEX SELLS 115

Chapter Seven LET ME ENTERTAIN YOU 131

Chapter Eight A LITTLE HELP 151

Chapter Nine YOU CAN'T DO THAT! 170

Chapter Ten UNDERLINE THESE PARTS 189

Chapter Eleven TURN-ONS AND TURN-OFFS 208

Chapter Twelve WORD ORIGINS 229

INDEX 242

INTRODUCTION

That sex, in one form or another, has been around since before the beginning of mankind is obvious. We wouldn't be here if it hadn't been. In the twentieth century we began to emerge from the effects of the Victorian Age where the repression of all things sexual and all feelings sensual was standard operating procedure. So it's no surprise that when the lid was finally taken off, beginning with the Kinsey Report in 1948 and continuing with the free-love movement of the 1960s and 1970s, we began to regard ourselves as the creators of libertinism.

Nothing could be further from the truth.

In 1992 New York City condoned women exposing their bare breasts in public as long as the action wasn't lewd. Agnès Sorel accomplished much the same thing in the fifteenth century by dressing to expose her breasts and set a trend. Nude beaches aroused curiosity this century. But in ancient and medieval times entire towns bathed together and nudity on the streets was commonplace. Oral sex, anal sex, and ménages à trois gained popularity during the twentieth century but by no means did we invent the practices. Indeed, compared to the ancient Greeks and Romans we are tame. In the 1990s a surgeon general was fired for advocating the teaching of masturbation in school. The ancient Egyptians group-masturbated to ensure the fertility of their fields.

While we wrestle with the question of whether or not prostitution is a victimless crime that should be decriminalized, early Christian leaders accepted the necessity of wayward women to forestall the immodest use of decent ones. We argue about whether homosexuality is biologically or environmentally determined. In ancient Greece it didn't matter; pederasty ruled the day. Feminists decry the existence of pornography as an abuse of women. Phallic and fertility symbols litter the caves of earliest man. And if AIDS is the plague of the twentieth and twenty-first centuries, then syphilis was the scourge for hundreds of years beginning in the fifteenth century, with "cures" that seldom worked and were often more torturous than the disease.

This book is arranged in chronological order. Because many practices evolved over a period of time, making specific dating unreliable, I chose to use two symbols to help with the chronology. The use of the < symbol before a date indicates that a practice or event was in place by that time. Similarly, the > symbol indicates that a practice or an event evolved from that time.

I invite you to explore the history of sex and its accoutrements. I offer my apologies now for omissions and the lack of depth in many of the subject areas. Space on paper is never kind to a writer. Every entry in this book could be expanded tenfold. Most entries merit their own book. Rather than feeling dissatisfied, I hope you'll use this information as a springboard to discover for yourself the color and the depth of this subject. You won't be disappointed.

Chapter One
THE TOOLS

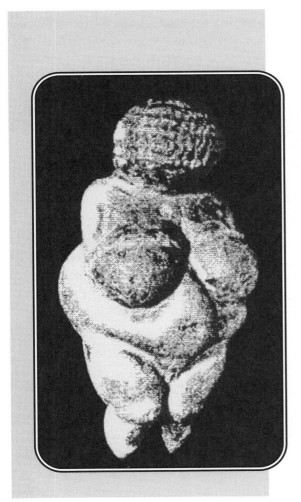

B.C.

c. 25,000 The Venus of Willendorf is formed by prehistoric man, most likely as a fertility goddess as opposed to mere female representation. Short, fat, bulbous, and grotesque by today's standards, the faceless figure is mostly breasts, belly, buttocks, and vagina. More than sixty of the unstatuesque statues are found throughout the Ukraine, Siberia, Central Europe, and France. Fertility symbol or not, the Venus proves that prehistoric man is taken with prehistoric woman.

c. 13,600 "The Cup of Roots," a mixture believed to produce sterility, is used from around the time of the Great Flood. The combination of Alexandrian gum, liquid alum, and garden crocus, mixed with wine to cure gonorrhea, is popular with the Jews. Jewish men are not allowed to drink it, since they are the seed bearers. The belief is that God's Chosen People must be fruitful and multiply. Jewish women, however, are free to imbibe.

c. 1850 Cervical caps, diaphragms, and jellies to prevent sperm from doing their job are mentioned in the Egyptian Kahun Papyrus. Crocodile dung is shaped into a tamponlike insert, and smearing the vagina with honey and natron slows the little guys down from swimming upstream. Three hundred years later the Ebers Papyrus advises soaking a pad of lint in a solution of fermented acacia shrub tips and inserting it into the vagina. Acacia tips produce lactic acid, an ingredient that will be used in spermicidal jellies three thousand years later.

<1700 Legend relates the problem of King Minos of Crete. His sperm is full of serpents and scorpions, making sex detrimental to his partners. He marries the daughter of the King of the Sun who happens to be immune to his contaminated come, but the union remains childless. A condom fashioned from a goat's bladder strains out the serpents, leaving pure sperm, and allows Minos to father eight children. Condoms aren't used widely, but the story is indicative that some type of condom exists.

c. 500 Miletus, a seaport city of Ionia, becomes the dildo-making capital of the Mediterranean. Made of wood or leather, these little helpers are needed by wives who are largely ignored by their husbands, and also by tribads, the Greek term for lesbians.

c. 500 The Pythagoreans define sperm as a "clot of brain containing hot vapor within it." With every ejaculation, man loses more of his gray matter.

c. 500 The Greeks have a version of a cervical cap: the inside of a pomegranate mixed with water and formed into a pessary. They also wear the womb of a lion in an ivory tube, or they wear an amulet containing the tooth of a child hung near the anus to prevent pregnancy. Men smear their male members with alum or gallnut mixtures, or they swallow a concoction made with the burned balls of a castrated mule to help out with their end of family planning.

c. 400 Why should a woman have sex? For pleasure? To have children? To please her husband? How about to keep from losing her mind? Or her health? Hippocratic doctors warn that a woman who doesn't marry, have sex, and give birth will eventually suffer from hysteria, throw herself against walls, or strangle herself. Some experts are convinced that a frustrated womb wanders about the body, distressing other organs. A few hundred years later, renowned Roman medical man Galen comes out against the wandering womb theory but does agree that the womb is the source of most women's ills.

c. 400 Bottoms up! At least for the Greek hetairai (high-class prostitutes). Anal intercourse is not allowed with wives, but the courtesans use the back door to prevent pregnancy.

c. 350 Wishing to keep the Greek population at a stationary level, Aristotle joins in with his version of birth control. Olive oil mixed with "oil of cedar, ointment of lead, or with frankincense" coats the womb so sperm won't stick. Olive oil is effective but not for that reason: the thickness of the oil slows down sperm.

<300 The best Roman form of birth control is not to have sex with your wife. But that doesn't mean abstinence. Even the most humble citizen has slaves, and slaves have no rights. Female slaves are a prime target but as pederasty spills over from Greece, male slaves are equally at risk of attracting their masters' attention. Women slaves are sometimes sent to work at brothels, with their earnings going to their owners.

c. 200 To prevent pregnancy a Roman woman wears amulets, uses a cervical cap of honey-soaked wool, or simply holds her breath at the moment her partner ejaculates. A rhythm method is also practiced. The problem with it is that the Romans have the safe and the fertile days reversed.

<100 An intact hymen is no prized possession to the Roman man. He doesn't want to break it when there's a god ready to do it. The Roman bride sits upon the phallus of Priapus in a holy ceremony in the hope that the god will make her fruitful. Only then is the husband

allowed his share. Over the years Romans lose sight of Priapus's godliness and put more emphasis on the licentiousness of the phallic symbol. Rome's not alone in its sacrifices to the gods. It's said that Cleopatra herself is a sacrificial victim, receiving the physical attentions of 106 men in one night. Other countries raise phallic symbols in their fields to ensure a good harvest. Some architects incorporate the erect pillars into their buildings. Smaller versions are worn as charms against evil. Even early statues of Christian saints to whom barren women can pray are equipped with oversized erections.

c. 100 Lucretius passes on a form of birth control learned by observing prostitutes. That feminine bump and grind does more than pro-

The Romans make sacrifices to their god, Priapus. Brides sacrifice their virginity by sitting on a stone phallus to ensure fertility.

duce pleasure, he says. It averts the semen "out of the direct course . . . and turns [it] away from the proper spot." What's good for the harlot isn't good for the wife. Lucretius says of this practice, "This our wives have surely no need of."

A.D.

c. 50 Historian and social commentator Pliny the Elder gives advice to men on birth control: "If the male organ is rubbed with [oil of gum of] cedar just before coitus, it will prevent impregnation." Women can eat parsley or mint or get a spider's egg with two worms in it, wrap it in deerskin, and wear it as an amulet before sunrise. Pliny also believes that menstrual blood kills vermin, ruins crops, tarnishes mirrors, and dulls razors.

c. 100 Dioscorides, a Greek physician, writes of fail-safe contraceptive methods. A woman can smear herself with menstrual blood or step over it, wear asparagus as an amulet, drink ground willow leaves mixed with water, put pepper into her uterus after sex, or insert a pessary soaked in peppermint juice and honey. For permanent sterility, she might try the bark of the white poplar mixed with the kidney of a mule, or for four days drink spleenwort leaves picked on a moonless night and cooked in wine.

Gesundheit! Was It Good for You?

c. 120 The Greek physician whose medical writings on obstetrics will be referred to for centuries prescribes the female version of coitus interruptus. Soranus teaches that as the man reaches his climax, his partner should hold her breath and draw back so his sperm isn't "hurled too deep into the cavity of the uterus." Immediately she should squat down and "induce sneezing." Douching also helps. Married couples trying to conceive should mate like animals. Sex from the rear position deposits the seed deeper.

c. 200 For the woman who wants everything from the man who isn't quite enough, the *Kama-sutra* gives instructions on how to increase the length and girth of a penis. The "armlets" that fit like tubes and the bracelets that form a ring around the penis "should be made of gold, silver, copper, iron, ivory, buffalo's horn, various kinds of wood, tin or lead, and should be soft, cool, provocative of sexual vigor," and studded with soft globules for the woman's pleasure. A more direct fix is also indicated: a man can perforate his lingam (penis) and insert small pieces of cane, gradually increasing the size. If the woman's yoni (vagina) is too large, anoint it with the liquid of the fruit of the *Asteracantha longifolia* and it will contract, but only for the night. Too tight? The roots of the *Nelumbrium speciosum,* the blue lotus, and powder from the *Physalis flexuosa* plant mixed with ghee (clarified butter) and honey will open 'er right up.

c. 230 The use of a sponge or a spongy substance to act as a cervical cap to absorb sperm is not only allowed by Jews but required for use by minors, pregnant women, and nursing mothers. It's the obvious choice over coitus interruptus, which is forbidden to Jewish men.

c. 590 Chinese women of the Sui dynasty take their pleasure with an olisbos made from a bamboolike plant that, when soaked in hot water, swells and hardens like a penis. Homosexual

Great Moments in Sex

WHO OR WHAT GOT WOMEN PREGNANT BEFORE MEN FIGURED OUT THEY WERE RESPONSIBLE

TRIVIA

- The Moon (Maoris of New Zealand)
- Eating the flesh of a human (Australia)
- Dragon's saliva (China)
- A ghost entering a bathing woman (Trobriand Islands)
- Squatting over the fire that cooked a fish given to the woman by the baby's father (Queensland, Australia)
- The child crawls into the womb, sperm then feeds it (Hudson Bay Eskimos)

women buy the double-header. Women also use an Exertion or a Burmese bell, a hollow silver ball inserted inside the vagina before having sex. The one-ball system depends on the male member to rock it back and forth. The Japanese version is "tinkling balls," which gain popularity in eighteenth-century Europe. One ball contains a drop of mercury; the second ball vibrates when shaken or struck. Both are inserted into the vagina, and slight thigh or rocking motions make life quite pleasant. Chinese men sometimes insert the Burmese bells into their penises. Rumor hints that potency is increased.

c. 655 Lady Wu Chao, consort to Chinese Emperor T'ai Tsung, introduces mirrors to enhance lovemaking. Large sheets of reflecting glass are placed around the couch where she and the emperor play during the daytime. They are removed when a general points out that many images of the emperor are a bad omen. After T'ai Tsung dies, Wu Chao takes over his empire and his bed and reinstalls the mirrors.

c. 700 Indian women fumigate their vaginal passage with neem-wood smoke to prevent conception. Hot coals are put into a spouted vessel over which powdered neem wood is sprinkled. The spout is inserted into the vagina. The smoke fills the cavity and readies it for intercourse. Fumigation is also used in Islamic countries and remains in use as late as the early twentieth century when some Jews in New York use the steam of stewed onions to bring about abortion or return the menstrual flow.

c. 900 Persian doctor Abu Bakr Muhammed ibn Zakariya al-Razi, considered the finest clinician of the Middle Ages, advises using suppositories before having sex. They can be made from cabbage, colocynth pulp, pitch, oxgall, the inner skin of a pomegranate, animals' ear wax, elephant dung, scammony, or whitewash. If a woman's period is late, "vigorous sexual intercourse" and violent movements are recommended to bring it on.

c. 900 In the Middle Ages, magic and mysticism are believed to play a role in contraception. Throughout Europe, birth-control methods include spitting three times in the mouth of a frog, holding a jasper pebble in your hand during sex, urinating on the urine of a wolf, and wearing the anus of a hare around your neck. Weasels don't fare well. The amputated foot of a live female weasel worn around the neck or the testicles of a male weasel bound to the thigh

Weasels as birth control? Their legs, testicles, and bones are used to forestall pregnancy.

of a woman who also wears a weasel bone nixes the procreative process.

1000> At the turn of the millennium there is relief that the world has not ended and the final judgment has been postponed. People enjoy more creature comforts, one of which is the mattress. For those who can afford one, a down mattress takes the place of the floor or a bench. Poor folks have to make do with mattresses filled with pine needles, leaves, and other miscellaneous stuffings that mildew quickly and provide hiding places for bugs.

c. 1000 India's Jyotirisvara Kavisekhara's *The Five Arrows of the God of Love* includes dietary guidelines to prevent fertility. Roots, flowers, fruit, or seeds combined with melted butter, sour rice water, or three-year-old molasses puts the kibosh on fruitfulness.

c. 1180 Egyptian physician Ibn al-Jami, in *The Book of Right Conduct Regarding the Supervision of the Soul and Body,* writes that a woman simply has to eat beans on an empty stomach to be pregnancy-free. Al-Jami doesn't note whether beans are detrimental to sperm or if a gaseous belly is detrimental to a sexual atmosphere.

c. 1200 The Chinese of the Yuan dynasty invent the happy ring. Made from the eyelid of a goat with the eyelashes intact, the ring is processed until the correct texture is achieved. In use, the happy ring is tied onto the erect penis so that the hardened eyelashes can make his partner happy.

Aw, Sit on It!

c. 1300 How many years do you want to remain pregnancy-free? Hold up that many fingers and then sit on them. European brides sit on their fingers while riding in the bridal coach. Another variation is for a divorced woman to touch her womb with her fingers to forestall fertility. In Bosnia, horsewomen thrust their fingers under their belly girdles.

c. 1500 Architecture gives a boost to middle-class privacy. Houses are built slightly larger and provided with private bedrooms.

1530 Paracelsus, a German physician, treats the venereal disease ripping through Europe with mercury, and it works—sometimes. The treatment is rubbed on syphilis chancres or put on plasters and then applied to the sores. Oral liquid doses are given but since mercury is poisonous, the adverse side effects leave a lot to be desired.

Great Moments in Sex

1543 Andreas Vesalius turns the medical field on its ear with the publication of *The Structure of the Human Body*. He's the first to accurately describe the female reproductive system, and also proves that men and women have the same number of ribs. It's been common knowledge that men have one less because Eve was made from Adam's rib.

c. 1550 The Chinese employ a *yin-chia* to help prevent venereal disease. Only the head of the penis is covered by this partial condom. Agar-agar jelly smeared over abrasions along with washing genitals before and after sex is also used to prevent infection.

c. 1560 Gabriel Fallopius gives his name to a part of woman's anatomy when he describes the tubes that carry the egg from the ovary to the uterus. The egg is fertilized in these fallopian tubes, though Fallopius doesn't realize it, since the egg hasn't yet been discovered. Fallopius also names the vagina and the placenta.

1564 Fallopius describes the condom in *De Morbo Gallico*. The first condom, designed as protection against syphilis which has reached epidemic proportions in Europe, is a linen sheath that fits over the glans and beneath the foreskin of the penis to keep it in place. It was tested on 1,100 men before publication, but Fallopius is unaware that his condom also prevents conception.

c. 1590 Penis rings are a must for the Chinese man-about-town. While a plain silk band wound tightly around the base of the penis keeps the big guy erect longer, fashionable men opt for an ornately carved ivory ring, usually depicting two dragons, with tongues twisted into a spiral forming a nub that massages the clitoris during sex.

c. 1596 Men of the Philippine Islands know how to take care of their women, according to

God must have taken Adam's rib symbolically. As of 1543, Vesalius proves that men have just as many ribs as women.

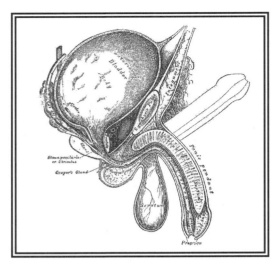

His

Francesco Carletti in his book *My Voyage around the World.* The penis is perforated about halfway up the shaft and a leaden stud is inserted "that passes through it from one side to the other. On top of the stud there is attached a star, also of lead, which revolves there and covers the whole member and projects a little beyond its edges. At the bottom of the stud there is a hole through which a wedge is passed so that it is firm and cannot emerge from the member." Painful at first, so it is said, it gives pleasure later on. Some observers believe it's a deterrent to homosexuality.

1600s Frenchwomen take matters into their own hands, separating sex for pleasure from sex for pregnancy with the employment of the sponge. Soaked in an astringent with a ribbon attached for removal, it's inserted into the vagina and followed with a douche after sex. This custom spreads across Europe and is carried to America. For French ladies who prefer to stay on the side of religion, doctors prescribe a migraine headache.

1668–1673 Anatomist Regnier de Graaf studies the human reproductive system. He describes the structure of the testicles and then moves on to the ovaries, which he names. Graaf, however, fails to penetrate the secret of the ovary, leaving the ovum yet to be discovered. He dies in 1673 of the plague.

1699 Dutch microscope maker Anton van Leeuwenhoek plays with his body fluids under the microscope. He uses his saliva and discovers bacteria in the mouth. Peering at his blood, he accurately describes red blood cells. Then he takes his own ejaculate (which outrages some when results are released) and discovers sperm. Van Leeuwenhoek believes he sees a complete individual in each tadpole-like sperm.

c. 1700 The condom is improved. It's now made from sheep gut, animal bladders, or fine skins, an improvement that most likely is created by a worker in a slaughterhouse. Casanova touts their effectiveness and calls them English overcoats. But because their primary purpose is still to prevent venereal disease, most married couples shy away from them, embarrassed by the implication.

c. 1710 Leave it to the French to invent the bidet. Though cleanliness is not a priority, the

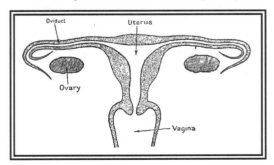

Hers

bidet serves a sexual function. French women use a sponge as a contraceptive and its efficacy is enhanced by the douche, which the bidet aids. There's also speculation that the newfound cleanliness makes oral sex more palatable.

Oops!

1767 In an unselfish effort to find out if syphilis and gonorrhea are the same disease, physician John Hunter injects his own penis with pus from a man known to have gonorrhea. The only problem is that the man is also an *unknown* syphilitic. When Hunter develops the hard chancre of syphilis *and* gonorrhea he declares the two diseases to be one and the same.

1785 Artificial insemination is reported in Paris by M. Thouret, the doyen of the medical faculty at the University of Paris. Thouret impregnates his wife with his own sperm using a tin syringe. The first third-party insemination is done in Philadelphia in 1884 on a chloroformed woman who is unaware that her sterile husband instructed the doctor to impregnate her with semen other than his.

1827 Finally the egg is discovered. With Regnier de Graaf's finding of the female follicles, doctors were convinced the human egg had been found. But when Karl von Baer examines a small yellow point contained in a dog's follicle, he finds the first mammalian egg. The idea of instant conception when sperm meets egg is crystallized.

1827 Japan's *kabutogata,* or hard condom, is made from tortoiseshell, horn, or thin leather.

This remarkable little device safeguards from venereal disease, prevents pregnancy, provides added pleasure for the woman because of the texture, and, in case he's not in the mood, the woman can use the kabutogata alone.

1828 Theresa Berkley invents the Berkley Horse. This London brothel keeper, known for her punishing talents, whips her clients with a cat-o'-nine-tails, leather straps studded with nails, and rods kept in water to ensure suppleness. The Berkley Horse takes flagellation to new heights. The customer is strapped onto this padded, adjustable ladderlike device, which has open spaces for the client's face and genitals, so that while he is being whipped by one mistress his penis can be massaged by another. The Horse is successful, whipping up a small fortune for Berkley. Berkley isn't alone in offering kinky specialties. Madame Gourdan offers the Salon of Vulcan, a room containing only a leather armchair that imprisons an unsuspecting client or lured innocent female and keeps the victim helplessly imprisoned until someone releases them—if they're lucky: one young girl remains trapped for days.

TRIVIA Ancient Jewish lore proclaims that the seed from a certain testicle determines the sex of a child. Boys are the product of the right-ball sperm while girls are produced by the weaker and smaller left.

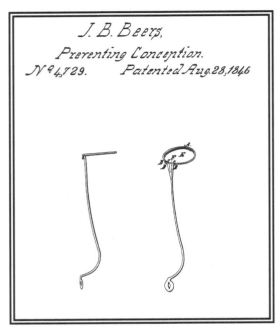

J. B. Beers,
Preventing Conception.
N⁰ 4,729.   Patented Aug. 28, 1846

John Beers's "wife protector" prevents pregnancy.

1830 The cervical cap is invented. Who invented it is debatable, but gynecologist Friedrich Wilde writes of the cap, which is custom-made for each woman. A wax impression is taken of the woman so the cap fits snugly. It's worn at all times except during menses, when it's removed and replaced when the flow stops.

1844 Goodyear develops the vulcanization process for rubber and puts an end to animal-skin condoms. Rubber condoms, which gain popularity in the 1870s, are sold discreetly over the counter and, for a time, through the mail, for about five dollars a dozen. But they're reusable. Condoms are washed out before and after use and are thrown away only when they crack or tear.

1844 John Humphrey Noyes, founder of the utopian Oneida Community in upstate New York, believes he has discovered *coitus reser-*

vatus. Although practiced in Asia for centuries, Noyes, who publishes this method in 1866, decides on this male continence for himself and his followers who are free to enjoy sex with anyone in the community. Unlike coitus interruptus, where the man ejaculates outside of the woman's body, coitus reservatus allows the man to pleasure his partner, but he then withdraws and does not ejaculate. Noyes defends this practice, saying, "It is as foolish and cruel to expend one's seed on a wife merely for the sake of getting rid of it as it would be to fire a gun at one's best friend merely for the sake of unloading it."

1845 What appears to be a coming-of-age ritual for native Australians is reported, though the practice is ages old. Subincision, performed in a ceremonial rite, marks the advancement of a boy to manhood. The penis is slit from the urethra along its entire length to the scrotum. A piece of bark is inserted to keep the opening from healing over. Though some anthropologists say this is a contraceptive method, there's no sign that it worked. The penis can still become fully erect, although it may be somewhat flattened. Urinating is done by squatting. The ceremony is performed when "the hair on the face of the young man is sufficiently grown to admit the end of the beard being tied," and certainly before marriage. Any man refusing the rite is not allowed into the men's camp or to marry. If he runs away with a woman, he's killed.

1846 John Beers, a Rochester, New York, dentist, receives a patent on his "wife protector," a diaphragm made of oiled silk and gold wire, which covers the opening to the uterus, thereby preventing pregnancy. The woman can insert the apparatus without the aid of a doctor.

Great Moments in Sex

1849 The medical community finally gets a handle on the fertility cycle of the human female. Unlike animals, women aren't fertile just before and after their periods. Ovulation occurs about ten days after menses. For the first time copulating couples have a chance to try natural birth control by practicing rhythm. The Catholic church grudgingly condones it. Its unreliability earns it a nickname: Vatican roulette.

1870s German doctor W. P. J. Mensinga develops a diaphragm, the first genuinely popular contraceptive. The soft rubber circle with a stiffened rim is folded and inserted lengthwise to cover the entrance to the uterus. The expense of having it fitted by a physician keeps it out of the hands of poor women who need it the most.

1879 Albert Neisser of Germany discovers gonococcus, the organism that causes gonorrhea. There's still no reliable cure, but Neisser's discovery makes it possible to determine if a person has been cured or is still a carrier.

1880s The commercialization of birth-control products begins. Powders, jellies, spermicides, and suppositories are offered as an alternative to homemade brews and devices that necessitate doctor visits.

1880 Dr. S. S. Lungren performs the first tubal ligation in the United States. It's a major operation done at the time of a cesarean operation to protect a woman from future high-risk pregnancies. Today most tubals can be done under local anesthesia.

1897 Vasectomies are used to relieve enlarged prostates. Soon the surgical procedure is performed on prison inmates to cut down on the frequency of masturbation. Finally the vasectomy is performed as a contraceptive measure on willing men only. Surgical sterilization is practiced but mainly for eugenic purposes. The operations are performed mostly on the mentally ill.

1899 The headache excuse becomes a thing of the past as the Bayer company introduces acetylsalicylic acid, or aspirin. It's put out first in powdered form; tablets won't reach the store shelves until 1915. In no time, aspirin becomes the world's most prescribed drug.

1906 German bacteriologist August von Wassermann devises a test to diagnose syphilis. He does this one year after fellow German Fritz Schaudinn discovers the organism that causes the venereal disease that has terrorized the world since the late fifteenth century. Within the year Wassermann develops a second test that shows if syphilis is currently present or if a person ever was a carrier.

TRIVIA

The standard man-on-top front-entry position is called the missionary position because traveling Christian missionaries felt it necessary to rid locals of their heathen positions and convert them to the "acceptable" Christian technique.

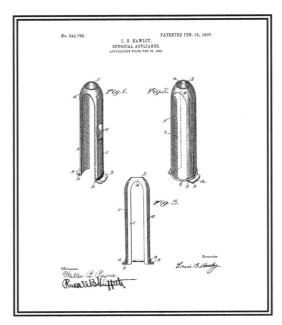

No. 844,788.   PATENTED FEB. 19, 1907.
L. B. HAWLEY.
SURGICAL APPLIANCE.
APPLICATION FILED FEB. 26, 1906.

Louis Hawley's penile stiffener gets it up when you can't.

1907 The first handheld vibrator is patented by Clarence Richwood. This vibrator is not battery-powered; it works with water pressure. The drawback is that the user has to be near a sink or a tub.

1907 Louis Hawley patents a politically correct penile stiffener. In this age of strict control of contraceptives, Hawley's tube-shaped splint is like the Japanese hard condom but has a hole in the tip that allows semen to enter the vagina. Therefore it's not a contraceptive device.

1909 After 605 tries, Dr. Paul Ehrlich discovers Salvarsan, an arsenic-based compound that actually kills the spirochete that causes syphilis. Ehrlich's magic bullet, known as "606," contains enough arsenic to kill the germ but not the patient. For his contribution, he receives the Nobel prize.

1922 Vitamin E is discovered by Herbert McLean Evans, head of the Institute for Experimental Biology of the University of California. Evans shows that the vitamin plays an important role in animal reproduction and hopes that it might be soon available to help correct human sterility. Later studies indicate that vitamin E increases fertility and may restore male potency.

1927 K-Y® Jelly is marketed for medical use though it won't be sold over the counter until 1980. The water-based jelly is safe for use with condoms and doesn't corrode them, like petroleum jelly.

1928 Dr. Ernst Gräfenberg creates the first effective intrauterine device for humans. The IUD, a ring made of silver and gold, is implanted by a doctor. But only about 25 percent of Gräfenberg's patients adapt to it. Inflammation and infection make the IUD unusable for most women.

1929 The first sex hormone to be isolated is estrogen, one of the body's tools that develops sexual maturity in women. Edward Doisy establishes that sexual desire and readiness are induced by the hormone.

1930s The development of liquid latex makes the condom much more popular, lower in price, easier to use, and now, they're disposable. Still the vanguard against infection, condoms are sold through vending machines. The thinness of latex gives back some of the feeling that men have missed.

1932 Testosterone is isolated. Produced in the cells of the testicles, the hormone causes

Great Moments in Sex

men to mature sexually. Adolph Butenandt, who identified the hormone, also learns to synthesize testosterone from cholesterol.

1935 The king of Assyria in the sixth century B.C. had it, and so did the ancient Egyptians and Chinese. Gonorrhea has plagued man throughout history. But this year sulfonamides are introduced, and finally a quick and sure cure is found. But only for a while. Within a few years the gonococcus develops a resistance to sulfa drugs.

1936 Can't get it up? Now there's surgical help for you. Doctors can remove a section of rib cartilage and insert it in your penis to create an erection. While the human boner is boneless, most male animals have a bone (in a whale it's over six feet long) to help with their erection. The doctors take a cue from the animal kingdom. But the operation isn't all it's cracked up to be. Infections and tissue damage make the operation unpopular.

1941 Penicillin is produced in mass quantities. Alexander Fleming discovered the wonder drug in 1928 but not until thirteen years later is it possible to manufacture large amounts of it. Both gonorrhea and syphilis are vulnerable to the drug. Neurosyphilis—once treated by giving the patient malaria so that the high fever would kill the spirochetes—is curable, too. The cure for gonorrhea is short-lived. It isn't long before the disease becomes resistant to it.

1944 Ernst Gräfenberg discovers a "zone of erogenous feeling" in women that is capable of inducing orgasm—and it's not the clitoris. Located inside the front wall of the vagina behind the pubic bone, along the urethra, the G-spot lies undetected until firmly massaged.

And then, WOW! Gräfenberg writes about the G-spot in 1950, but it isn't until the 1980s that the information filters down to the public and private experimenting begins. Guys don't have to be jealous. The male counterpart is the prostate gland, which can be manually stimulated through the anus.

1945 Researchers in Germany find that the average man has five erections every night, each lasting about twenty-five minutes. The only problem is that men are asleep at the time. The hard-ons happen during REM (rapid eye movement) sleep. Don't believe it? Take the stamp test suggested by Dr. Sherman Silber in his book, *The Male: From Infancy to Old Age*. Simply wrap a roll of six postage stamps—or more or less, as required—around the base of the penis and tape the ends together. If the stamps tear, it means you've tossed and turned a lot during the night. But if one of the perforations is neatly torn, you've grown.

1945> Dr. Arnold Kegel develops exercises designed to help women suffering from incontinence. Known as Kegel exercises, they are performed by simply contracting the pubococcygeus muscles as if you're trying to stop the flow of urine. The exercises increase sexual pleasure by keeping the muscles toned. And, yes, men can do them, too.

1948 The Polaroid Land camera, able to produce a black-and-white photo in under a minute without relying on a third party to develop it, goes on sale. Intimate photos for the masses are just a snapshot away.

1950 One more improvement for the condom: the reservoir tip is added. Stanley Penksa

The Tools

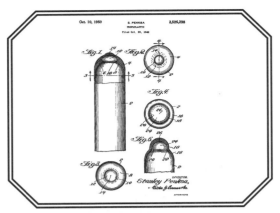

If you wonder where the semen went, it's in the reservoir tip of Stanley Penksa's newly designed condom.

secures a patent on the prophylactic with a pocket at the tip. Now that the semen has a place to go, there's less breakage.

1952 Lewis Twyman's sex harness receives a patent. A series of belts worn around the woman's waist with stirrups suspended from the back of the belt, this device enables a man to climb aboard in bed and lessens the chance of his slipping out. Later harnesses are intended to help cardiac patients by relieving stress on body parts, which lessens the exertion on the heart. Other fun harnesses consist of handles that let the man direct movement or that fit either partner and hold a dildo or vibrator in place.

1959 John Briggs invents a penile splint made of rubber (or leather or plastic) that fits over the penis of an impotent man or a man who has a problem remaining turgid. Looking like the real thing in form, the cover is slit lengthwise on one side in case of an erection.

1960s The concept of the IUD has been around ever since ancient Arabs put stones into the uteri of camels to prevent pregnancies on long trips. There are a couple of attempts to produce an effective IUD in the early part of the twentieth century but it isn't until the 1960s, when New York gynecologist Jack Lippes produces the Lippes loop, that IUDs achieve a 99 percent effective rate with minimal risks. In the 1970s the Dalkon shield results in death for some users, tainting all IUDs. It takes a few years before public confidence restores its popularity.

1961 The innovation that is to have the most dramatic effect on the human sex life is put on sale. The Pill, the first oral contraceptive, is 99 percent effective and works by disrupting ovula-

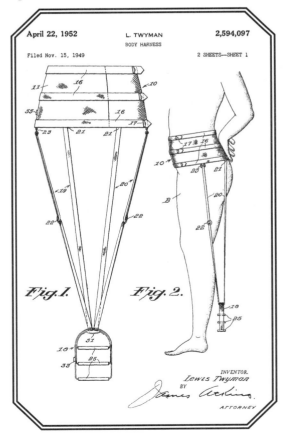

The sex harness for women helps men in bed.

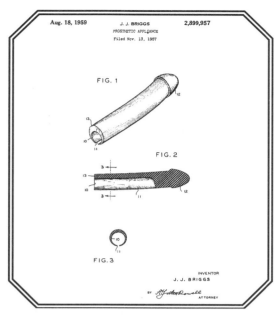

Aug. 18, 1959   J. J. BRIGGS   2,899,957
PROSTHETIC APPLIANCE
Filed Nov. 13, 1957

FIG. 1

FIG. 2

FIG. 3

INVENTOR
J. J. BRIGGS

BY
ATTORNEY

The penile splint keeps men erect.

tion the same way pregnancy does. It has some side effects—nausea, dizziness, headaches, edema, breast tenderness, and menstrual irregularities—but millions of women decide they are far outweighed by having control over their sexuality. Enovid-10® by Searle is the first pill to hit the market. Developed by Gregory Pincus and John Rock with the financial backing of millionaire Katharine McCormick and the emotional support of birth control advocate Margaret Sanger, the pill is taken daily. But unlike other methods, it's completely disassociated from the sex act, allowing total spontaneity. Put all this in the context of the youth movement of the 1960s and the sexual revolution is under way.

1966 The technological advancements of the space age finally reach the field of fake phalli.

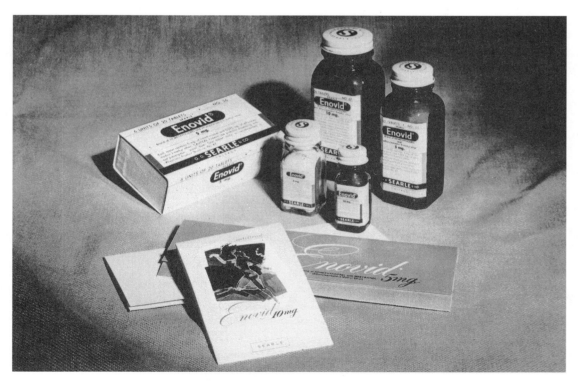

The Pill offers women control of their sexuality.

Brilliant in its simplicity, the one-piece torpedo-shaped plastic vibrator runs on batteries. Designed by Jon H. Tavel, it's cordless, so it can go anywhere. The vibrator becomes the most popular sex toy of the flower power generation.

1969 The Pill offers women 99 percent effective contraception. Vasectomies offer men 100 percent effectiveness. And this year men don't have to be hospitalized to get one. The Margaret Sanger Research Bureau in New York City offers outpatient surgery.

1970 If Charles P. Hall had set out to design a piece of furniture especially for the sleazy 1970s swinging singles set, he couldn't have done a better job. Hall invents the water bed. He fills a plastic bladder with water, then adds a heater after chilling himself one experimental night. Designed for comfort, it is seized upon by the singles set as the ultimate playpen. Hugh Hefner installs a king-size water bed in his mansion. Las Vegas hotels and no-tell motels put them in their suites. The average John and Jane Doe buy them, too, but misfortunes follow. The overweight beds cause some floors to collapse, and electrical outages are not unknown when the beds leak.

1970 Kinesics, the science of body language, is the study of nonverbal communication, and psychologists will teach you how to improve yours to get what you want. Women are alerted that walking provocatively, running their hands through their hair, touching their own breasts or thighs, and checking their makeup are a few signs that let men know they're interested. Men are just as easy to read: they fuss over their appearance, rearrange their clothes, lower the pitch of their voices, or hold eye contact a little

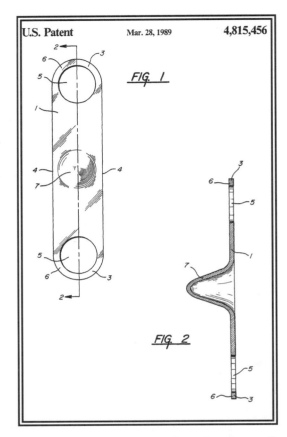

This AIDS-preventing oral condom has end loops that slip over the ears for a snug fit.

longer than necessary. Although kinesics is applied to all areas of life, it makes cocktail parties more interesting while it's in vogue.

1974 Help for the man who can't get it up is now available through a fluid-activated cylindrical implant. The implantee produces his erection by squeezing a bulb in his scrotum, which inflates the cylinder in the penis; this lifts the penis to erection, and we're ready for action. The device is capable of producing two erections a day for about twenty years. A release valve lets everything become flaccid once more.

Other implants include one-piece units that are activated when the head of the penis is squeezed; two-piece units housed all in the scrotum; and other non-inflatable yet malleable rod-type implants that are flexible enough not to be noticed when not in use. Nothing is without its disadvantages: infections, erosions, movement of the implant within the body, scarring, and malfunctions all have to be dealt with.

1983 The modern contraceptive sponge is introduced. Marketed under the brand name Today, the polyurethane sponge is soaked with spermicide and is 85 percent effective for twenty-four hours. Depending on how passionate a sex drive you have, at a dollar a sponge this method can be costly. The sponge accounts for 28 percent of over-the-counter contraceptive sales. In 1995 the sponge is pulled off the market because of bacteria problems. By 1999 Allendale Pharmaceuticals reintroduces the popular contraceptive. The sponge remains the same though the price has risen to two dollars, proving that when it comes to sex inflation affects more than just penises.

1987 Oral condoms are invented as an answer to the rise in sexually transmitted diseases, including HIV and AIDS. These condoms are pieces of latex that fit over the mouth for use during oral sex.

1989 Researchers in the 1970s verified that humans were equipped with a vomeronasal organ (VNO) located in the nose. This year Dr. David Berliner unearths his old research on the human skin compounds he isolated in the 1950s and realizes they might be human pheromones. He sends them to neurophysiologist Luis Monti-Bloch who tests the substances on VNOs, and the results are astonishing: seems that humans respond sexually to one another based on smell. Over two hundred chemical components can be found in male and female odors in sweat, urine, breath, saliva, skin oils, breast milk, and sexual juices. Women come out smelling better on this one. Those ladies who have sex at least once a week have more regular menstrual cycles, fewer fertility problems, and easier menopause. The reason? Studies show they benefit from the smell of the man.

1989 John Friedmann receives a patent for his Disposable Internally Applied Penile Erector, which consists of a hollow naillike tube inserted into the urethra for support. A plastic cap attached to the tube fits over the head of the penis and a latex sheath rolls down the member to keep everything intact.

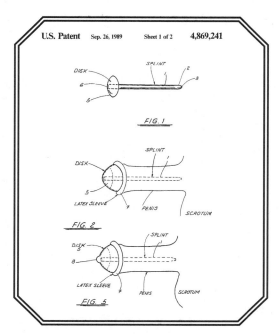

The Penile Erector fits into the urethra for an uplifting experience.

1990 Norplant is the first truly innovative birth-control product to be introduced in the United States since the 1960s. Six match-type sticks surgically implanted under the skin of the upper arm in a fifteen-minute operation take care of contraception for the next five years. Norplant, like the Pill, prevents ovulation and increases cervical mucus, which blocks the sperm. The first response is enthusiastic. As its side effects become apparent—40-pound weight gains, month-long periods, and an hour-long removal procedure—its popularity wanes.

1992 It's been in use in ninety other countries for the last twenty years. This year the Federal Drug Administration finally approves Depo-Provera as an injectable birth control. One shot gives three months of protection using the same method the Pill and Norplant use. Adverse reactions include a 5-pound weight gain, irregular bleeding, depression, and a loss of libido.

1993 The female condom goes on sale. A soft polyurethane tube with a flexible ring on either end, it fits into the vagina, cloaks the inside walls, and hangs outside the vagina, never allowing skin to touch skin. At $2.50, compared to $1.00 for a male condom, it doesn't achieve the expected popularity. A failure rate of 26 percent and a squeaking sound when the action starts turn most women off.

The sexual organs are the true seat of the will, of which the opposite pole is the brain.

Arthur Schopenhauer

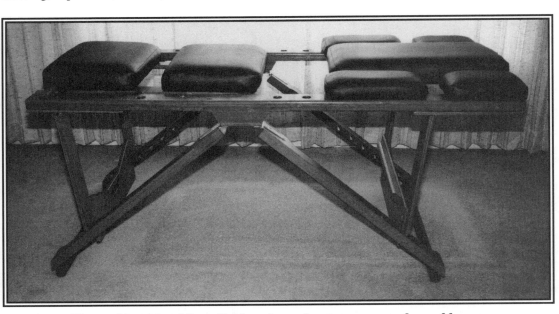

The multipositional Love Table reduces the stress on muscles and bones, making sex even more pleasurable.

Great Moments in Sex

1995 Men don't go through menopause like women, but their testosterone levels begin to dip about one percent a year after age forty, which can lead to a reduction in sex drive, the loss of the angle in an erection, and impotency. With baby boomer males reaching age fifty in droves, testosterone replacement therapy in the form of transdermal patches catches on. Replacement therapy pumps up muscles as well as penises, though, on the down side, evidence shows that it can stimulate existing prostate cancer.

1995 Virtual reality never felt so good. In its pioneer stages teledildonics uses a lightweight spandex suit and gloves filled with electronic conductors and goggles plugged into a computer system. Play with someone else (limit two, please—for now) or play with a computer that will replicate the latest sex god or goddess for your enjoyment. The epitome of safe sex in more ways than one, teledildonics is AIDS safe and a great way to explore sexual alternatives and fantasies without risk. Are you a man who'd like to know what it's like to be a multi-orgasmic woman, or a woman who would like to get that big bang feeling? It's possible, or at least it will be. The sensations produced by the body suits are still pretty basic. Some say teledildonics is nothing more than electronic masturbation. When it's perfected, no doubt, the "in" thing will be jacking in and jacking off.

1996 The Love Table is introduced by BodyCare Products. Invented by retired massage instructor Mac Fry, the flexible table is designed to support body parts and reduce muscle stress during lovemaking. Optional items include a playboard, armrests, thigh supports, a spacer, and a headrest to ensure perfect coupling.

1997 An orgasm pill may be in the future. Researchers find that women are able to withstand 40 percent more pain when slight pressure is applied to the inside of the vagina. This knowledge leads researchers to isolate a chemical that produces orgasms in women. The hope is that it can be turned into a drug for chronic pain sufferers. The rest of us will have to get our orgasms the natural way or pray for a backache.

1998 Viagra, the first oral medication for impotency, becomes available in April for men who lose the ability to have or maintain an erection because of hardening of the arteries to the penis. An erection is possible within twenty minutes after swallowing Viagra. It becomes the most successful prescription introduction in history with 120,000 scripts written in one week. At $10.00 a pill, and with five thousand male baby boomers turning age fifty every day, Pfizer's stock gets an erection, too.

1998 The Food and Drug Administration approves the Morning After Kit for women. The $20 kit includes high-dosage birth-control pills that prevent pregnancy up to seventy-two hours after intercourse.

The Tools

Chapter Two
THE HISTORY OF SEX

B.C.

c. 8,000,000 Ramapithecus, perhaps man's earliest ancestor, climbs down from the trees and discovers that by standing on two feet he can increase his hunting, gathering, and run-ning skills. By standing erect, Ramapithecus also plays the first game of "I'll show you mine if you show me yours." Sex, which was always had from the rear position, gradually progresses to other options.

c. 3,000,000 The Pliocene era sees Australopithecus fully erect—on his feet, that is. The vertical posture causes man to become the first animal with protruding fleshy buttocks. Full frontal viewing demands the female become more attractive to the male—one rea-son for the loss of body hair. This—or because the anus is now hidden between those fleshy cheeks where fecal matter can be trapped, lead-ing to insect and bacterial infestation, not to mention an odoriferous unaphrodisiac smell—promotes the front-entry position of sex. The menstrual cycle replaces estrus, allowing sex year-round, enabling Mama Hominid to pro-duce more little baby hominids so the race doesn't die out. It's during this age that pair bonding begins. The nearly monogamous pat-tern allows males to bond more easily with each other. Jealousy and frustration levels are lower,

Neanderthal man—not much to look at but a skilled hunter.

which increases hunting skills necessary to take care of the females who are taking care of the brood.

c. 350,000 Peking man becomes a cave dweller, establishing the first permanent residence, and forces a type of community to evolve. Posturing for claims on the better caves may help to develop the idea of family. At this point the man has no idea that he's responsible for impregnating the woman.

c. 75,000 Neanderthal man is a skilled hunter and does take care of the sick (although he resorts to cannibalism on occasion), but he doesn't live long. Life expectancy is thirty years. Neanderthal men outnumber women, mainly because so many women die in childbirth. Although population growth is sufficient to allow the human race to survive, infant mortality is extremely high. Only one in five children survives long enough to become a teenager.

c. 8000 Agrarian life develops at the end of the Pleistocene era. Man farms and takes control of his environment. Although men assume paternal responsibility, it's thought that women become pregnant through mystical means. All bloodlines are matrilineal. Woman is seen as possessing mystical powers: she bleeds monthly without any harm to herself and blood *is* the stuff of life. Though neither sex is really dominant, "god" is pictured as Magna Mater, the Great Mother.

c. 3500 Quite possibly while tending his flock, man notices that female animals don't get pregnant unless a male animal is introduced. Man finally puts two and two together and real-

izes that he's responsible for paternity. Pregnancy is no longer a magical mystery. It moves into the realm of cause and effect, with man being the cause. Though some cultures believe that parts of the baby come from each parent—the bones and brain from the father, the flesh and blood from the mother—other cultures view women as mere receptacles. In either case, male supremacy rears its head. Man has learned to control his environment and now he's responsible for procreation! How much greater can you get? Woman just doesn't compare, and the descent of her status begins. More importantly, matrilineal bloodlines are replaced with paternal lines. It is now *"my* child." And since having sex with more than one man can confuse the idea of "mine," monogamy for women takes on new importance while men's sexual license is unhampered. Also taking a back seat: Magna Mater. Mythology is thrown topsy-turvy, with female deities taking on an evil role or replaced by male gods.

c. 3500 Egypt's pharaohs find a way to keep it in the family. All inheritance passes through the mother to the daughter, even though it's the son who inherits the throne (daughters do assume the rule if there is no son). In order to get his share of the wealth, it's common for a brother to marry his sister. This option is available to the common man. The problem is, such joinings usually produce only daughters. Sons, supplied by unrelated second wives, later marry their half sisters to shore up their claim to the throne. And so the system perpetuates itself. It's also not unknown for sons to marry their mothers, as did Akhenaten, Tutankhamon's father. (Tut himself was born of a later marriage and married his half sister.) For the common folk monogamy is the norm: you can marry only as many women as you can support. Divorce is available to both husbands and wives. Adultery on the woman's part is the only grounds for which no property settlement is required.

c. 2350 Life in Sumer is equitable for women, with a few exceptions. Adulterers are forgiven their wanderings, but adulteresses are put to death. Once a woman is married, she's expected to produce children. If she doesn't, she's divorced. And she had better want children and lots of them. Any woman who doesn't is drowned.

c. 1750 Temple prostitution thrives in Babylon where sex with one of these women is considered an act of worship. This practice is carried on in other societies, including Cyprus, Egypt, Lydia, Syria, and Phoenicia, but Babylon plays it to the hilt. It's considered a duty for *all* women to honor the goddess Mylitta by waiting at her temple until a stranger pays to have sex with her. These are the rules: Once a woman sits down on the steps at the temple she may not go home until she has performed the sex act. She has no choice in who her partner is. Because payment is made in silver, which is considered sacred, she must accept the offering, no matter how small it is. This is a onetime offer. Once her obligation to the goddess is fulfilled, that's it. You can never buy her again. Says Herodotus of this practice: "Those that are endowed with beauty and symmetry of shape are soon set free; but the deformed are detained for a long time, from inability to satisfy the law, for some wait for a space of three or four years."

c. 1725 Hammurabi, the king of Babylon, codifies the laws. Chiseled into an 8-foot-high piece of black diorite, the Code of Hammurabi contains 282 paragraphs dealing with civil law. In respect to family matters, premarital sex is given the green light because of religious obligations. Once married, a woman is expected to produce children. If she's barren, her husband is allowed a concubine for the purpose of begetting children. He may choose the woman or, if the wife is smart, she'll go out and find someone without his asking. This helps to eliminate any emotional attachment the husband might have. The concubine enjoys the same rights as the wife, except that once the child is delivered, the contract is up without obligation to either side. While men are allowed to drown unfaithful wives, prostitution flourishes for male enjoyment. During a war, if a husband is taken captive, the wife is allowed to live with another man, but she must go back to her husband when he returns.

c. 1700 Abraham founds Judaism, focusing on monotheism and enforcing a strict moral code and family values. Women are considered possessions, attaining status only through motherhood, since it is imperative for the Chosen People to multiply. Chastity is of the utmost

Jewish men have multiple wives and concubines, but Jewish women are stoned if their virginity is in question.

importance. Any bride whose virginity is questioned must pass inspection. If she fails, she is stoned to death, as is any woman accused of adultery. Polygamy is permissible, not for pleasure but because secondary wives and concubines add to the number of offspring.

c. 1275 Moses ascends Mt. Sinai to receive the Thou Shalt Nots from on high, including number seven: Thou shalt not commit adultery. The Ten Commandments aren't a suggested moral code; they are the law of the Jews. Judaism sees the family as the basis of society and marriage as the basis of the family. Since women are possessions of their husbands, adultery on their part is viewed as a violation of property, and the punishment is death. Polygamy and prostitution (with foreign women, since prostitution is forbidden to Jewish women) still exist for the convenience of men. If a husband dies, his brother or nearest male relative is expected to marry his wife in order to carry on the bloodline.

c. 1200 The custom of veiling a woman's face originates in Assyria. Only "respectable" women are allowed to do so. Failing to wear a veil or a woman of lesser rank wearing one both merit the same punishment: flogging. The veil must be opaque enough to hide one's identity, and any man who recognizes a woman through her veil and doesn't report her is also flogged. Physical punishment is common in Assyria. A husband who catches his wife and her lover in flagrante delicto has the option of killing them both or merely castrating the lover and cutting off his wife's nose.

c. 1100 In the Vedic period of India sex is considered a natural act for both men and women and *kama,* the pursuit of pleasure and love, is one of the Four Aims in life. Marriage is by forcible abduction, purchase, or consent, with consent being disreputable. Being stolen or bought and paid for is looked upon as a compliment. Polygamy is fine. It raises your respectability if you're able to care for many wives. Phallic worship prevails in ancient India, as it does in modern India. Siva is the deity; the phallus is its icon. Temples are adorned with symbols of *yoni* (the male) and of *linga* (the female). Girls are educated along with boys, and women are permitted in society. Both of those practices will end with the coming of the Muslim influence around 500 B.C. At that time purdah—the exclusion of women—begins, and women are expected to obey humbly.

c. 900–600 Sparta flourishes. A society unlike any other, it emphasizes the creation of the perfect warrior—and lots of them. In order to achieve this, celibacy is considered a crime, premarital sex gets the state's thumbs-up, and since boys and girls are separated for training, homosexuality isn't frowned upon. Men are advised to marry at age thirty, women at twenty; the bride is carried off forcibly. Those men who prize their bachelorhood too long are often physically set upon publicly by groups of women. Once married, the state's eugenics program encourages husbands to lend their wives to men who are stronger and more vigorous.

753 Rome is founded, legend says, by Romulus and Remus, the twin sons of Rhea Silvia, a Vestal Virgin. The Vestal Virgins play an important role in Rome from day one. Six daughters from the leading families are chosen to guard and tend the eternal fire of Vesta, the goddess of the hearth. Plucked from their families at about age ten, they dedicate the next thirty years of their lives to the fire, living in

Aphrodite arises from the foaming semen of Uranus, whose testicles were cut off by his offspring.

celibacy until they retire. Should the fire go out, they are whipped. Sex is out for them. The Vestals are considered daughters of the state and to lie with any Roman would be incest, a crime punishable by death. Occasionally they are blamed and punished for political and military disasters. And occasionally one of the Vestals loses her virginity and is dealt with severely. Plutarch says that "no spectacle [was] more horrible." Now unchaste, she is put into a litter that is cloaked, fastened, and carried to the forum, where a waiting crowd follows her to an underground chamber. Here a bed, a lamp, and a small supply of food await her as she is forced down a ladder. Once she is ensconced in the tomb, it is sealed and the Vestal is buried alive.

c. 750 The Greek poet Hesiod writes *Theogony*, a genealogy of the gods and goddesses, which contains the story of the creation of Aphrodite, the goddess of love and sexual intercourse. Uranus (Heaven) mates with Gaea (Earth) and produces a race of Titans, some of whom have fifty arms and one hundred hands. Uranus isn't too fond of them and condemns them to Tartarus, the netherworld, which irks Gaea. She advises the Titans to kill their father, and Cronus accepts the challenge. With sickle in hand he mutilates Uranus by cutting off his testicles and throws them into the sea. From the blood that falls upon the ground come the Furies. But from the semen that spills into the water and foams arises Aphrodite, the goddess of love and sex.

c. 625 Corinth, a Greek port city, becomes a center of prostitution. Ship captains eagerly dock here for a little R&R with the devotees of

help God. Ironic, since the only way to get more men is to have babies with women. Zoroaster admits that in a perfect world man would not need sex, but considering the task at hand, celibacy is unnatural and evil.

c. 600 The first five books of the Old Testament are compiled. They form the Pentateuch, supposedly the dying testament of Moses to the Chosen People. In the beginning is the story of Adam and Eve, cribbed from Sumerian mythology, but with a twist. Eve becomes the fall guy and is cast as the evil temptress, a role she'll play throughout history.

c. 594 Athenian lawmaker Solon sets up the first state-licensed brothels. Believing that prostitution is an essential service, he initially stocks the *dicteria* and places a tax on the world's oldest profession. Slow in the beginning, the ser-

Aphrodite who hand over their fees to the temple priests. As a result the Temple of Aphrodite becomes immeasurably rich, owning more than a thousand temple slaves. Besides having their own holiday, the courtesans are not only tolerated by citizens but looked upon as public benefactors.

605 Zoroaster founds Zoroastrianism in Persia. Although the religion doesn't catch on quickly, many of its tenets are adopted by later religions. Zoroaster speaks of an inherent difference between good and evil. In Zoroastrianism, woman doesn't fare too well. She is seen as evil, the "Demon Whore" who chose to embrace Satan (an event from which sprang menstruation). God is engaged in a 9,000-year battle with Satan and needs man, who is good, to help defeat evil with good thoughts, deeds, and words. Man's duty is to bring forth more men to enlarge the army to

vice catches on and ancient Greeks are tantalized on the street by a variety of young bare-breasted or sheerly dressed women. Solon introduces laws for nonprofessionals: Any man married to an heiress must do the deed at least three times a month. Violation of a free woman costs the accoster 100 drachmas. Anyone who catches an adulterer in the act may kill him on the spot.

565 Although the principles of Tao (pronounced "dow") have been around for at least a thousand years in the Orient, Lao-tzu composes its basic principles in the 5,000-word book, *Tao T'e Ching*. Basically, Tao teaches the need to be in harmony with *ch'i*, the essence of the universe. Tao, meaning "the way," is the path with interaction between *yin* and *yang* propelling one forward. Woman is the lesser yin while man is the lesser yang, and their interaction is essential for harmony. Tao teaches that vaginal secretions are yin essence and sperm is yang essence and the yin benefits the yang. In fact, yin essence is so important to the power of man that Tao says it is best to have ten women in one night. Before men get too excited, a word of caution: there are no wham-bams here. Pleasuring a woman is so important that sexual skills are highly prized and taught. Coitus reservatus (stopping before ejaculation) and coitus obstructus (pressure applied by fingertip to the spot between the anus and the scrotum along with a breathing technique causes the semen to be absorbed into the body rather than ejaculated, a trick that separates orgasm and ejaculation) are not only suggested but demanded, since any excessive spilling of semen is considered a waste of yang. The same principle puts masturbation in a dark light. What to do with all that semen? Save it for one woman to have children. But beware.

Ejaculate at the wrong time of the month or day and your baby will have a dubious future.

c. 500 Pederasty, a type of homosexuality, blossoms in Greece. After a boy completes his schooling he's taken under the wing of an older man who guides him morally and intellectually. Youths range from age twelve to twenty, while "guides" are usually in their thirties. The Greeks believe a fine body implies a fine mind. It's a source of status for an older man to be a mentor to a good-looking boy, and it's a great compliment to a boy to be in the company of a distinguished man. It is primarily a love of the mind that Plato heralds in his *Symposium*. That this "Greek love" can establish and retain such a

foothold for about two hundred years is understandable. Girls aren't educated as the boys are. The sexes are separated, and women are looked upon with disdain. Add to this that it is the custom for an older man to marry a younger girl—and this during the Golden Age of Greece when intellectual and philosophical pursuits are the order of the day—and there is no mind lock with a woman. If procreation is a way to pass on one's genes, then pederasty is a way to pass on one's mind. Not all Greek men are pederasts. Some are blatantly heterosexual, although strict heterosexuality is seen as effeminate. (Only a weak man would want to be with weak minds.) There are rules that guide pederasty. Only boys who have gone through puberty are touchable; underage boys are jail bait. The relationship ends when the youth is capable of growing a beard. Effeminate dress and manners are considered shameful.

c. 500 When Greek men decide to take a break from the boys, unless they want to make a baby with the wife, it's off to the prostitutes. Greece has several types from which to choose. The lowly *pornai* are found in common brothels and are bought by the hour, day, week, or even a year by one man, or he could time-share her with one of his friends. Having a party? You'll want an *auletride,* a woman who specializes in dance and music and, after a few glasses of wine, sticks around for a few more party favors. The best, most respected women in Greece are the *hetairai.* Members of the citizen class, the hetairai are women who have fallen into disrepute or who are not about to put up with the treatment the ordinary Greek housewife gets. They are educated and can talk philosophy with the best of them. They are witty, charming, beautiful, well groomed, and cultured, not to mention sexually gifted. The hetairai are so well respected that the Greek men don't mind being seen with them in public. But it costs. The hetairai are renowned for the high prices they charge. In fact, it's a source of contention with Greek men. But the hetairai know they can make money only while their beauty is in top form, so they get it while the getting is good. Prostitution is so popular in Greece that it's heavily taxed. Once the average Greek woman decides it's time to come out of the house and betters herself, the day of the hetairai will wane. But that will take a few hundred years.

c. 500 Meanwhile back in Rome women enjoy a more equal standing with men. Husbands are still the head of the house. They even play judge and jury if the wife commits a crime. Virginity before marriage is a must for women, and childlessness is condemned, not by law but by public opinion. Adultery on the woman's part can bring death, especially if the husband catches her in the act. Indeed, by law, a man must divorce an adulterous wife. But times are starting to change. As Rome expands its empire and imports customs, life will never be the same.

c. 500 Sexually speaking, until this time Chinese women had parity with their men. They enjoyed freedom of choice in marriage and were able to divorce. Widows could remarry. But the Confucian *Book of Rights* is changing all that. The operable word for women, who are now considered a biological necessity, is "obey." Their primary function is to produce sons to care for ancestral graves and carry on the tradition of the family. Confucianism takes hundreds of years to evolve. The end result is the loss of women's power and authority. Polygamy, which in other societies is reserved for the nobility who can afford it, is common in the middle class on up. When a man marries, along with his wife he gets her sisters and servants as well. The *Book of Rights* does provide for the care of wife and concubine, prohibiting favoritism and insisting that even as they age the husband must have sex with his partners at least once every five days. To help keep attentions equitable it is suggested that no husband touch his wives outside of the sex act lest it lead to spontaneous lovemaking. Hand-to-hand contact is evaded with the use of a bamboo tray to pass items to and from each other. Prostitution exists not so much for sex, which the men get enough of at home, but for social intercourse and an evening of merriment. For the common woman premarital chastity is a must, although once she is married, the boredom of seclusion often leads to clandestine affairs.

451 Rome organizes its laws and produces the Twelve Tables, which affect both public and private life. Women are somewhat emancipated, being able to marry by simply living with a man without religious ceremony. This protects any inherited property she might have from going to her husband. All she has to do is return to her father's house for three nights every year. The husband is still the undeniable despotic ruler of the family. He can still kill or sell his children, although a thrice-sold son is free from his father's rule.

c. 450 After centuries of being sequestered in the back of the house and shunned by men in general, Greek women begin their revolt against the men's club Greece has become. Taking a cue from the hetairai, women are educated and put more emphasis on their physical attributes than on their broodmare capabilities. Abortion and infanticide are practiced more, and aided by the Peloponnesian Wars, population figures fall drastically. Men assist in what will become the downfall of Greece by postponing marriage. During wartime, bigamy is allowed to boost population numbers, but it's of no use. The weakened state falls to the barbarians and the Romans.

338 The Sacred Band at Thebes is annihilated at the Battle of Chaeronea. Thirty-three years earlier the band had been formed, composed entirely of pairs of homosexual lovers who pledged to stand by each other until death. The older *heniochoi* (charioteers) and their younger *paraibatai* (companions) are considered the premier fighting force in the Hellenic world.

215 Rome passes the Oppian Law during its war with Hannibal. Women are forbidden to own more than a half ounce of

As Rome's laws are loosened, orgies become a part of life.

TRIVIA

WHAT IT TAKES TO BE EMPEROR

More than a few Roman emperors exhibit peculiar sexual quirks. Tiberius (42 B.C.–A.D. 37), a bisexual, has a retreat in Capri where a special room is set up for sexual escapades. He fills the room with perverts and women and watches their antics. If they aren't entertaining enough, he has books of positions he directs them into. Another of his pleasures is his "little fishes," children who are taught to play with his genitals underwater while he bathes. Older "fishes" perform fellatio on him.

Caligula (37–41) likes to have sex with his sisters as well as with other women and men. His idea of foreplay is to remind his lover while kissing her neck that "Off comes this beautiful head whenever I give the word." Then there are dinner parties where he surveys his guests' wives, chooses one, retires with her to the bedroom, then returns to the party and delivers a critique.

Nero (54–68) likes to play with boys. One boy of whom he is particularly enamored he has castrated and dresses like a woman and then marries him. He also marries another man, this time playing the woman's role himself. At night he imitates the sounds of "a maiden being deflowered." Then there's his heterosexual side. Bored with "routine" sex, he ties women and men to stakes, dons wild animal pelts, and cages himself. Released from the cage he attacks their genitals until his lust is sated.

Domitian (81–96) seems sedate compared to his three predecessors. Never tiring of "bed-wrestling"—his word for intercourse—he plucks out his lovers' pubic hairs one by one.

gold, to drive chariots through the streets, and to wear dyed clothes. The money used to import or make these luxuries is needed for the national defense. Fourteen years later the war ends but the Oppian Law remains in effect until women take to the streets in open rebellion. Cato warns that this is a portent of things to come, but Valerius backhands women while repealing the law: "What of women, whom even trifles can upset?" He'll soon eat his words. Laws are passed allowing women to manage their own dowries, divorce their husbands, and practice birth control, including abortion and infanticide. The shift from sex for baby-making to making whoopee is on.

191 Magna Mater comes back to Rome as Cybele is officially enshrined on the Palatine Hill. Worship of the goddess borders on the barbaric and ribald, with wild dancing and music building up to a frenzy, ultimately leading to the male candidates for priesthood castrating themselves and presenting their severed male members on the altar of the goddess. From that night on, they serve as sacred eunuchs, clad in female attire. In 186 B.C., Rome deals with the

Dionysian cult. Hearing from inside informers about the night-held bacchanalia rituals where, says Livy, "everyone found his own particular vice catered for," the authorities arrest seven thousand participants and sentence hundreds of them to death. Subsequent rules make it impossible to worship, and the cult gradually fades away.

c. 167 Full circumcision is practiced by the Jews. The ritual has been performed since the time of Abraham as a sacred covenant with Yahweh (Gen. 17:10–11): "This is my covenant, which ye shall keep, between me and you and thy seed after thee: Every man child among you shall be circumcised. And ye shall circumcise the flesh of your foreskin; and it shall be a token of the covenant betwixt me and you." It is during the time of the Maccabees that a law is enacted to remove the entire prepuce. Circumcision is practiced in ancient Egypt and in African tribes, but as a rite of puberty. The Jews use circumcision as indelible identification and perform the operation (with flint stones in ancient times) eight days after birth. Until this time the portion taken was small enough that Gentile women couldn't tell the difference.

c. 150 Over in Palestine is an extremist Jewish sect called the Essenes who passionately observe the written and oral law (they consider it sacrilegious to have a bowel movement on the Sabbath). The first century A.D. Jewish historian Josephus tells us that the Essenes are misogynistic and find women "polluting," especially during the menstrual cycle. Since a man can't tell which woman is having her period and because women are lascivious and "none of them preserve their fidelity to one man," it's better to shun them all of the time. A few Essenes are married, but sex is for procreation only and all sensual pleasure is denied.

A.D.

9 Rome has a problem. A rapidly declining birthrate in an age of debauchery is leaving the empire without enough citizens to fuel its ranks within the army and without. Emperor Augustus has laid down some laws to deal with the situation. Making adultery a matter for the civil courts, he rules that a husband *must* divorce his wife if she commits adultery or face prosecution himself. The adulteress is banished to an island, deprived of a percentage of her wealth, and her lover. If he's married, he's exiled to a different island. Single men are let off the hook. As for philandering husbands, regular visits to the local hooker are okay, but dalliances with a mistress are cause for prosecution for "unnatural vice." This year Augustus decrees that widows must remarry within two years of the husband's death. Divorcées are given eighteen months. Confirmed bachelors and childless couples are penalized by losing all or part of their inheritance. The Romans find loopholes. Men get betrothed to underage girls and wait years for them to reach marrying age. Augustus shortens the engagement time allowed. Then the divorce rate soars. As historian Will Durant notes, "Immorality continued, but it was more polite than before."

14 Roman Emperor Tiberius decides to uphold the ancient Roman rule of not executing virgins. But not so fast. Just because your hymen is intact doesn't mean you're off the hook. Tiberius decrees that all virgins to be executed will first be raped by their executioner.

c. 20 The great Jewish philosopher Philo of Alexandria interprets the story of Sodom as homosexuality. The Sodomites "not only in their mad lust for women" committed adultery and "forbidden forms of intercourse," but "men also mounted males without respect for the sex nature which the active partner shares with the passive." Other religious elders came to this conclusion but Philo puts the last word on it. The word "sodomy" is used to denote homosexual intercourse, although in later years it comes to mean all unnatural sex, including anal and oral sex between men and women.

c. 25 Jesus Christ begins preaching. Besides turning the other cheek and the meek shall inherit the earth, Jesus preaches a new morality based on chastity. Those who leave their parents, wives, or children, and even those who make themselves eunuchs and devote themselves to God are praised. His tender nature appeals to women, and his classless teachings have people from all walks of life listening. He's crucified about five years later. Christianity takes off with the preaching of his disciples.

c. 40 Saint Paul picks up the banner of Christianity and helps spread the word, adding his own flavoring to the blend. Like Christ, he preaches that chastity allows more time and energy for devotion to God. Paul sees women as subservient to men in all ways. "Man was not made from woman, but woman from man; and man was not created for woman," he says, "but woman for man." Celibacy is the operative word for Paul. Realizing that not all men can keep that lifestyle, he allows marriage because it's preferred to fornication and adultery and because "it is better to marry than to burn." But sex is for procreation only. One advantage this

religion offers women is that it sets the same ideal standard of fidelity for both sexes. In reality, men are still forgiven their trespasses more easily. Marriage becomes indissoluble except for those who are stuck with a pagan partner.

c. 100 Almost as popular as Christianity is Mithraism. Mithras is the god of light. Devotion to him includes abstinence and a good deal of self-control. Mithraism, with its homosexual undertones, filters through the Roman army whose soldiers take a pledge to wage a lifelong war against evil. The religion endures for another two hundred years, until Constantine decides to throw his weight behind Christianity.

c. 100 Introduced as a guide to proper behavior for Manava Brahmans, the Code of Manu is later adopted by the entire Hindu community. Composed of 2,685 verses, the code includes rules for relationships between men and women. Although women are to be cared for, dressed and fed well, they are also the source of dishonor and strife. Men are advised "therefore [to] avoid women." Sex is considered a natural act, but men must strive to control their desires. The priority for men is to have children (mainly sons), for "then only is man a perfect man." That eliminates all forms of birth control. Abortion becomes a capital crime. Marriage is a must for everyone. An unmarried man is an outcast, and a virtuous woman is a disgrace. The thought of not marrying is so repugnant that child marriages are performed, after which the bride returns to her parents until puberty. Marriage is for eternity. Men can divorce only if the wife is unchaste. And adultery? Forget about sinning against your wife; that's impossible. An adulterer sins against another man, for which crime Manu says, "Let the adulterer be placed in an iron bed well heated, under which the executioner shall throw logs continually, till the sinful wretch be there burned to death."

c. 195 The Christian theologian Tertullian logs on with his viewpoint. He's a firm believer that the Second Coming is at hand, so there's no logic in making more babies. Not fond of women, he becomes even more bitter with age, describing them as "the gate by which the demon enters." On the other hand, he's no friend of homosexuality. "So far as sex is concerned, the Christian is content with the woman." He condemns parents who let their daughters go about unveiled. A custom at some Christian services is agape, symbolized by a kiss between men and men and women and women, or, sometimes, between men and women. Tertullian believes it leads to sexual indulgences. The church agrees with him and sets standards for kissing. The lips should never be open, and if any sexual pleasure is derived, kissing should never be repeated. By the third century agape is done for. The church accepts marriage in order to keep a rein on promiscuity. Husbands and wives, though, are encouraged to be chaste.

c. 200 The Tantric sect emerges in Asia and India. Hedonistic in creed, Tantrists believe that if the world was created by a divinity, then everything in the world is to be worshiped as divine. Rather than putting women in a subordinate role, both Buddhist and Hindu Tantrists see women as a way of purification. Sex is the most powerful force for man and animal. Indeed, sexual excitation is an indication of divine presence. Highly secretive because they believe their teachings and powers can be used to do

harm, all instructional literature is so obliquely written only a few can understand it without guidance. Sex is used in rituals as are magic and chanting *"Om mani padme hum,"* which literally means "The jewel is in the lotus," or "The penis is in the vagina." Initiation is with a *dakinis,* a female spiritual leader. Initiates are taught to worship their own erect penis. Once past the first stage, couples meet with their gurus and swap partners (the religious experience just doesn't happen with your own mate) for an evening of five enjoyments: the eating of fish, meat, and cereals, the drinking of wine, and sex—which probably makes this church service a lot more fun than singing in the choir.

242 Mani of Ctesiphon, at the coronation of Shapur I of Persia, announces himself as the Messiah and founds Manichaeism. Considered a heretic, Mani preaches that Satan was man's creator and Eve his masterpiece. Men have light within them (women do, too, but not as much), and it is their mission to bring more light into their lives to move closer to God. In order to do this, they must become vegetarians and refrain from sex, sorcery, and worshiping false gods. Mani's teachings spread into the Roman Empire, but after thirty years he's crucified, his skin stuffed with straw and then hung from a gate.

309 The first church council to deal with sexuality is held in Elvira (now Granada), Spain. Thirty-seven of the eighty-two canons passed by this council pertain to the regulation of sexual behavior. Along with reaffirming that nonprocreative sex is prohibited, homosexuality is put on the list of damnables with deathbed communion denied to men who philander with boys. Penalties are meted out to adulterous women

Great Moments in Sex

St. Jerome enjoyed sex in his earlier days. Later, he found lust "obscene."

and prostitutes. The council looks into its own house as well and demands "absolute continence" from all members of the clergy, insisting that they not live with their wives if they're married.

313 Constantine the Great, Roman emperor of the West, accepts Christianity and permits all Christians freedom to worship without persecution, thus allowing the religion to spread.

325 The Council of Nicaea tries to incorporate and stabilize Christian teachings. Along with settling the debate over whether Jesus is God (yes) and setting the time for Easter, the council excludes those who voluntarily castrate themselves from the priesthood. The question of celibacy for priests is put on the table but the 318 bishops opt for the status quo: a man may not get married once he enters the priesthood, but those

who are can keep their wives. The church sees marriage for clergy and any children born to them as a threat. By not allowing sexual activity, it exempts priests from scandal. Also, the children are likely to inherit their father's estate rather than the church. Besides, devotion is to the church and to God, not to a wife and children. As usual the church frowns upon sex that isn't for procreative purposes and demands fidelity from both the husband and the wife. Prostitution is denounced, and the ideal is lifelong chastity for both sexes.

c. 382 Coming in on the side of celibacy for the Christian church is Saint Jerome, theologian and moralist. Although at one time he was sexually active (while a hermit and in abusive self-denial, he is overrun with memories of desire and hallucinates that his room is filled with tempting dancing girls), he now views lust as obscene, fit for animals but not mankind. Womankind is "filth." Childbirth is dirty. Marriage is carnal and to be condemned. Love exists but it is asexual. An intolerant anti-Semite, Jerome insists on celibacy for all men, especially clergy. Women should join convents or live as virgins at home. Saints Ambrose, Augustine, and Jerome become the Big Three thinkers of the early church.

386 Pope Siricius issues what is believed to be the first papal decree prohibiting priests from having sex. It has little effect.

c. 400 Saint Augustine, a Catholic, comes up to bat with his theological philosophy. Augustine enjoyed the ladies in his youth, even keeping a concubine with whom he had a child. At age thirty, at his mother's insistence, he becomes engaged to a ten-year-old girl and during the two-year waiting period for her to reach "maturity," he converts to Christianity. Like Jerome, Augustine turns his back on sex but not with the acridness of his contemporary. Augustine preaches that Eve tempted Adam, Adam acted with Eve, and through this act, the rest of mankind is tainted with original sin and sexual desire. Since children are a product of the sex act and the only way to have sex is to feel a little lusty, that sin of desire is perpetuated in every offspring. Augustine, too, links sexuality to animallike behavior but stops short of condemning it, for God wants his children to be fruitful and multiply. In his view, married procreative sex is far better than fornication or adultery. While not entirely in the woman's corner (he ponders if women will become men in the afterlife), he does admit that the penis might be responsible for sin, but only during sex.

476 Rome falls. For all its glory, the empire isn't up to the crises that befall it. Its poor economy, despotic government, class struggle, and the lack of a moral compass for its people lead to its demise. Roman citizens marry later in life, if at all, and limit their family size. Epidemics, wars, and contraception take their numbers down until the importation of barbarians is necessary to maintain sheer numbers. Illiteracy is rampant. The economy is in such tatters that most of the Empire is on a local barter system. In the midst of this comes Christianity, offering a moral code in a lawless society and stability in a state of chaos.

c. 500 The Franks formulate Salic Law. Women receive some protection from the rules. Immodestly stroking the hand of a woman brings a fine of 15 denarii, 35 denarii for the upper arm. If you grab those pert breasts, it's 45 denarii. And there's no discount for cash. Adultery committed by the wife gets her the death sentence; for hubby it's not a problem. The man of the house also gets to divorce his wife whenever he likes.

c. 500 The Babylonian Talmud, a compilation of the oral law of the Jews, is finished. Amassed over the last few centuries by scribes and rabbis, it is considered the word of God and pertains to all areas of life. Unlike Christianity, the Talmud doesn't degrade sex. Lifelong chastity, considered sinful, is avoided by early marriage. Sex and related functions—menstruation, childbirth—render one unclean until she/he performs a purification rite. Though childbirth confers perfect womanhood, the new mother is unapproachable and unclean for forty days after giving birth to a boy, eighty days for a girl. The Talmud condones polygamy but makes adultery a capital crime.

517 The bishops of the Frankish kingdom extend the boundaries of incest. Added to the list is a brother's widow, a wife's sister, a stepmother, first and second cousins, the widow of an uncle, and a stepdaughter. Of course, closer kin are also verboten. In 596 King Childebert II makes marriage to a stepmother a capital offense. Spiritual kinship makes the list in 721, including godmothers and godfathers. From the ninth to twelfth centuries marriage within seven degrees (if you have a common ancestor during the previous seven generations) is prohibited. That makes it tough on royalty, who are obliged to marry their own kind. Most of them are related. Finally, the Lateran Council of 1215 limits incest to the first four generations commencing from a common ancestor.

534 Byzantine Emperor Justinian develops the Justinian Code of Law, which he expands and amends throughout his reign. The emperor believes that natural disasters are punishment for immoral conduct, and he deals with transgressions severely. Using Christian principles as an outline, he combines them with Roman law and produces some of the following laws: Divorce is forbidden unless one spouse enters a nunnery or a monastery. Abortion is also a valid reason for ending a marriage. (Justinian's wife, Empress Theodora, later convinces him to extend the grounds for divorce for women to include impotency, bringing a lover to live in the house, making his wife commit adultery, and being held captive for five years.) Men are punished with death for adultery while accused women live out their lives in a convent. A husband is allowed to kill his wife's lover, but he has to warn her first. A rapist earns the death penalty, with the victim inheriting his property. Hardest hit are homosexuals: before execution they are castrated, tortured, mutilated, and paraded before the public.

567 Homosexual activity in monasteries leads the Second Council of Tours to support the Benedictine rule of not allowing two monks to sleep together. There is no evidence that homosexuals gravitate to monasteries. Rather, because monks and priests can't marry, the situation may foster this sexual expression. By 693 the Council of Toledo feels that homosexuality is too prevalent in Spain. Accused clergymen are expelled and damned. To this, the king adds the punishment of castration.

c. 600 Priests hearing confessions can now make use of penitentials—popular manuals listing the appropriate penance for various sins. Penitentials first appear in Ireland, but they soon spring up throughout Europe. A sampling

of atonements: Seven years' penance is recommended for adultery, three to fifteen years for anal or oral sex, and three years for fornication. Coitus interruptus interrupts your life for two to ten years. A wet dream requires seven days of fasting unless you helped the wet dream along manually—then your diet is restricted for twenty days. Punishments are meted out for various methods of stimulation depending on your age, whether the sin is a one-time experience or habitual, and whether you play an active or passive role. Bestiality confers one to ten years of penance. Any position other than the missionary gets the big frown. The punishment for homosexual activity depends on what you do and with whom. "Licentious kissing" without ejaculation earns eight special fasts, while a habitual fellatio offender gets seven years. Interfemoral sex (rubbing the penis between the passive partner's thighs) is a two-year no-no. And lesbian sex or a woman masturbating brings three years of mea culpa-ing. Forms of penance include dieting, fasting, prayer, attending mass, displaying public contrition, and giving money to the poor.

c. 600 Life for the Vikings is pretty straightforward, as are the penalties for misbehavior. Marriages are arranged by parents. In the case of an unsanctioned elopement, the husband becomes an outlaw and the wife can be legally slain by her relatives. Divorce is allowed to both spouses if either one of them cross-dresses—specifically if a woman wears trousers or a husband wears his shirt open at the breast. A husband can divorce his wife for other reasons but they'd better be sound. If they're not, he can be killed by her relatives. Polygamy is allowed until the thirteenth century but adultery for women isn't. Her paramour can be killed by her wronged hubby. Other than that, life goes on.

c. 600 What makes a marriage? That's the question the Catholic church starts tussling with and continues to debate until well after the twelfth century. Based on Augustine's teachings, marriage is the sinless vehicle for people to have sex as long as it's for procreation. But does sex make the marriage? Or is it mutual consent to a contract? The debate rages on, with consent getting the nod. After all, the Second Coming is just around the corner, and the Second Coming means the end of the world. Who needs children if the world's not going to be here? And if you're not having children, who needs . . . ?

c. 610 Muhammad has a vision of the archangel Gabriel, who informs him that Muhammad is the messenger of Allah. This is the first of many visions, during which the entire Koran is given to Muhammad, a piece at a time. The prophet announces himself to the Arab peoples and establishes a new morality and faith. In pre-Islamic times Middle Eastern society is matrilineal. Women are able to have more than one husband, and they can divorce a spouse simply by turning their tent around so that the door faces the other way, a sign to the husband that he's no longer wanted. But Muhammad, in trying to elevate and protect women, switches to a patrilineal society, although the sequestering and subjugation of women mostly happens after his death. Polygamy, not polyandry, is allowed as a moral obligation to take care of widows of warriors. Men may divorce. A waiting period (*'iddah*) for a woman after divorce to make sure she's not carrying her ex-husband's baby is initiated. Out of respect for his wives, Muhammad requires

them to wear veils, and this becomes mandatory for all women later. Women gradually are eliminated from Islamic society, with their remaining purpose in life to bear children. At its height Islam will spread to Syria, Mesopotamia, all of Persia, and into Africa and much of Spain.

c. 618 The Tang dynasty period in China is a good one for the emperor. The number of wives and concubines in his seraglio is so extensive that some ladies do nothing except organize his sex schedule, keep track of menstrual cycles, and watch for signs of pregnancy. Etiquette and Tao philosophy dictate who gets seen and when. The concubines of lowest rank are frequented the most often and before those of ascending rank, the correct way to build up yang. The empress is seen once a month, hopefully when she's fertile and the emperor's yang is strong. A strong yang is essential for strong, healthy, intelligent heirs to the throne. The yang of the emperor's subjects is in pretty good shape, too, thanks to polygamy. Only the poor, who can't afford multiple wives, remain monogamous.

c. 651 The 114 chapters of the Koran are compiled, setting down moral guidelines for the followers of Islam. The lifestyle includes polygamy for men, who may have as many as four wives as long as they can treat them fairly and impartially. If not, monogamy is the rule. Divorce by the husband is allowed but discouraged. A wife may divorce her husband but with less ease, and she must return her dowry to her husband. Celibacy is not allowed; marriage is a must. Concubinage is strictly forbidden. Adultery by a man or a woman is punishable by one hundred lashes. Sex before marriage is forbidden. If you have problems with that, try fasting to help you through the hot times. A marriage must have the consent of the bride and groom, and the only stop sign on the honeymoon is if she has her period. There's no sex during the menstrual cycle and none afterward until she completes a purification ritual.

c. 743 Walid II develops the harem-eunuch system in Islamic territory. The harem is a sanctuary for women during menstruation and childbirth. But as the *purdah* develops, the harem evolves into a place of seclusion. To guard women, eunuchs become a necessary appendage, once their appendages are cut off. The Koran forbids the making of eunuchs, but Christians and Jews supply them at a high price.

c. 796 The Council of Fréjus declares that a bride and groom should be of the same age. It has long been the custom for mature men to marry young girls, often with the betrothal taking place years before the wedding to allow the bride time to grow up. Since love doesn't enter the equation in marriage, it isn't necessary for the engaged couple to have anything in common save property or wealth that needs to be expanded or protected. Members of the nobility secure their lands and titles with marriage as early as possible; one young girl is married, widowed, married, widowed, and married again before she is eleven. In some cases the bride is older than the groom. The council warns against these matches because the father or older brothers of the immature groom may take advantage of the new wife. After the council's decision the marrying age for girls is fifteen.

c. 875 *Jus primae noctis*—right of the first night—is established in Scotland. The lord has the right to the maidenhead of his vassal's bride on her wedding night. Husbands come second. This practice spreads throughout the feudal states, though in some areas, husbands are allowed to buy back their brides by paying a "virgin tax."

c. 1000 The Chosen People have been fruitful and multiplied enough. Polygamy, which was permitted to increase the numbers of Jews, gives way to monogamy. The emphasis is now on preserving the Jewish race. After delivering two children into the world, one's duty is considered fulfilled. Divorcing a woman against her will is also forbidden.

1059 The Lateran Council tries to put teeth into its ruling that priests should be celibate. After excommunicating priests who are sexually active, the church forbids parishioners to attend the services of priests who are married or keep concubines and still continue to practice their religious duties. This doesn't sit well with bishops who are unwilling to break up the priests' families. Plus married priests are accepted in many areas. It's the single, celibate ones who are scrutinized and suspected of philandering. The papal view is that priests should live by a higher moral code. And there's the question of control. If priests' children are allowed to inherit parishes it will diminish the power of the papal seat. Of course, it's a better idea than the one suggested in 1018—that priests should be slaves of the church and children automatically disinherited. The Lateran Council accepts the bishops' viewpoint and rescinds its order to parishioners.

You Use It, You Lose It!

c. 1066 Where once a monetary fine was the penalty for English adulterers, the stakes for an on-the-side romance increase during the eleventh century under King Canute and William the Conqueror. Cheating men ante up out of their wallets, but unfaithful wives lose all they possess, plus their noses and ears. The cutting off of appendages reaches a climax under William the Conqueror, with castration as the recommended punishment for men.

1069 During a war with Russia, Boleslaw II, king of Poland, faces a morale problem within his army's ranks. The left-behind wives of his officers are whiling away their lonely hours with the staff left to serve them at home. When rumors reach the front, the officers run home, many to find their wives pregnant. Boleslaw responds by abandoning the servant-sired chil-

dren in the forest and forcing the ladies to wet-nurse puppies. As an added punishment the women have to carry their furry "offspring" at all times. If a dog is man's best friend, then a puppy must be woman's. Carrying the cuddly creatures becomes a fad and soon no one can tell who is being punished.

c. 1100 Byzantium is home to a cult that practices devotion to the Virgin Mary. The idea is picked up by Saint Bernard of Clairvaux who founds abbeys across Europe dedicated to the mother of God. The church isn't too pleased with the devotion to Mary but for the first time since Eve, women are offered a new role model. No longer does woman have to be seen as a temptress. Now she can identify with the

Madonna. The status of women gets a slight boost. Men don't mind. Those afraid of the wrath of Jesus can get around it by asking his mom to intercede.

c. 1100 Meanwhile in southern France the Albigensian heresy gains strength. Known as Cathari, this sect believes that life is evil. Children are forbidden, but sex isn't. Only the perfecti, the church elders, practice celibacy. Any sexual activity that doesn't result in procreation is allowed. Though redemption is merely by purification and abstinence, it's a practice that's usually put off until you're on your deathbed. Homosexual and heterosexual anal intercourse is the preferred sexual activity. The French refer to the heresy as *bougerie*. In time the English pick up on the French word and change it to *buggery,* meaning anal intercourse.

c. 1100 The Aztec civilization emerges. Another society that has an insatiable need for warriors, polygamy and concubines are allowed, but women are expected to remain faithful. Penalties for sexual transgressions are harsh. Marriage has to be with someone outside the clan. Anything else is considered incestuous and punishable with death by hanging. Men can have their flings, but not with married women. Adulterers are looking at the death penalty also. The worst treated are homosexuals and transvestites. The passive partner is tied to a log; his entrails are removed and buried in ash. Then he is set on fire. The active partner is covered with ash, tied to a log, and left to die. Heterosexual anal intercourse is practiced, however, most likely as a form of birth control.

c. 1100 Putting on the gloves to debate what constitutes a marriage are Gratian, an Italian

> *Give me chastity*
> *—but not yet.*
>
> Saint Augustine

monk, and Peter Lombard, bishop of Paris. Gratian proposes that consent enters a couple into *matrimonium initiatum* (begins the marriage), but *copula carnalis* (sex) ratifies it *(matrimonium ratum)*. The church isn't too pleased with this interpretation, since it would invalidate the marriage of Joseph and Mary at the time of the birth of Jesus. Lombard says no, no. Marriage is achieved *per verba de praesenti,* by consent in the present tense. "I *will* marry you" is a betrothal—a promise that is binding but breakable. "I *do* marry you" is consent. Say it and you're hitched permanently. Just like Joseph and Mary. The church smiles and accepts Lombard's view.

1123 Still can't get those priests to stop marrying! This year the Lateran Council pushes one step further: It forbids marriage to any priest once ordained. But it doesn't say anything about keeping a concubine.

c. 1174 Eleanor of Aquitaine, queen of France (and later queen of England), promulgates the rules of courtly love. This game between married noble ladies and their wanna-be lovers has its foundation in Arabia, where the mystique of veiled women allows men to write love songs to their fantasies. European women are much more

**Succubi cause men's wet dreams in order to steal semen, then turn into incubi
and invade women's sleep to deposit the seed.**

socialized so that mystique is created by putting a woman on a pedestal. The basic principle is that love cannot happen between a husband and wife because marriages are arranged and held together by duty. Love is achieved through four steps. First, the lover worships his lady from afar, hiding around corners to catch a glimpse of her, almost stalking her. He declares himself to her and enters the second stage—waiting until the lady makes up her mind. She rebuffs him, for frustration and tension build love. With humility, perfect courtesy, and gentleness, he does everything he can to change her mind. When and if she accepts him, he becomes her suitor, a status that can last for years, until he becomes her lover. Love is categorized. Pure love is the melding of minds and hearts but

no physical possession. Mixed love is pure love with sex added. Licentious desire, sex for the sake of having sex, is evil and unwanted and termed False love. Once this love game is consummated it makes them guilty of adultery. But cuckolding the husband is part of the game. All of this goes on at a time when the church is at the zenith of its power.

c. 1250 The church has a new spokesman against the evils of sex in Thomas Aquinas who, legend says, once drove a would-be seductress out of his chambers with a flaming piece of wood and then used it to burn a cross into his door. Aquinas sees a woman as a man gone wrong, a genetic defect. Woman needs man for everything. Man needs her only to re-create himself and, even in sex, is the active partner (the one on top). Therefore, women must defer to men. Thomas also sees any other than the man-on-top-get-it-over-with-quick-we're-only-making-a-baby sex as a sin against God and against nature. His tsk-tsk list includes hetero-sexual oral and anal sex, various positions, bes-tiality, and masturbation. He gives the church reason to hate homosexuality, using the logic that if sex is for procreation, then homosexual-ity is heretical. Prostitution is tolerated simply because it allows men to leave decent women alone. Masturbation rates lower than dreaded fornication because there's no chance for a baby to be made. With Thomas's logic, rape becomes less of a sin than whacking off because there's a chance for conception.

1275 At the age of fifty-three Angela de Labarthe declares that she has had sex with the devil and has given birth to his child, a monster infant with a wolf's head and serpent's tail. Angela is promptly burned at the stake. The devil is a symbol for evil and temptation. But over the years he has taken on form and his home now has a location. Thomas Aquinas declares that hell is in the bowels of the earth. Satan appears as a man, a monster, an animal, prowling everywhere, lurking in the shadows, wreaking havoc, and creating evil. The fear of Satan is greatest at night when his servants turn themselves into succubi, beautiful women who invade the sleep of men, cause wet dreams, take the semen, then turn into incubi (male succubi), invade women's sleep, and deposit their seed. There are cults devoted to Diana—the goddess of women, identified as an incubus by Pope John XXII—who worship four times a year. During their nocturnal ritual, a man posing as

the devil straps on a metal phallus and has sex with witches. Belief in the power of sorcery spreads. When the Black Death rolls around in the next century, it creates mass hysteria. Over the years thousands of women are executed for witchcraft.

1295 Marco Polo returns to Venice after a twenty-six-year journey to the east, telling tales so astounding that he's asked to recant them on his deathbed. The stories of strange lands where prostitution flourishes and virginity is an impediment to marriage are not believed and earn Polo the nickname "Marco Millions." Polo spends a year in a Genoese jail, where he dic-tates a book describing his journey through Lebanon, Mesopotamia, the Persian Gulf, Kashgar, the Gobi Desert, and Shangtu, where he and his father and uncle were guests of the great khan. The khan's officers, he relates, rounded up one hundred young girls from whom forty were chosen and checked to make sure they didn't snore, have bad breath, smell, or have imperfections. These women were put into His Majesty's service, "where they are to perform every service that is required of them, and he does with them as he likes." Polo never recants his tales, only confessing that he hasn't told half of what he saw.

c. 1300 Prostitution flourishes in Europe. Brothels find no lack of employees among women unable to support themselves or whose creditors have forced them into service. Parents barter their daughters to pay off debts. Most brothels are licensed and taxed, adding valu-able revenue to the towns. Important customers are often treated free of charge. When Hungary's King Sigismund and his men visit Ulm, he's so pleased he publicly thanks his

Rubber duckies aren't the only things that make bath time fun. Mixed bathing in Europe is an opportunity for socializing as well as cleansing.

hosts. The church considers the needs of the common man and looks upon these visits as venial rather than mortal sins—at least until the sixteenth century when the syphilis epidemic changes all of this.

Rub-a-Dub-Dub, the Whole Town's in the Tub

c. 1300 Public bathing is nothing new in Europe where bathhouses are heated a few days a week and locals are informed by town criers when the water reaches the right temperature. Laws are set to establish what condition of undress people can take to the streets in, since many show up in various states of nudity. The site of socializing, haircutting, drinking, gambling, and flirting, the baths are staffed by maids clad in see-through white dresses who scrub the patrons' backs, wash their hair, and pat them dry. Affronted moralists get their way only when officials realize the baths help spread epidemics and close them down.

c. 1300 In the Inca civilization the emperor enjoys one right denied to his subjects: the right to marry his sister. This ensures royal descent. Should his sister prove to be barren he marries another sister or a cousin. Should any other Inca marry his sister, he's punished by having his eyes plucked out. Polygamy is the rule for everyone including the king, who usually has a few concubines stored away as well. While virginity at marriage is no big deal for either the man or woman, once a person is married, adultery has its consequences based on class distinction. If an upper-class woman has a romance with a commoner, they are both executed. People from different provinces are tortured for their trysts. Locals can get it on, but the husband maintains the right to kill his wife as long as he does it in cold blood; murder in the heat of passion is a serious crime, and the penalty for it is execution. Another punishable transgression is rape, for which a heavy stone is dropped on the man's shoulders for the first offense; death is the punishment for a second rape unless the victim agrees to an immediate marriage. Homosexuals are put to death but that's not enough to satisfy

SEE FOR YOURSELF!

TRIVIA

Queen Christina of Sweden (1626–1689) is rumored to be a hermaphrodite. She helps fuel the rumors by hunting, excelling in archery, and wearing her hair short. Frustrated by not being able to quell the gossip, she purposely tips over her carriage and tumbles to the ground with her skirts above her waist. Those who run to the queen's rescue are invited to "Come closer and convince yourself that I am no hermaphrodite." After abdicating the throne, she dresses in male attire and leaves Sweden under the name of Count Dohna.

Inca law. To be sure that the behavior doesn't spread, the homosexuals' families are also killed and their houses burned.

c. 1300 Things aren't too different in Russia than in the rest of the world. The woman is under her husband's thumb, but should she rebel and kill him, she's buried alive up to her neck and left to die. Girls are married off at age twelve, boys at fourteen. Virginity is a must. During the marriage ceremony the father of the bride gives the husband a *durak* (a whip) to remind the wife who wears the pants. The Russian church is morally strict. Sex during Lent, the forty days before Easter, is a big *nyet*.

1347 Queen Johanna of Naples founds a bordello in Avignon. Customers are warned that bad manners, disturbances, or scaring the girls will result in punishment. Girls are medically checked weekly; they are given food, shelter, clothing, and a wage and must spend time in prayer. Jews and heathens are not allowed on the premises—only "good Christian men." Hours are curtailed during Easter week.

1382 John Wycliffe, an English reformer and doctor of theology, translates the Bible into English to make Scripture available to any Englishman who can read. In his translation he uses the word "sex," the first time it appears in the Bible:

> *"Of alle thingis havynge sowle of ony flesh, two thow shalt brynge into the ark, that maal sex and femaal lyven with thee."*

c. 1400 In an era when marriage is a uniting of holdings, divorce is forbidden, and separate sleeping quarters replace communal bedrooms,

Pope Leo X dies in the throes of passion.

adultery abounds and the Age of Bastards begins. Women achieve equality with men in movement, socializing in pubs, and riding to the hounds. Men promote their sexuality with skintight trousers that show off "swollen members." Though modesty is a must for maidens, illegitimate children are accepted by society as well as families.

c. 1400 The Greek experience is revived in Italy by the Renaissance man, who takes a keen interest in the male body but becomes more bisexual than homosexual. Sodomy laws are in effect, but Florence and Bologna are rife with gay activity. Nobles sleep with pages, artists with their apprentices. Laity and clergy alike question or ignore rigid church dogma in

favor of the hedonistic life. Well into the next century bishops include their mistresses at papal functions. Pope Leo X dies while in the throes of passion with a boy. Pope Paul III earns the moniker "the prince of sodomy." And Spain lightens its punishment for homosexuality. Instead of being castrated and stoned, offenders are simply burned at the stake. Switzerland still dismembers and then incinerates them.

1415 At a time when the papacy is in contention (there are three popes), Pope John XXIII is deposed for "notorious incest, adultery, defilement, homicide and atheism." Some of the charges are trumped up, but while a cardinal at Bologna, he's said to have seduced two hundred virgins, matrons, widows, and nuns.

1453 When the Ottoman Empire replaces the Byzantine Empire rumors of Turkish harems leak out to the Western world. Little truth is contained in the fantasy of a sultan lounging on overstuffed pillows while being fed figs and dates by half-clad beauties. The sultan's mother is in charge of the seraglio. Black eunuchs stand guard and wait for the sultan to make some insignificant gesture toward one of the women. She is then bathed, shaved completely, perfumed, and clothed. When summoned, she enters the sultan's bed from the bottom, slithering her way under the covers until she's face-to-face with him. Whatever money he's carrying is hers, regardless of the sum. If she gets pregnant and delivers a son, she's well taken care of for life. The Turkish harem exists into the twentieth century.

1484 Pope Innocent VIII earns the sobriquet "the honest." He's the first pope to acknowledge his illegitimate children. Father to at least a son and daughter, he celebrates the marriages of his children and grandchildren in the Vatican.

1484 Convents aren't only for nuns who devote themselves to the Lord's work. They also harbor poor women and unmarried daughters. So convents aren't always the chaste places the name implies. This year a convent in Ulm, Germany, is searched. Love letters are confiscated and medical examinations show that most of the nuns are pregnant.

1492 Giulia Farnese, a married woman, gives birth to a daughter. The father is not her husband but Rodrigo Borgia, known to the world as Pope Alexander VI. The papal lothario has fathered a few other offspring, most notably Lucrezia and Cesare Borgia.

1496 All Parisians afflicted with *la grosse vérole,* later known as syphilis, are ordered out of the city. Coming in on the heels of Columbus's return voyage, the origin of syphilis is debated for centuries by the medical profession. It could be the one thing Columbus imported that he shouldn't have or perhaps it had been around as a pox in Europe but in a less virulent form. In either case, invading armies make sure it sweeps through Europe. The French call it *le mal de Naples* because their soldiers are infected during a war with Naples. Italians call it *il morbo Gallico,* the French disease. Poor man, king (Henry VIII, Charles VIII, and Francis I), and pope (Julius II) alike are infected. England is struck in 1496, India in 1498, Poland in 1499, Russia and Scandinavia in 1500. Prostitution is no longer seen as a necessary outlet but as a conduit for the epidemic's spread.

It's Not Just for Procreation Anymore

c. 1520 Martin Luther's reformation is under way. Among other, more serious points of contention with the church in Rome, Luther doesn't believe in celibacy for priests. He views continence as direct opposition to what God has in mind and sees chastity, male and female, as dangerous. Marriage for any man, he says, is as necessary as eating and drinking. And sex isn't just for making babies; it's a part of life. As liberal as he is on this point, when it comes to adultery, his strictness overshadows Rome's. Adultery is a reason for divorce, as is a woman denying sex to her husband. Luther takes away the little progress that women have made, subjecting them to their husbands again. The good wife obeys her husband, listens quietly, and doesn't argue. She cooks. She sews. She raises children. As Luther ages, his temper and tongue grow more caustic. Before he dies he refers to the pope as "a Roman hermaphrodite."

1529 While up on charges of violating the Statute of Praemunire, Cardinal Wolsey is accused of infecting England's Henry VIII with syphilis by whispering in his ear.

1534 John of Leyden, an Anabaptist, takes over the town of Münster. Using Luther's teachings as his foundation, John employs the Old Testament stories of Solomon and David to justify his acceptance of polygamy. Saying "better many wives than many whores," he marries four women and proclaims polygamy the going game in Münster and himself the king of Zion. Within a year the town is recaptured by conservative forces. John and two of his assistants are tied to stakes, their bodies shredded with red-hot pincers, their tongues pulled out, and daggers driven into their hearts.

1536 John Calvin brings his reform to Geneva, Switzerland. Like Luther he favors marriage of clergy although he advises marriage should be avoided as long as they are able to be celibate. Austerity is the key word for Calvin. Simplicity in life, dress, and habits is a must, which lays the groundwork for the Puritan movement. Worldly pleasures and temptations are to be conquered. He rids Geneva of drinking, gambling, and the district devoted to prostitution. Adulterers are driven through the streets and out of town in disgrace. Calvin's views spread to Scotland, the Netherlands, and England.

1545–1564 Rome asserts itself through the Council of Trent, sessions of which sit on and off during this time. Despite the preachings of Luther and Calvin, marriage, Rome insists, is a sacrament that requires banns to be published and parental consent given. Clerical celibacy is no longer a question to be dealt with. It's celibacy for the clergy and chastity for everyone else, with sex only after marriage and only for making babies—period. Furthermore, enough of this Renaissance stuff. All these nude paintings and sculptures—no more. Anything that incites lustful sensations is wrong. Writing or publishing obscene literature is a capital offense in Italy. And prostitution is disgraceful.

1545 Henry VIII shuts down England's brothels. Parliament gave the official thumbs-up to them in 1161. Fear of syphilis and the reformation make this an easy decision for the king. Paris closes its houses in 1560. Germany's Frauenhaus in Ulm, Basel, and Nuremberg are also closed.

Young male sopranos are castrated before their voices and their interests change.

Great Moments in Sex

c. 1550 The Sistine Chapel's papal choir uses *eunuchi*. That's not a type of pasta, it's castrated male sopranos. Women aren't allowed to lend their voices to the best choir in the Western world. Castrati, as they are later called, are recruited once their voices reach full soprano range but before puberty sets in and changes them. One hell of a sales pitch convinces boys that singing for God is better than being able to have children. Or their parents make the decision for them and are remunerated handsomely. The papal choir isn't the only choir that uses castrati. Falsetto singers are so popular that France commercializes the making of deballed singers and exports them to Italy and Spain.

1566 In addition to making homosexuality a capital crime, Pope Pius V expels prostitutes from the Papal States. Businessmen complain that the decree will depopulate the city, so Pius closes his eyes to a small red-light district, but he offers assistance to any woman who wants out of the world's oldest profession.

1585 – 1590 Pope Sixtus V wants to stamp out lascivious conduct. To show that the word "tolerance" is not in his vocabulary, he makes a young woman watch while he hangs her mother, who sold her into prostitution, and he burns a priest and a young boy accused of homosexual acts.

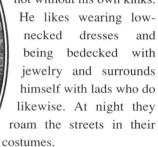

Hedonism lurks behind society's prim facade in the seventeenth century.

1588 Legal prostitution ended in France in 1560. To make sure hangers-on get the point Henry III decrees all harlots must leave Paris within twenty-four hours or face a public flogging and have their heads shaved. In Toulouse, officials are even more serious. Harlots are stripped, bound, put in an iron cage, and dunked in the river three times. Should they survive they spend the rest of their lives in jail. Henry's not without his own kinks. He likes wearing low-necked dresses and being bedecked with jewelry and surrounds himself with lads who do likewise. At night they roam the streets in their costumes.

c. 1600 Manners and gentility are chic this century in Europe. But behind the prim facade lurks an age of hedonism. Sex is a natural appetite and this age is an all-you-can-eat meal. Rationalism dictates that since marriages are business affairs, romantic dalliances are where you find love. A husband always has something on the side, and if a wife has her husband's unexpressed approval, so does she. To all appearances the home remains a congenial place for raising legal offspring. Virginity is a must for sexual tension, acting as a fox to the hounds. In vogue are discreet masquerades, where masked soon-to-be-lovers tease with whispers, squeezes, and kisses. When he wins her approval, they make l'amour, she with her mask on, he with his off. Such bawdy affairs can bring scandal to blue bloods. If caught, men are seen as lecherous, but envied. Women are tarts, and they are shamed. Frenchwomen must be especially careful. If she becomes an embarrassment, her hubby can abduct her and put her in a convent. He has two years to decide whether or not he wants her back.

1620 The Puritans arrive in America with their own moral code. Any good in a person is far outweighed by the evil that lurks within. Sex is natural but it's a temptation to overcome. Premarital sex brings damnation, spiritually and physically. What God is going to do to your soul is foreshadowed by what the church elders are going to do to your body. Flogging, branding, pillorying, banishment, public confession, monetary fines, and the death penalty await fornicators, adulterers, sodomites, homosexuals, and perverts. And no sex on Sundays even if you're married. Despite their dour outlook Puritans are realists. They never deny that passion exists or that sex feels good. Celibacy never enters the equation, though sex is for procreation. It's hard going for the new colonists. Men outnumber women, and sin is rife.

1633 English Puritan William Prynne publishes his *Histriomastix, the Players Scourge,* attacking the immorality of the theater. He states that all actresses are whores, an unfortunate remark, since Queen Henrietta Maria, wife of Charles I, is rehearsing a part in a court masque. Prynne is barred from practicing law, fined 5,000 pounds and sentenced to life imprisonment but not before he is pilloried and has both ears cut off. He is released from prison in 1640.

1635 France tries its hand at curtailing prostitution again. Though royalty and the upper class are serviced, Louis XIII outlaws prostitution, decreeing that prostitutes should be "whipped, shaved, and banished." Pimps are sent to the galleys for life.

1639 Mary Mandame is the first woman in the American colonies to be forced to wear a badge of dishonor. A citizen of Plymouth, Massachusetts, Mary is charged with "dallyance diverse tymes with Tinsin, an Indian." For her anti-Puritanical behavior she is sentenced to be "whipt at a cart tayle," and to "weare a badge upon her left sleeve during her aboad" in town. Failure to wear the badge will get Mary "burned in the face with a hott iron."

1650 The Congress of Franconia adopts a resolution that demands bigamy in Germany. The Thirty Years' War depletes the population by nearly seven million, and leaves Germany and its women wanting for able-bodied men. The Franconia legislation allows every male "to marry two wives; and each and every male is earnestly reminded, and shall often be warned from the pulpit, to so comport himself in this manner." Men under sixty are not allowed to enter monasteries. Taxes are imposed on single women. This is one law that men don't mind obeying. By 1700 Germany's population has returned to prewar numbers and monogamy returns.

1657 Japan builds a new capital, Edo, which includes Yoshiwara, a district dedicated to prostitution. In Japan the oldest profession has long been supervised by the government and isolated in walled-in areas on city outskirts. Shimabara, near Kyoto, is the largest quarter where *yujo*s practice their trade. The ambience of these quar-

Great Moments in Sex

ters is also a lure. Men enjoy the elegance, restaurants, festivals, and entertainment as well as physical fun.

1700 The eighteenth century sees a change in marriage. Keeping a family costs money, and men postpone nuptials, sometimes permanently. Later marriage reduces procreation time, so families become smaller. And men begin to marry women their own age. Love hasn't fully entered the marriage ceremony yet, but mom-and-pop businesses have, and men are looking for helpmates. Not everyone is saving his or her virginity for the wedding night. Traveling becomes more common, and itinerant businessmen, who may not pass this way again, feel no need to be cautious about one-night stands with local women. Maids do more than clean their masters' manors. Toward the end of the 1700s romance blooms and it becomes important to feel some emotion for the person you marry.

c. 1700 A homosexual subculture emerges in London. The big city affords anonymity, and its size allows some establishments to cater exclusively to that clientele. These pubs and coffeehouses, known as "molly houses," are found in other large English cities such as Bath, York, and Bristol. Sodomy laws are in effect but are seldom enforced. Male lovers meet in parks and walks. Masters take liberties with their servants. Gay aristocrats use their wives as cover. He-whores act like women in private but revert to masculine roles in public. The word "effeminate" once referred to heterosexual men who preferred the company of women. As homosexuals become fancier, the definition swings to them. Overt homosexuality isn't confined to England. France and the Netherlands have gay subcultures, too. Lisbon is the site of transvestite balls. In the latter half of the eighteenth century London becomes the capital of lesbianism.

1714 Adulterous Roman Catholic men no longer must name their paramour when confessing their trespasses. The requirement is done away with after too many priests contact the named women for their own pleasure.

1772 Count Donatien Alphonse François de Sade, a.k.a. the Marquis de Sade, is given the death penalty for poisoning prostitutes with an overdose of cantharides (Spanish fly) and assaulting a prostitute. De Sade brings the woman to his garden pavilion where he strips her, beats her, and cuts her with a knife. The next day he reopens the wounds. She manages to break free and runs to the police. The Count entered the army at the age of fourteen and regularly saw floggings, rapes, and assorted tortures, which may account for his perversion. After being condemned, he flees to Italy and stays there until 1777 when he returns to Paris. He's arrested again and jailed, only to escape a year later. Recaptured, he's sent to the Bastille where he writes the novels that make him infamous. His family succeeds in getting the death penalty overturned, but they have him placed in the Charenton Lunatic Asylum, where he is committed as an incurable in 1803. He dies there in 1814.

c. 1776 Ben Franklin pens an open letter to King George III in his newspaper, the *Pennsylvania Gazette,* complaining of the prostitutes exported to the colonies. It's England's custom to clear overcrowded prisons by sending criminals to the colonies. Franklin proposes sending American rattlesnakes to live in the king's royal gardens as a fair exchange.

Off with His Head!

1777 Louis XVI and Marie Antoinette, who were married in 1770, are finally able to consummate their marriage. Until now Louis had a problem with the tightness of his foreskin that made lovemaking painful. Various advisers, anxious for an heir, persuade the king to have the quick, simple operation that would rectify the situation. He does so this year. The next time Louis's head goes on the block, it's far more serious. He's guillotined in 1793 during the French Revolution.

1778 The last person to receive the death penalty for bestiality in Sweden is beheaded and burned at the stake. The usual penalties range from flogging to the aforementioned chop-and-light. Although bestiality isn't confined to Sweden, the Swedes do take a dim view of it, executing over six hundred people in the last forty years. It isn't just the act that repulses Swedes. Mating with animals is high on the list of things to do at witches' Sabbaths. The belief is that anyone who happens to witness the act of bestiality, whether innocently or not, also sins. The ultimate fear is having an animal born with the offender's facial characteristics. His wife dreads having the animal's body fluids mixed into hers through sex with her husband and giving birth to a baby with animal features. The animal that receives the offender's attention is put to death.

1792 Mary Wollstonecraft publishes *Vindication of the Rights of Women,* demanding respect for women. Wollstonecraft advises fellow females to give up their subservient, weak-willed ways, which encourage male domination. She finds fault with the educational system, which doesn't prepare women for jobs that would allow them financial freedom and independence. She demands acknowledgment of women's desires, asserts that they are as strong as men's, and they deserve to have physical satisfaction during sex. Any woman in an unhappy marriage is nothing more than a legal prostitute. Though she rails against the double standard of chastity, she is a rationalist at heart. Marriages, she declares, should be made with the head, not the heart.

1792 Another religious import from England arrives in America: Ann Lee and her Shaker sect. The death of each of her five children soon after birth and a near-death experience during her last pregnancy have convinced her that sex is the source of all evil. Ann renounces the "lusts of the flesh." She has a few visions, in one of which she sees Adam and Eve making love, and decides that celibacy is the answer. Marriage is condemned, so any couple who wants to join the Shakers must disavow their marriage and live as brother and sister. How do you get more Shakers? Converts. There will always be converts. Ann declares that God is hermaphroditic and is capable of reproducing himself without all that revolting touching, as was man before the Fall. What brings attention to the Shakers is their ritual dance. Starting off slowly during services, the leaping to and fro, spinning, trotting, clapping, and convulsing till the early morning hours is said to be an outlet for pent-up sexual energy.

1798 Thomas Malthus publishes his *Essay on the Principle of Population,* warning that overpopulation will strip the earth of its resources. The human race needs to take steps now to control its numbers. He cites the poor as the major problem but doesn't see contraception as the answer. A firm believer in continence, Malthus promotes chastity, an end to early marriage, restraint after marriage, and an end to the welfare system to get things under control. If not, Mother Nature will step in with disease and famine. He loves the free enterprise system but says that raising the salaries of the poor makes it possible for them to have more children they can't afford. His ideas aren't taken seriously at first. But by 1801, when the population census is higher than statisticians predict, politicians jump on the Malthus bandwagon. In the late nineteenth century, neo-Malthusians use his work to promote birth control.

c. 1800 The same mind-set that gave rise to the right of first night is prevalent in the American South. Plantation owners take it one step further. Not content with the first night, they take any night they please. White wives are pure, untouchable, and accorded all southern gallantry. Sexual fulfillment comes from the black slaves, who are considered wild animals, less than human, but above the ape. This idea is based on the seventeenth-century belief that blacks are descendants of Noah's son, Ham. One reason for owning slaves is to create more slaves. Blacks are bred with blacks. But lighter-skinned blacks sell for more money on the auction block. Mulatto girls bring a good price when sold for prostitution. Never mind that many bear a striking resemblance to the overseer or the plantation owner. They are whipped, bought, and sold, and their families are torn apart as if they are complete strangers. Southern men defend these practices, saying that in the South, unlike the North, there is little public prostitution, no free-love communities, and no polygamy problems. Only the Civil War puts an end to the widespread abuse of black women.

1804 The French Revolution has shredded families and morals alike. Now Napoleon needs social order, so he reestablishes the Catholic church in his country to achieve his goal. Under the Napoleonic Code husbands have full authority over wives, children, and property. An unmarried woman has full civil rights, but when she says "I do" she relinquishes everything. Adultery is forbidden to both husband and wife but while she can divorce him only if he brings a concubine into her home, he can divorce her, put her in solitary confinement, or, if he catches her in the act, kill her. Once again marriages are arranged by parents. Romance and love matches are out. Although Napoleon believes polygamy for men would be fine, he won't allow it. He also won't allow divorce after ten years of marriage. By 1826, divorce, for all practical purposes, is abolished and stays that way until 1884. It takes an act of Parliament to grant a divorce, a time-consuming and expensive effort. Only 317 divorces are granted between 1801 and 1859.

**The French in love? Better be.
Divorce is nearly impossible.**

1806 A higher class of streetwalker appears in Philadelphia. Where once twenty-five cents would get a man any affection except for the final act, these new ladies of the evening stroll the avenues in pairs, well dressed and carefully groomed. When propositioned, they will take the customer home for two dollars.

**Queen Victoria's advice to women on sex:
Lie back and think of England.**

1837 The lady whose name is used to describe an era of repression unlike any seen before takes the throne after the death of her father. Queen Victoria, a prim, proper mother of nine and devoted wife of Prince Albert, doesn't begin the Victorian era. That swing started at the beginning of the century. But she does personify it. Where Puritans regard sexuality as something to overcome, Victorians repress sexuality altogether. It's not "nice girls don't do that." It's "good people don't have those feelings." Women require no sexual satisfaction. Men are expected to control themselves. You don't answer to God; you answer to your neighbors. The key word is respectability. The only time a woman gets close to sex is to become pregnant. Women's health is put in jeopardy because doctors can't examine them unless a chaperon is present, and then the exam is conducted through clothing. Since even normal sex is wrong, any deviation is an abomination. Men are told from the pulpit and by pro-

fessionals not to press their wives for sex. Victorian manners trickle down to the lowest classes and spread across the Western world. What happens to all that repressed energy? It rears its head. What men won't force upon their pristine wives is had with prostitutes. And they can always travel to Italy, where love is less inhibited.

1842 Joseph Smith, the founder of the Mormon church, advocates polygamy for his followers, saying multiple marriages are divinely inspired. How do you get women to go along with it? By saying that virgins, prostitutes, and spinsters are all barred from heaven whereas marriage is for eternity. Only 25 percent of Mormon communities practice polygamy, and there are women who leave in disgust. But most women defend the practice. A man can marry as many women as he can support, and he must treat all wives equally. There's no courtship, no romance. A simple agreement secures the engagement. Adultery, promiscuity, and contraceptives are forbidden. The practice of polygamy isn't publicly confirmed for ten years and comes to an end in 1890 when Utah is considered for statehood.

1857 New Orleans has a problem. Prostitution is so rampant that the city fathers have to do something about it. So they do: they tax it. All prostitutes must have a license. One brothel owner, Emma Pickett, isn't happy about paying the city government. She sues, and the courts find for her. The ladies celebrate for a week.

1864 In an effort to check the epidemic spread of gonorrhea and syphilis, the English Parliament passes the Contagious Diseases Act, making known prostitutes and any woman suspected of prostitution subject to medical checks. This law applies only to garrison towns in an effort to control venereal disease, which is rapidly infecting the army. Victorian repression has made prostitution a booming business. Women are plucked off the streets for behaving suspiciously and given a medical inspection that is so unhygienic that doctors are accused of causing more cases than they cure. Johns are let off the hook; they are not compelled to seek treatment, and most go home to infect their wives and unborn children. Women who are diagnosed positive are sent to Lock Hospital for three months and registered as prostitutes when released, even if they aren't. Proper ladies cry out against these laws (two more are enacted in 1866 and 1869), saying that vaginal examinations are an affront to a woman's decency. Brothel owners rise up against the gentry. They see the law as protecting their self-interest. It's no surprise when the upright ladies win. The law is repealed in 1885.

1874 The Women's Christian Temperance Union is formed in Cleveland, Ohio. The ladies are disgusted. It's bad enough that home-brewed alcohol has been replaced by store-bought bottles, on which men can squander a family's hard-earned money. But these evil men, their passions excited by foul spirits, come home and take advantage of their wives. If women have to conform to society's expectations, then so do men. Understand that these women don't advocate a loosening of strictures for themselves. After a couple of generations of Victorian morality, women have accepted a lack of sexuality. They want men to be like women: pure, gentrified, and above reproach. It makes sense for the WCTU to join forces with the suffrage movement. After all, men make the laws that affect them. A parallel movement rages in England where their motto is "Votes for Women and Purity for Men."

1878 Pope Leo XIII puts an end to employing castrati in the papal choir at the Sistine Chapel. Perhaps he's read Deuteronomy (23:1): "He that is wounded in the stones, or hath his privy member cut off, shall not enter into the congregation of the Lord."

1884 Friedrich Engels writes *Origin of the Family Private Property and the State* to show how capitalism keeps women subservient. Monogamy is a man's way of making a woman his property, and it gives him the ability to create children "of undisputed paternity" who inherit from the father and perpetuate the system. Capitalistic sex is an act of economic dependency, since marriage is required for it. Sex should be based on the feelings between a man and woman, as desire is natural. Self-denial is absurd.

1885 W. T. Stead, editor of the *Pall Mall Gazette,* writes a series of articles on prostitution in London. Focusing on white slavery (enforced prostitution) and child prostitution, the articles raise a furor. Stead and his staff of reporters research the articles on the streets. To illustrate a point, Stead buys a thirteen-year-old virgin from her parents (he sends her to the Salvation Army in Paris for safekeeping). Stories of sound-proofed brothels dedicated to deflowering virgins, of slum children sold by their parents, of children three to five years old chloroformed before being violated, and of police involvement in the slave traffic shock the sensibilities of readers. The *Pall Mall Gazette* sells more papers than ever and irritates the police. Parliament hears the outcry from voters and passes the Criminal Law Amendment Act, which has been languishing for years. To get even with Stead, police get the parents of the child he purchased to file charges against him. The editor spends three months in jail; his reporters serve one to six months. Stead later dies on the *Titanic*.

1885 England passes the Criminal Law Amendment Act. Besides raising the age of consent and making brothel keeping and pimping illegal (prostitution itself is exempt from the law), it criminalizes homosexual oral sex. The law applies only to male homosexuals. Queen Victoria refuses to consider that women participate in such a thing.

1898 Japan passes its Civil Code of 1898. Trying to entrench traditional family values, the code puts an end to concubinage, which elevates the position of the wife. It also takes women in general down a couple of pegs by extolling the virtues of premarital chastity, obedience, and submissiveness to husbands. Segregated from school age on, men are considered superior to women. To show who wears the pants in the family it's considered good form for the husband to berate his wife in front of guests. Adding to emotional distance are the small living quarters shared with the groom's parents. Couples must share their bed with children, and paper-thin walls don't add to privacy. Sex is a quick sprint with little or no foreplay, usually from the rear position to keep the noise down.

1916 Margaret Sanger opens the first birth control clinic in America in the Brownsville section of Brooklyn. As a girl whose mother bore ten children and died young, and later as a maternity nurse who saw countless botched abortions, early deaths, and unwanted pregnancies, she became convinced that birth control information should be disseminated to women. Sanger tours Europe to find methods of contraception and

brings them back to the United States. On the clinic's first day, 140 grateful women stand in line outside the door. Within the first month, it's closed down as a "public nuisance" and Sanger is arrested. During the next decade she sways public opinion and opens a second clinic in 1925. With religious groups against her, she's arrested again. Finally in 1930, the court rules that doctors may advise *married* women on the use of contraceptives. Sanger dedicates her life to the issue of birth control, founding the International Planned Parenthood Federation in the 1940s and working with Gregory Pincus in the 1950s to develop the Pill.

1917 When the Bolsheviks take over Russia they institute Karl Marx and Friedrich Engels's philosophy of sex. Monogamy is a male capitalistic tool used to enslave women for the purpose of having children to whom they can leave their property. Women are oppressed by men when they should be contributing their talents to the state. Sex should not be equated with marriage but with reciprocal non-binding love. Only civil marriages are recognized, and the wife does not have to take her husband's name. Marriages are easily annulled if there are no children. When there are, a court decides. Houses are built without kitchens since women are in the workplace and everyone is supposed to eat at state-owned restaurants. Lenin warns that sexual license in the name of Marxism can go too far. Apparently it does. By 1930 the emphasis returns to the family and the suppression of sex, since all that exercise can rob a body of energy needed for the state's work. Divorce laws are tightened, abortion is made illegal, and kitchens are installed in houses. By the 1950s, sex is so repressed that Nikita Khrushchev is shocked when he sees the can-can performed on an American movie set.

1920s The first youth rebellion takes place on college campuses as flappers toss away their corsets, bob their hair, raise their hemlines, drink with the boys, tell off-color jokes, smoke, and party till dawn. Sheikhs, only too happy with their new women, don raccoon coats, drink hard, and become overtly romantic. The college crowd has a new weapon in its sexual arsenal: the automobile. Its rumble seat is perfect for the new pastime—necking and petting parties. Hickies are as numerous as raised eyebrows. Preachers take to the pulpit to condemn bobbed hair, disgraceful women, and lascivious dances. Religious groups say that youngsters are damaging "the stability of our American civilization." The older generation is aghast. But the college campus is the place to be.

1922 Baltimore opens the first public clinic in the United States to treat venereal disease. The social stigma keeps many sufferers from seeking treatment, exacerbating the problem. While wealthy whites can afford the physicians who are willing to attend them, most doctors and hospitals refuse to see VD sufferers of any class or race. In 1922 alone the Baltimore clinic helps 13,000 patients who come in for forty weeks of painful injections of arsenicals and heavy metals. Because the clinic treats mostly poor people, and because the government draws its statistics from the clinic's records, syphilis is viewed mainly as a problem among black people.

Flappers take to short hair, short skirts, and rumble seats.

1937 The *New York Times* creates a "Sex crimes" entry in its index to categorize the nearly 150 articles it published about the subject this year. Loosening mores and a higher reader interest in sexual offenses are reflected in the number of newspapers and national magazines publishing these stories.

1942 Nazi Germany makes all homosexual activity a crime punishable by death. Sodomy has been a crime since 1871, and the Nazis have sporadically campaigned against deviance. It isn't until Ernst Röhm, one of Hitler's inner circle and a known homosexual, is ousted and executed that the sentence for thousands of gays is death in a concentration camp. Hitler also sets up a school for future brides for his Schutzstaffel (the SS). These Aryan girls must have fair complexions and be at least five feet eight. The goal is to legalize only eugenically correct marriages.

1947 Indian leader Mahatma Gandhi admits that in order to test his celibacy he takes nude women to bed with him. In 1906 the married Gandhi decided that sex interfered too much with his life's work, so he took the vow of *brahmachari* and became celibate.

1950 The Chinese Marriage Law appears to put women on a more even par with men. But the state uses the law to get information by setting up complaint meetings where women are urged to vent their feelings against their husbands and the husbands' relatives and to tell family secrets. This tears the fabric of the traditional Chinese family and causes many women to lose face and commit suicide or be killed by their husbands.

As in the USSR, communism puts sex on the back burner, teaching that the state comes first. By 1955 the damage to the family is so severe that party members once again extol the virtues of being a "family woman."

1960s Openly rebelling against the establishment and the undeclared war in Vietnam, baby boomers usher in an era of free love. They set out to rid themselves of racism, classism, sexism, the double standard, and their parents' approval, and they develop a do-your-own-thing mentality. Sex is fun, to be had as often as desired with whomever you please and pleases you. Saving yourself for marriage is passé. Experimenting with positions, clitoral stimulation, and oral sex becomes fadlike. Hedonism is the newest sport and it's played out on college campuses. The institution of marriage seems to be on its last legs as couples opt to live together, the divorce rate soars, and alternative lifestyles are accepted. The boomers number 73 million

Mahatma Gandhi practices celibacy by sleeping with nude women.

Great Moments in Sex

strong. Their sheer numbers are enough to drive the cultural change.

1967 England decriminalizes sodomy. Consenting homosexuals are free to make love in private without fear of arrest. But they can't join Her Majesty's military service.

1970 Following the example of the civil rights movement and the women's movement, homosexuals come out of the closet and demand equal rights, using "Gay is good" as a slogan. Staging protests, demonstrations, and parades, activists introduce the plight of the homosexual to middle America. While personalizing homosexuality helps its acceptance, there's a rapid rise in violence against gays, sometimes with little or no penalty for the criminal.

1976 So what does the Vatican think of everything that's going on? Not much. Pope Paul VI issues the *Declaration on Certain Questions Concerning Sexual Ethics,* which allows no justification for gay behavior, masturbation, or any sexual relations outside of marriage. Ten years later the Vatican holds the line that homosexuals must reorient themselves or lead sexually inactive lives.

1984 Gaetan Dugas, a.k.a. Patient Zero, dies. The Centers for Disease Control in Atlanta estimates that Dugas, an extremely handsome and physically fit airline steward from Canada, is one of the first half dozen homosexual men to get and transmit AIDS in North America. Diagnosed with Kaposi's sarcoma, a skin cancer associated with AIDS, Dugas brags that he has at least 250 sex partners a year, many of whom he finds in bathhouses in San Francisco,

New York, and Los Angeles. Forty of the first 248 AIDS victims are connected to Dugas. Even when he's informed that he's responsible for infecting others, Dugas refuses to stop having unprotected sex. AIDS becomes a worldwide epidemic. Initially thought of as a gay disease, AIDS soon strikes the heterosexual community. In 1986 the surgeon general recommends offering sex education to schoolchildren nine years old and up that includes guidelines on AIDS protection. By 1993 over a half million Americans carry the disease.

1985 What syphilis did to brothels in the sixteenth and seventeenth centuries, AIDS is doing to the homosexual bathhouses. Bathhouses are popular gathering places where gay men meet and have sex. At first warnings are posted against the dangers of oral and anal sex. After years of heated debate, San Francisco closes its bathhouses. New York orders bathhouses, sex clubs, and porno shops to stop permitting on-site sex or be shut down.

1986 After a one-year study, the attorney general's Commission on Pornography releases its findings in a 1,900-page report, claiming that pornography causes sexual violence against women and children. Recommendations of the commission include aggressive enforcement of antipornography laws, extending laws into new areas, and lifetime probation for child pornographers. In 1970, another government commission found no relationship between porn and violence. This year's panel insists that during that time the rise of cable TV, the availability of X-rated videos, the accessibility of pornographic material through the Internet, and the proliferation of adult bookstores changed the outlook. The attorney general's commission, composed of

seven men and four women, come under attack for their right-wing views even though they urge the elimination of restrictions on porn for adults.

1994 President Bill Clinton calls for the resignation of Surgeon General Joycelyn Elders after she endorses teaching masturbation to school-children. Speaking at the United Nations on World AIDS Day, the surgeon general is asked if she would promote self-satisfaction to discourage school-age children from trying riskier forms of getting off. "With regard to masturbation," she answers, "I think that is something that is a part of human sexuality and a part of something that perhaps should be taught." Elders's string of

"misstatements" during her fifteen months on the job has right-wingers and even the president's own staff calling for her removal.

Sometimes a Cigar Is Not Just a Cigar

1998 President Bill Clinton redefines sex. Former White House intern Monica Lewinsky testifies that she and the prez had ten sexual encounters which included her performing oral sex on him, that he touched her breasts and genitals, and that on one occasion they briefly had genital-to-genital contact, that he used a cigar as a sexual aid, that she had oral-anal contact with him, that he brought her to orgasm manually twice, that she gave him a blow job while he was on the phone with a member of Congress, that her navy blue dress had semen stains on it (DNA results showed the match was 1 out of 7.87 trillion Caucasians), and that they had phone sex on ten to fifteen occasions. The president denies all this under oath, saying that he had no "sexual affair," no "sexual relationship," and no "sexual relations" with her. He does eventually admit to having "inappropriate intimate contact," under the definition of sex as provided in a sexual harassment lawsuit brought against him by Paula Jones. Clinton argues that "any person, reasonable person" would agree with him that oral sex falls outside that definition: since he did not reciprocate the oral sex, Lewinsky had sex but he didn't. Of course, in his later grand jury testimony Clinton also argued about the meaning of the word "is" and about the definition of "alone."

Chapter Three
THE EXPERTS AND THE MANUALS

B.C.

c. 450 Parmenides is one of the first to suggest that lesbianism is biological, natural, and inherent. The Greek philosopher who has an adult male lover, feels the same way about male homosexuality.

c. 400 Plato expounds on the origins of the human race in his *Symposium*. In the beginning there are three sexes: man, woman, and hermaphrodite, each born in a set of two. Primeval human is round with his back and sides forming a circle. He has four arms, four legs, and two privy members, and he moves at a fast pace. Zeus is irritated when primeval humans try to reach heaven. He punishes them by splitting them in half, creating the human form. We spend our lives looking for our other half. "When one of them meets with his other half . . . these are the people who pass their whole lives together . . . and the desire and pursuit of the whole is called love."

c. 350 Women are incomplete men, Aristotle claims. The breakdown begins with menstrual fluids, which lack "the principle of the soul." Semen is a hot soul substance. If the semen remains hot enough inside the cool mother's body, it becomes a boy. If it cools and its goal to become a boy is frustrated, it becomes a girl. A clitoris is an incomplete penis. By the way, women don't need to have an orgasm to become pregnant because they don't emit semen.

c. 200 Chinese "pillow books" are sold in the marketplace as gifts for newlyweds; they're tucked under the bride's pillow. They teach as many as forty-eight positions—some of them improbable—plus the importance of kissing, foreplay, and the need for the man to prepare the woman for sex. Anal sex and oral sex are accepted. The books also stress the importance of not wasting semen, which is considered to be man's vital essence.

Dream a little dream . . . and, Artemidorus says, you may be prosperous, in love, in danger, or just horny.

2 Ovid writes *The Art of Love,* a primer on how to win the woman of your dreams, what to do with her when you get her, and how to get another one. In keeping with Roman law, Ovid warns men away from married women, though he admits that "stolen love" is "the most pleasant." Find a partner at the gladiator games or at fashionable places where opening a conversation is easy. Once contact is made, love letters help, as do covert looks and private signals that convey your passion. Compliments are a must, as is bending over backwards to please her—do you want to go to bed with her or not? Be well groomed. This applies to women as well: "I hardly need warn you to let no rankness as of the goat be beneath your arms, nor your legs be bristling with rough hair." Once the first kiss is given, it's green to go. Techniques and positions are explained, as is the importance of foreplay and a slow buildup. And never come before your partner. Should you wish to have another lover, use different rendezvous points. You don't want your lovers to bump into each other.

A.D.

c. 50 The Stoic philosopher Seneca warns Romans against behavior that is contrary to nature, including hot baths and banquets after sunset. He condemns men dressing effeminately and older men trying to look youthful, because men do these things to appeal as the sexual object of other men. He believes a married woman who has only two lovers is a remarkably faithful wife.

77 In *Natural History,* Pliny sends out the alarm against a menstruating woman. Wine turns to vinegar, seed becomes sterile, and fruit falls from trees under which she stands. She'll blunt razors, rust metal, and take the polish off ivory and mirrors. With just one look, swarms of bees die at once. At least she can get work as an exterminator.

c. 90 Plutarch says it is whorelike for a wife to initiate sex. On the other hand, if a husband takes to rolling in the hay with a lover or a maidservant, the wife shouldn't be upset. She should be relieved he's expressing his licentiousness with another woman.

c. 100 Artemidorus beats Freud to the punch with his book *The Interpretation of Dreams*. Freud uses dreams to uncover the past. Artemidorus uses them to predict the future. With sex dreams, much depends on whether the dreamer plays the active role—doing as opposed to being done to. Dreaming of sex with a willing wife means profit in business. With a prostitute, you'll suffer a minor embarrassment. Dreaming of entering a whorehouse and being able to leave is a good sign. Get stuck in a brothel, you're dying. Make love to a beautiful unknown woman and you'll accomplish something major. If she's ugly, it means the opposite. Having sex with yourself (not masturbation) denotes a major illness or great pain (you can't have sex with yourself without great torture). Kiss your own penis, you'll have kids. Not married? You will be. Sex with a corpse means death for you. Screwing animals? As long as you're the active partner, you'll receive a benefit from that animal. If the animal's the active partner, wake up! Something awful is about to happen. Most important, Artemidorus reminds us, sometimes a sex dream just means you're horny.

c. 116 The final word on women's health is written by Soranus, the leading gynecologist and obstetrician of the day. Flying in the face of common belief, Soranus says intercourse isn't necessary for women to be healthy and there's nothing wrong with virginity. Plus, childbearing isn't all it's cracked up to be. Repeated deliveries make a woman old before her time and lead to premature senility. Periodic abstinence isn't a bad idea. He also believes a woman must have a sexual appetite in order to conceive. Therefore, if she's raped and becomes pregnant she must have enjoyed it, if only on a subconscious level.

c. 170 The famous physician Galen believes oral sex is unnatural although he does understand how men can find fellatio pleasurable. However, cunnilingus is much more disgusting.

c. 200–400 Indian sage Vatsyayana et al pen the *Kama-sutra* to serve as an instruction manual for the Indian bon vivant. It provides instructions on how to kiss, hug, bite, embrace, seduce, perform oral sex, and have intercourse in over thirty positions, many of which require acrobatic ability (the sage Suvarnanabha recommends that they be tried in the buoyancy of water). The manual also gives guidelines on etiquette, home decorating, cooking, obtaining power and wealth through love, and the use of aphrodisiacs. Practical advice on how long a honeymoon couple should take to consummate the marriage (ten days), whether a woman should make the first move (no!), and the importance of matching the size of the penis (the lingam) to vagina (yoni) is also included. The *Kama-sutra* becomes the best known Indian manual and is one of the first to recognize the importance of love. The *Kama-sutra* exempts true lovers from the many rules that are given and suggests that they rely on their instincts.

Thank the Lord for the Nighttime

c. 200 *The Instructor,* by Clement of Alexandria, instructs early Christians on the proper time for sex. Daytime is reserved for devotion to prayer. After supper it's time to cuddle, coo, and copulate—as long as passion and voluptuousness are omitted.

c. 650 Chinese physician Sun Szû-mo includes a chapter entitled "Healthy Sex Life" in his medical work, *Priceless Recipes.* He warns that men over forty lose their potency and once they do, "countless diseases will descend on [them] like a swarm of bees." There is hope in learning the Art of the Bedchamber. A man who abstains from sex too long suffers from boils and ulcers. To bring good health, nurture your vital essence by copulating with ten women in one night without having an orgasm. Don't forget foreplay. If you can get the number of partners up to twelve women in one night— remember, no semen emitted—you will remain young and handsome forever. Keep working your way up. When you get to ninety-three women in one night, you attain immortality. And the respect of every other man on the planet.

c. 900 The supposed conversation between Emperor Huang Ti and his chief female adviser, Su Nü, forms part of the text of the *I Hsin Fang,* a Chinese medical book. Su Nü talks about the five signs of female satisfaction: (1) A flushed face and hot ears indicate she's thinking of making love, which means a man can begin thrusting. (2) Her nipples harden and her nose sweats. Lust is aroused. Thrusting should be limited to five inches. (3) When she lowers her voice and moans, you can thrust at your own pace. (4) When the vulva is fully wet, you may use any thrusting method. (5) When she wraps her legs around you and holds on to you, you should thrust deeply. Western civilization has to wait until the twentieth century to learn these things.

c. 1100 Islamic theologian Ghazzali clarifies why women are less than men. Because Eve ate the forbidden fruit, God punished women in eighteen ways. Among them are menstruation, childbirth, having to marry a stranger and leave her parents, not having rights over her body, being unable to divorce, and having to wait three to four months after a divorce or husband's death before she can remarry. Ghazzali also blames women for all the misfortunes and woes that befall men.

1184 Andreas Capellanus, or Andrew the Chaplain, sets down the rules of courtly love in *Treatise on Love and Its Remedy.* In the first of its three parts, this work explains what love is, how it can be aroused, and who can love (nix on peasants; they rut like animals). The second part lists thirty-one rules for lovers including the following: When made public, love rarely endures. When one lover dies, a two-year period of widowhood is required. It's forbidden to love a woman you wouldn't marry. A new love chases away an old one. One woman can be loved by two men, or one man by two women, but one cannot be in love with two people. The third part informs readers that the first two sections were written in jest. Sex is reserved for marriage only. Women are incapable of loving because they are substandard. Many believe that Andrew wrote the third part because he was a chaplain and an ambitious one.

c. 1400 The Japanese send their daughters into marriage well prepared by giving them the marriage manual of Kaibara. Kaibara, a Confucian scholar, tells women that to have a happy life a wife must live in submission with her husband as her lord, serving him "with all worship" and never disobeying him. The separation of sexes is crucial. No friendship or intimacy must be formed with any other man, nor should she be discontent or jealous. It's no wonder Japanese men don't mind getting married.

c. 1500 *The Perfumed Garden,* written by Shaykh Nefzawi, a Tunisian, is an expanded *Kama-sutra,* covering positions, aphrodisiacs, sex rites, contraceptives, anatomy, and useful information. For example, having sex on an empty stomach ruins your eyesight. Sex on a full stomach is injurious to the intestines. Alum in the vagina prevents semen from reaching the uterus. Used too frequently, it causes sterility. Taking a glass of honey with twenty almonds nightly stimulates a man's sexual power. Nefzawi informs women of the different types of penises. There's the Housebreaker, which rubs the vulva two or three times before plunging in. The Impudent becomes erect when it

wants to, even if it embarrasses its owner. The Weeper sheds tears easily. The Stumbler can't find its way in. And the Sleeper gives the appearance of being stuck in the fast-forward position but, when it gets what it wants, it goes to sleep. Vaginas get classified, too. The Silent one takes it anytime without making a sound. The Swelling One swells when a male member gets near it. The Large One belongs to plump and fat women. The Humpbacked has a large mound of Venus. Nefzawi writes the book out of a desire to serve mankind.

**It's courtly love for the upper classes.
Peasants rut like animals.**

1566 *The Yellow Emperor and the Plain Girl* is a Chinese sex manual that is a compilation of ancient sex manuals. Written in the form of a dialogue between the Yellow Emperor and the Plain Girl, the handbook includes positions (nine of them), thrusting techniques, varying sizes of male members, how to conceive, the benefits of sex, and the importance of not wasting semen. The Plain Girl has all the answers for the Emperor, who practices the lessons he's taught and lives to 120 years of age at which time he and the Plain Girl ascend into heaven together.

1642 One of Europe's first standard works on sexuality, *Geneanthropeia,* written by medical professor Johannes Benedict Sinibaldi, is published in Italy. In it he warns of the dire consequences of masturbation, including gout, constipation, a hunchback, and bad breath.

1684 *Aristotle's Masterpiece* is published in London. Composed mostly of folklore, it reasserts the need for both partners to be pleasured in order for conception to occur. Good thoughts are necessary during sex, since one's thoughts can influence the health of the baby. It also advises a man not to withdraw immediately after ejaculation if the couple is trying to conceive, lest they lose "the fruit of their labor."

1696 Dr. Nicolas Venette writes *Tableau de la Vie Conjugale.* The best season for sex is spring, he says. Winter's too cold. You'll freeze your balls off. Summer and fall are okay, but not as good as spring. Premature baldness is found in men with high sex drives because their craniums dry up. Want a lascivious woman? Look for one with flabby breasts. And men with large noses usually have the longest penises.

1709 Women take note: Passionate lovemaking is a no-no. It acts as a contraceptive. That's what Musitanus writes in *Women's Diseases,* citing Spanish women who "move their whole body during intercourse from an excess of voluptuousness." This accounts for the sterility of Spanish women.

1746 Ben Franklin shares his wisdom in *Advice to a Young Man on Choosing a Mistress.* Don't go after young women. An older woman is much better. She can't get pregnant. She's more experienced. From the waist down you can't tell the difference between her and a young woman. And most important, she'll be grateful.

1758 Science joins the church in giving masturbation the big no with the publication of Swiss physician S. A. Tissot's *On Onanism, or a Physical Dissertation on the Ills Produced by Masturbation.* Tissot interprets the story of Onan (see Trivia, page 171) as masturbation, strengthening the church's position. But Tissot's condemnation of masturbation isn't based on sin. Priming the pump by yourself increases blood pressure inside the skull, he says, paving the way to insanity. Along with a trip to the asylum you'll also receive pimples, constipation, hemorrhoids, blisters, body odor, blindness, deafness, tumors, itching, impotence, or a painful permanent erection. Now, leave yourself alone.

1788 A fascination with masochism and sadism—especially in England—results in a series of flagellation manuals for brothel owners to make sure their customers' needs are met. *Venus Schoolmistress,* for example, separates clients into those who want to be whipped, those who want to do the whipping, and those who prefer to watch. Other manuals suggest types of clothing, assorted rods, and scenarios for customers to choose from.

1812 The most influential medical writer of the time, Dr. Benjamin Rush, chief surgeon of the Continental army, publishes *Medical Inquiries and Observations upon the Diseases of the Mind* in which he draws a direct link between masturbation and insanity. All diseases can be attributed to the decrease or increase in nervous energy. Masturbation accomplishes both. Rush isn't against sex. Lack of it produces, among other things, tremors, hysteria, and nocturnal pollution (wet dreams).

c. 1830 Dr. Claude-François Lallemand coins the term "spermatorrhea" to denote a condition brought on by too many wet dreams. Lack of physical strength, mental focus, and logic, poor work habits, and tiredness are some of its symptoms.

Benjamin Rush contends masturbation causes insanity.

1830 Attacked for his beliefs, reformer Robert Dale Owen writes *Moral Physiology* to defend himself and take a few pot shots at prudes who believe sex shouldn't be seen or heard. Those who are steeped in righteousness and who feign offense in public at anything remotely sexual, he argues, can usually be found doing unsavory things in the dark. Sexual repression leads to unnatural practices and to the "solitary vice." Owen advocates self-control and limiting family size, most notably through withdrawal.

1830–1840 Alexander Walker publishes his trilogy on women: *Beauty, Intermarriage,* and *Woman Physiologically Considered,* the last of which details Walker's thoughts on women and sex. By nature's design women are more sexual than men, and it is for this reason that they must be subdued. Too much excitement can lead to masturbation and nymphomania, as can erotic literature, theater, balls, or anything else that stimulates the imagination.

A Victorian doctor is astonished when a female patient confides that her husband has the "fatal habit of applying the tongue and lips" to her genitals. Alarmed, the doctor orders him to stop at once because it not only endangers her health but is sure to give her husband cancer of the tongue.

TRIVIA

Walker believes women should be involved in sex but warns that moderation is key for both sexes. Both men and women have limited resources and overusing them leads to an early death for men and erotomania and death for women. Celibacy isn't an answer, either, especially for women, who suffer hysteria, insanity, and death if they do without sex.

1832 Dr. Charles Knowlton publishes *The Fruits of Philosophy,* an account of contraceptive practices in America. Knowlton advises a post-coital douche of alum and a vegetarian astringent such as green tea. While trying to sell his book in Cambridge, Massachusetts, the following year, he is arrested and jailed for three months. *The Fruits of Philosophy* is also published in England and becomes a test case for obscenity in 1877, when reformer Annie Besant and Charles Bradlaugh are arrested for publishing an inexpensive edition of the book. The solicitor general calls it "a dirty, filthy book . . . to enable persons to have sexual intercourse, and not to have that which in the order of Providence is the result of sexual intercourse." Found guilty, they are let off on a technicality, but Besant loses custody of her daughter as a result of the case.

1834 Sylvester Graham, known for inventing the graham cracker, writes his *Lecture to Young Men on Chastity, Intended Also for the Serious Consideration of Parents and Guardians.* This essay warns "that excessive sexual desire" leads to general debility and heaviness, indigestion, increased susceptibilities of the skin and lungs, headache, impaired vision, urinary difficulties, weakness of the brain, epilepsy, insanity, and an early death of offspring to mention a few. Graham later adds that every ejaculation a man has lowers his life expectancy.

1848 Self-appointed experts Mary and Thomas Nichols attack the institution of marriage in their book, *Marriage.* Too many people are stuck in unhappy unions which fosters prostitution, they write. Unhappiness in women manifests itself in uterine tumors. Their solution is an equal world with individuals entering into love relationships and staying in them as long as love endures. A woman's children may have different fathers but since a child is the best "keepsake" a man can give a woman, he or she becomes part of the love scenario.

1849 French forensic psychiatrist Claude François Michéa tries a reverse thought process on what causes aberrations. Instead of sexual perversions causing brain or nervous damage, the damage or other biological disorder causes the sexual perversion. He attributes homosexuality to a recently discovered rudimentary uterus some men have.

for any reason other than procreation, you are making her a prostitute. Sex should be had no more than once a month and never during menstruation or pregnancy. The average family includes six to ten children. Do the math. It's quite possible that nearly half of a twenty-year marriage could be spent in celibacy.

c. 1896 German physician Magnus Hirschfeld puts forth his idea of what causes homosexuality. All people are born bisexual, Hirschfeld charges, but as we grow we lose our desire for the same sex. This natural progression results in heterosexuals. A second group grows but doesn't lose the primary desire. These folks are bisexual. Still another group emerges. These develop normally physically but the feeling center fails to recede properly, creating a third group that desires only members of their own sex. Hirschfeld sees homosexuality as a variant and works to repeal laws that punish the behavior.

1897 Dr. Albert Moll writes that homosexuality is a biological variation of the sex drive and should be treated as such. Moll, though, is a Darwinist who believes in natural selection. So while biologically determined homosexuals should be accepted as a mere variant, learned homosexuality tampers with the plan of nature and must be corrected. By 1911, Moll is using association therapy to treat homosexuality, replacing same-sex associations with opposite-sex associations.

1897 Sexologist Havelock Ellis publishes *Sexual Inversion* in which he states that there are feminine men and masculine women and though they may be abnormal, homosexuals should be allowed to go on with their lives,

achieving whatever good works they may be capable of doing. He cites his experience with his wife, who has a female lover (Ellis is sexually dysfunctional and incapable at this point in his life of having sex, though he'll get it up later in life). Ellis writes other books advocating love relationships and the acceptance of divorce. He joins other authorities on the reason women have a hymen: it's nature's way of ensuring a healthy species. Only a man with a strong penis is capable of breaking through, screening out the too young, too old, and feeble.

1900 Sigmund Freud revolutionizes sexuality beginning with his book *Interpretation of Dreams* and continuing with *Three Essays on the Theory of Sexuality* (1905–1915), lectures, and articles such as "Fetishism" (1927). He's considered brilliant, but Freud is a product of the Victorian age and steeped in a male Jewish culture, although he does not practice his faith. He develops the notion of infant sexuality, an explanation of children's sexual feelings toward their parents, resulting in an Oedipus or Electra complex. Girls develop penis envy when they discover they're lacking a penis and blame their mother for bringing them into the world "insufficiently equipped." A woman survives penis envy by marrying a father figure and using his penis, power, and authority. Unfortunately, women are rigid and unchangeable by age thirty and never achieve as much character as men because they lack penises. While little girls masturbate and receive pleasure through the clitoris, a woman who has matured correctly achieves vaginal orgasms, he says, pronouncing the two events as separate. He goes further, deeming women who achieve only clitoral orgasms "frigid." Women are stuck with this notion until 1966 when Masters and Johnson prove Freud wrong. Freud explains that clothes are sexually exciting because they cover "the hidden parts," increasing curiosity and stimulating the desire to undress the other person. As for fetishes, fur is arousing because it symbolizes, among other things, pubic hair. A man's coat, hat, and tie are phallic symbols.

1902 Iwan Bloch, a German dermatologist, advocates the study of sex through biology, psychology, and cultural, social, and historical influences. In *Beiträge zur Aetologie der Psychopathia Sexualis,* Bloch uses all of these plus religion to explain sexual deviations. Since every sensory organ can be erogenous and stimulated, and since everyone has sensory organs, it is not surprising that there is perversity. In fact, he wonders why more people don't behave deviantly.

1903 Otto Weininger rejects the notion that women are sexless creatures devoid of passion. In his *Geschlecht und Character* Weininger

SMALL BOOBS? BIG BRAINS!

In 1964, Professor Erwin O. Strassman studies 717 infertile women and reaches the conclusion that the smarter a woman is, the smaller breasts she has. Big breasts, he concludes, are associated with a lower IQ.

states women are inferior because they live to satisfy their needs. So polygamous is this female sex that in order to be considered human, she must repress her sexuality totally. For good measure, Otto puts Jews in the same "inferior" category because they exhibit female characteristics.

1904 Dermatologist Prince Albert Morrow studies sexually transmitted diseases in Europe and the United States and concludes that they are more prevalent than reported. In *Social Disease and Marriage* he sympathizes with the wife and children who are infected by a husband who contracts the disease from prostitutes. Morrow crusades against a double standard that holds prostitutes liable but not their customers and urges the reporting of venereal disease as a containment measure and as protection for the innocent.

1918 England's answer to Margaret Sanger is Marie Stopes, who opens the UK's first birth-control clinic. Before she does, she writes *Married Love,* espousing that women should be able to enjoy the sexual experience as much as men. Furthermore, if a woman is pregnant, the husband should find other ways of sexually stimulating her. Stopes studies sex to end her own ignorance. Married in 1911, it took her over a year to realize her marriage hadn't been consummated. Much of the response to her best-selling book is from women who confide that they can't be free to enjoy sex unless they are free from the fear of pregnancy. Their pleas for help inspire her to open a clinic.

1919 One result of Margaret Sanger's journey through Europe in search of birth-control methods is her book *Family Limitation.* Sanger reiterates her main message: a "woman's body belongs to herself alone," and methods of preventing pregnancy should be a woman's right. Along with detailed information on what can be used and how, diagrams are also included to carefully explain their use.

1920 A theory as to why women menstruate is put forth by German professor A. Gerson. Primitive woman, while being chased by primitive man, became so aroused that the uterus began to swell in anticipation and then bled. The blood accumulation, having nowhere to go, sought its only outlet. He describes this as *uterine hyperemia.*

1923 Gynecologist Robert Dickinson uses his notes on over 5,000 patients to write *A Thousand Marriages* and *The Single Woman.* His medical books increase knowledge about frigidity, frequency of intercourse (two or three times a week for married women), venereal disease, and masturbation (married women do it more often than single women). Dickinson also confirms physiological changes during female orgasms by observing the vagina through a penis-shaped glass dildo while women masturbate.

1926 Dr. Theodoor Van de Velde presents *Ideal Marriage,* the first popular sex manual. Van de Velde stresses the importance of foreplay. Why? Because women are *supposed* to have orgasms. He goes one better: "Every considerable erotic stimulation of their wives that does not terminate in orgasm on the woman's part represents an injury, and repeated injuries of this kind lead to permanent—or very obstinate—damage to both body and soul." Van de Velde includes ten positions and encourages couples to try the "genital kiss" (oral sex) as part of foreplay. Don't take the oral sex too far. If it results in an orgasm, it's pathological.

1928 Margaret Mead's *Coming of Age in Samoa* becomes a best-seller as Americans hungrily read of young girls growing up in the South Pacific. Mead is later accused of publishing faulty information, but her account of females readily accepting their sexuality and garnering as many partners as they can before they marry under the accepting eye of their culture makes Americans dream of tropical days and balmy nights. Mead becomes America's best-known anthropologist.

1928 In an attempt to find out if marriage contributes to sex problems, Dr. G. V. Hamilton conducts a study of two hundred men and women. Although marriage fares better than he thinks it will, only 48 percent of those interviewed are "reasonably satisfied" with their marriage. He also finds that men whose wives are physically like their mothers were more satisfied than those who married women unlike their moms. To women it didn't matter if hubby looked like dad or not. Only 29 percent of men and 13 percent of women had committed adultery while 16 percent of men and 13 percent of women condoned the practice. While virginity at marriage didn't affect whether women would be monogamous, innocent men were likely to keep their marriage vows than those who had sown their wild oats.

1929 Twenty-two hundred women respond to Dr. Katharine Davis's survey, part of her study of the sex lives of women. Most of the women of the Roaring Twenties feel that their husbands' sex drives are greater than or equal to their own. Only 3 percent say they'd appreciate hubby getting it up more than the average frequency of once or twice a week. While masturbation is thought to be "morally degrading," 65 percent of unmarried women and 40 percent of married women morally degrade themselves. The vast majority use some type of contraception. Over 9 percent have had at least one abortion.

1939 Wilhelm Reich was once a well-respected member of the International Psychoanalytic Association, but his ideas are now so far out that he's expelled from the organization. Reich replaces Freud's concept of the libido with energy, which he believes can be measured and contained. This "orgone," when captured, can be transferred back to the body to increase orgiastic potency and cure illness. He invents the orgone box, slightly larger than a coffin, in which one sits. The orgone is collected and directed back to the genitals where it restores potency. Yeah, the American Medical Association doesn't think so, either. The Food and Drug Administration forbids him to sell orgone boxes. Reich dies in prison where he's sent after defying the ban.

1948 Alfred C. Kinsey's *Sexual Behavior in the Human Male* is published to gasps of shock, horror, and awe—and to sighs of relief. Containing information from 5,300 in-depth interviews, the Kinsey report shatters several long-held beliefs. Among the more shocking revelations: between 92 percent and 97 percent of the male population have masturbated; 86 percent have had premarital intercourse by the age of thirty; 69 percent have engaged in intercourse with a prostitute; 50 percent have had extramarital affairs; nudity is more acceptable among higher class individuals than among the lower classes; at least one-third of the male population has engaged in some homosexual activity; and farm boys are more likely than city boys to have had sexual relations with animals—sheep, calves, goats, and chickens—though college-educated farm boys (27 percent) are more likely to have practiced bestiality than those with a grade school education (15 percent). Published at the high price of $6.50, the first 10,000 copies sell out quickly and eventually 275,000 copies sell in the United States alone. Kinsey is denounced in religious circles for undermining the public morals, but he shrugs off the attacks and goes on working.

1953 Kinsey's back, this time with *Sexual Behavior in the Human Female*. Blamed for leaving out factors like love and motherhood, Kinsey puts forth some interesting findings on the sexual activities of women. Women are sexual creatures from birth to death, with the onset and cessation of menstruation only being landmarks in life. Sexual activity in marriage does wane with age, but it's not the woman's fault. The guys have a harder (or softer) time upholding their end of the bargain. Yes, women masturbate—not as often as men, but when they do, it results in orgasm 95 percent of the time. Only 2 percent of women interviewed are classified as frigid—that is, incapable of experiencing orgasm. Members of the fairer sex also have sex dreams, 20 percent which end in a wet dream. Some 25 percent of married women admit to having had extramarital affairs, but unlike men, they leave animals alone; animal sexual contact is found to be insignificant.

1962 Helen Gurley Brown writes *Sex and the Single Girl,* the first frank how-to-catch-a-man guide. She doesn't mince words. She offers a complete list of where to meet men, how to charm them with your sex appeal, how to dress enticingly, how to have an affair, and what to cook for your lover. She tells women how to spot a homosexual man (no sense wasting time), how to tell if a man is a good lover, and why you should have an affair with a married man. The book becomes a best-seller instantly and launches Helen Gurley Brown's career as editor of *Cosmopolitan* magazine.

1963 Betty Friedan sends a questionnaire to members of her Smith College graduating class, and the responses form the basis of her ground-breaking book, *The Feminine Mystique*. Friedan contends that the ideals and hopes of women are trashed because they are totally defined in the roles of wife and mother. She points the finger of blame at advertisers, women's magazines, psychiatrists, and politicians for creating the fallacy of what woman's happiness should be. Her book becomes a bible for the burgeoning women's movement.

1966 Masters and Johnson's *Human Sexual Response* becomes a best-seller even though it's written for the scientific community. The authors observed, measured, inspected, and recorded the reactions of copulating couples in their laboratory. They then divided the sex act into four stages: excitement—the penis comes to attention and the vagina sweats; plateau—the balls increase in size by 50 percent, the vagina swells, and the clitoris retracts (it's heavy breathing time, folks); orgasm—the point of no return for men and the vagina contracts; contractions vary in number for both sexes, but they occur at intervals of four-fifths of a second; resolution—he falls asleep, she catalog-shops. The daring duo has more news for readers: Freud was wrong—there's no physiological difference between a clitoral orgasm and a vaginal orgasm. Ejaculation and orgasm are two separate processes for men, and if they learn to control the first, they can have several of the second. Men still can't live up to the mighty clit, though. Women are multiorgasmic, capable of up to twenty orgasms an hour.

c. 1967 The founder of Rational Emotive Therapy, Albert Ellis, lends a hand to bring about the sexual revolution. Ellis believes sex is a basic function that should be had freely before marriage and that accepting one's sexuality gives a person a sounder psychological base. Ellis is also a proponent of group marriages, though he doesn't believe that's a realistic possibility.

Sexual pleasure, wisely used and not abused, may prove the stimulus and liberator of our finest and most exalted activities.

Havelock Ellis

1969 Dr. David Reuben's book, *Everything You Always Wanted to Know About Sex (But Were Afraid to Ask),* answers all of your questions. Over one million people want answers when the hardcover book comes out; more than four million buy the paperback. Reuben uses an up-front, humorous question-and-answer format to explain how big a normal penis is, why women have only two breasts, why women can have more orgasms than men, why some people are undersexed, whether there are any aphrodisiacs that work, whether a penis can disappear, how S&M works, and what dildos, transvestites, and fetishes are. He also explains prostitution, birth control, abortion, venereal disease, menopause, and sex for the elderly. Suddenly everyone's more sexually savvy.

1969 "J" writes *The Sensuous Woman,* a guide to becoming a more thrilling lover and getting some satisfaction for yourself, too. This how-to book for women is so hot that author Terry Garrity doesn't use her name. Covering a wide range of topics, from masturbation to anal

sex, "J" assures her readers that if they love sex at forty, they'll love it at eighty. You can even learn how to tell if a man is good in bed based on how well he kisses: if he kisses with dry, pursed lips and only pecks away, forget him, he's a dud.

1970 In *The Female Eunuch,* Germaine Greer calls for the liberation of women but sees men as equally constrained. Instead of trying to usurp the power of the phallus, Greer wants women to gain their own power through knowledge of their bodies, minds, and history. To feminists who want to disassociate the enjoyment of sex from the penis she says, nonsense: "The orgasm is qualitatively different when the vagina can undulate around the penis instead of vacancy."

1971 If there's a *Sensuous Woman* there has to be a *Sensuous Man.* Written by "M"—Terry Garrity, author of the *Sensuous Woman,* and her brother John Garrity—the book guarantees that even short, bald, bowlegged stutterers can become superb lovers. "M," one of the "world's most expert lovers," shares manly advice on kissing, touching, premature ejaculation, and handling the "woman's-lib type." He also tells men where to meet women and how not to be discovered if they're having an affair with a married woman. Also detailed are techniques of lovemaking such as the Velvet Buzz Saw, the Sliding Pond, the Alternating Flame, and the Feathery Flick.

1971 Husband-and-wife anthropologists George and Nena O'Neill advance the idea of extramarital affairs within a marriage in their book, *Open Marriage.* The O'Neills believe that an open marriage based on mutual respect and

Great Moments in Sex

unlimited love allows you to embrace others without harming the marriage. The constant influx of love only serves to renew and strengthen the marital relationship.

1972 Sex and all of its fun aspects are featured in *The Joy of Sex*. Out of fear of losing his British doctor's license, the author of the manual, Alex Comfort, only admits to editing the book, which is set up like a cookbook in four sections: Starters, Main Courses, Sauces and Pickles, and Problems. Comfort defines "normal" as anything two consenting adults want to do. A variety of positions, oral and anal sex, teasing, talking, foreplay, and a lot of love and care are all ingredients of a healthy sex life. Although they aren't a must, Comfort urges couples to experiment with tactile accoutrements like leather, silk, feathers, masks, G-strings, and nipple rings. You can role-play, get into bondage, or use her armpit instead of her vagina. Comfort follows up *Joy* with *More Joy of Sex* and sells over 8 million copies in twenty years.

1974 *Sexual Behavior in the 1970s* contains the results of a survey commissioned by the Playboy Foundation. With the sexual revolution in full swing, the findings of this study mirror new attitudes. Seventy-five percent of single women under twenty-five had lost their virginity. And the missionary position isn't the position they are most likely to use. In fact, 11 percent of single men said they hadn't used it in a year. More in favor was the female on top. Oral and anal sex are on the upswing. Mate-swapping and group sex are more talked about than practiced. And the use of animals has dropped since Kinsey's day. Also dropping is prostitution. Who needs it? Permissiveness is associated more with higher education, liberal political leanings, higher income, and nonreligious people.

1976 Riding the wave of feminism, Shere Hite publishes *The Hite Report,* a study of female sexuality based on the responses in two thousand questionnaires. Men are more surprised than women to find out that only 30 percent of the respondents regularly achieved orgasm through intercourse while 29 percent never did. Of the 82 percent who said they masturbated, 95 percent reached orgasm easily. Oral sex was favored by many, with 42 percent of the women reaching climax. On the downside, women complain that most men are not concerned enough with pleasuring them and that sex too often ends with the male ejaculation.

1980 Diminutive, foreign-accented Dr. Ruth Westheimer takes her sexual therapy practice to the airwaves in her radio show, *Sexually Speaking*. The show begins as a taped segment but evolves into a call-in format, taking questions from listeners who want to know how to deal with premature ejaculation, being "preorgasmic" (Dr. Ruth's version of frigid), a crooked penis, virginity, not having enough time for sex, and a host of other problems, which she fields with unabashed straightforwardness. Never a proponent of swinging or extramarital affairs, and always emphasizing safe sex, Dr. Ruth adds television shows, a newspaper column, books, and even a board game to her techniques for educating Americans about sex.

1984 Advice columnist Ann Landers asks her female readers, "Would you be content to be held close and treated tenderly and forget about 'the act'?" Over 90,000 responses reveal that 72 percent would be content. Twenty-eight percent still insisted on the full wham-bam.

1988 Surgeon General C. Everett Koop writes *Understanding AIDS,* an eight-page booklet, which is mailed to 107 million U.S. households at a cost of $17 million. The brochure is a primer on AIDS, how it is contracted, and how to prevent it. Outside a monogamous relationship, Koop advocates abstinence, but also endorses the use of condoms, realizing that celibacy is not an option for most Americans.

1993 *The Janus Report* surveys nearly 3,000 American men and women. Though it's criticized for its self-selected and biased sample, it comes up with some interesting statistics: Three-fifths of married people say sex improves after marriage, with 54 percent considering themselves very active or active, compared to 47 percent of single people. When it comes to initiating sex, 54 percent of men said they like to, while 67 percent of women want the lead. Half of all men said that a wide variety of techniques is a must, and 58 percent of both sexes believed that talking dirty is normal. While orgasms are great, 76 percent of women said it wasn't necessary for both partners to come at the same time. Masturbation is natural, with 44 percent of married men and 16 percent of married women doing the hand jive weekly. Career women whack off more often than nonworking women (21 percent). The great majority (88 percent of men and 87 percent of women) believe oral sex is normal. Most people lost their virginity between ages fifteen and eighteen. And even though everyone sounds happy, one in three men and one in four women have had extramarital affairs.

1994 *Sex in America,* a survey conducted by University of Chicago researchers, is hailed as the first truly scientific survey by some and scoffed at by others. Based on face-to-face interviews, one of the survey's most controversial findings is that, over a lifetime, the typical man has only six sexual partners and a woman has two, bringing hoots from more liberal camps. The study reveals that vaginal sex is the favorite sex act, with oral sex a distant third. The number two spot is watching your partner undress. Seventy-five percent of married men and 85 percent of married women say they have never been unfaithful. Oral sex is more popular among whites than blacks, with both partners preferring to be on the receiving end. Who masturbates? The people who have the most sex. Apparently the more you're getting the more you want.

Chapter Four
SEX SYMBOLS: THE WOMEN

B.C.

c. 1500 Egypt's Hatshepsut becomes the first woman supreme ruler when she overshadows her half brother–husband, Thutmose III. In addition to ruling a vast empire, she builds a

number of monuments to herself, including the temple at Deir el-Bahri. Hatshepsut pleases her countrymen but her off-the-throne husband isn't happy. When she dies, he retakes the throne and promptly hacks her name and images off the monuments.

c. 1013 She's taking a bath and minding her own business. King David just happens to see her. Who is she? That's Bathsheba, he's told, the wife of your loyal soldier, Uriah. Does David just get an eyeful and walk away? No. He sends for her, beds her (he is her king, after all), impregnates her, has his faithful warrior killed in battle, and marries her. Bathsheba gives birth to Solomon. Although the Lord isn't too kind to David after this, it's Bathsheba whom history paints (literally) as a wanton temptress and seductress.

c. 500 The hetairai of Greece take center stage. Known for their beauty and intelligence, many of them become famous. There's Clepsydra, given the name of a Greek hourglass

A bathing Bathsheba catches King David's eye.

because she's so much in demand that she uses one to time her sessions with lovers. The line forms at Cyrene's door because she knows twelve ways of having sex. Theoris and Archeanassa amuse Sophocles and Plato respectively. Danaë and Leontium tutor Epicurus in pleasure. And Themistonoe maintains her practice until she's bald and toothless. A few of the hetairai rise to remarkable stature. They're discussed below.

c. 500 Another hetaira, Thargelia, pleases Cyrus the Great of Persia and accompanies his son, Xerxes, on his invasion of Greece. There she works her wiles on Greek military leaders and sends back reports. Legend says she's so good that Ionia is delivered to the Persians peacefully.

c. 450 "Superior in beauty to any woman that had ever been seen" is Lais of Corinth. Extremely choosy, she has sex with Diogenes, the philosopher, for free. But when she visits the studio of Myron, a sculptor, and disrobes, the old man is so overwhelmed that he offers her everything he has if she'll spend one night with him. She sizes him up, puts on her robe, says no thanks, and leaves. Myron's determined. He shaves, bathes, cuts his hair, puts on his best clothes and jewelry, and the next morning finds her again. "My poor friend," she tells him, "you are asking me what I refused to your father yesterday." Her philanthropy and beauty are honored after she dies. The Greeks build her a tomb fit for an emperor.

c. 450 Golden-haired beauty Aspasia gives up the world's oldest profession to run a school of rhetoric that attracts the likes of Socrates, Euripides, and Anaxagoras. When Athenian leader Pericles shows up, he falls for her, takes her as his mistress, and divorces his wife. However, a law he made allowing Athenians to marry only other Athenians prevents him from marrying her. She lives with him and her influence is a matter of heated debate. The enemies of Pericles bring her up on charges of impiety toward the gods. Her jury is composed of 1,500 men to whom she's not allowed to speak because she isn't a citizen. When the trial seems to be going against her, the usually stoic Pericles appears, pours out his heart, and cries. The jurors acquit her.

c. 300 Phryne's body is so incredibly beautiful that the artist Apelles is inspired to create his masterpiece, *Aphrodite Anadyomene,* when, at the festival of Poseidon at Eleusis she strips in front of the crowd and walks into the sea. Her artist lover Praxiteles uses her as his model for a statue of Aphrodite. She is usually modest, is always covered in public, and only makes love in the dark. She's immeasurably rich. Phryne offers to rebuild the walls of Thebes if it contains the inscription "Destroyed by Alexander, restored by Phryne the courtesan," but she's turned down. Any man with a modicum of power is at her feet. This ticks off their wives, who convince Euthias to charge her with making fun of the Eleusinian mysteries, a charge that carries the death penalty. She is defended by her orator lover Hyperides, who throws caution to the wind and rips her clothing off to her waist, giving the judges a tit show of a lifetime. They gawk, gape, ooh and ahh, declare her a divinity, and dismiss the case.

c. 300 Plutarch declares that Lamia got her name, meaning bloodsucker, because she's depraved. But Lamia, an *auletride* (a dancer who's also a prostitute), knows how to swivel those hips well enough to become the mistress of King Ptolemy of Egypt and later of King Demetrius of Macedonia. A woman like Lamia doesn't come cheap, so Demetrius levies a tax on Athenians to buy her soap. No problem. The Athenians like her, build her a temple, and elevate her to the status of a goddess, Venus Lamia.

238 When in Rome, do as the Romans do. Do Flora. She's so popular and rich from her trade that she specifies a large amount of money to be used every year to celebrate her birthday, which initiates the Floralia games. During the nude games, prostitutes dance naked on stage and a good time is had by all.

c. 60 Clodia, who is not a prostitute but the wife of Quintus Caecilius Metellus, governor of Cisalpine Gaul, makes male blood run hot in Rome. She goes about town unchaperoned, refuses to crouch down in her carriage or lower her eyes, kisses her friends in public, and invites male friends to dine with her while her husband is away. Outspoken on the rights of women, Clodia throws aside her matrimonial vows and takes lovers one after another, all of whom become her enemies when she tires of them before they tire of her.

c. 50 Cleopatra, queen of Egypt, is not exceptionally beautiful, but she is sensuous, exotic. She's a short brunette with blue eyes, is said to be fairer in complexion than her subjects, and has nice boobs. She meets Julius Caesar after being unrolled from a bundle of rugs at his feet. Mark Antony is introduced on a golden barge where she's resting on a couch draped in luxurious veils. Her meeting with Octavian, who defeats her armies, takes place in her bedroom

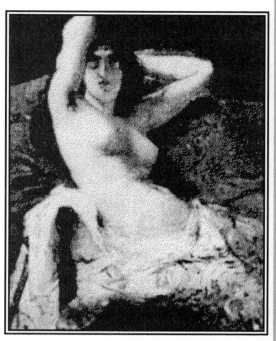

Cleopatra: Caesar and Mark Antony fall for her, but Octavian tells her to kiss his asp.

where she's lying naked. Caesar and Mark Antony fall for her. Octavian doesn't. He wants to take her back to Rome as a captive. Cleo won't have any of that. She does herself in by letting a mud asp bite her arm.

A.D.

c. 30 Salome does her dance of the seven veils for her stepfather, King Herod. She swirls and twirls so seductively that Herod promises to deliver anything she wants. John the Baptist's head, she replies, encouraged by her mother, Herodias, who was criticized by the Baptist for marrying Herod, her brother-in-law, after her husband died. The saint's noggin is delivered to her on a silver platter. Salome proves that dancing is one way to get a-head in life.

TRIVIA

IN THE GARDEN OF EDEN WITH ADAM AND LILITH

When God creates Adam from dust, he also creates a twin—Lilith. She and Adam are supposed to introduce sex into the world and fill it full of little Liliths and Adams. But Adam and Lilith have a problem. She refuses to be subservient to him. She won't assume the submissive position during sex, even when God forces her. She leaves. Adam still wants her. God sends three angels to bring her back but Lilith refuses. From then on, she's seen as the partner of the devil, responsible for harming babies and causing wet dreams. In the meantime, God goes back to the drawing board and creates Eve, this time from Adam's rib so her complacency is ensured. At least for a while.

c. 40 Messalina, the young wife of Emperor Claudius of Rome, is a nymphomaniac. Her saliva-dribbling husband, thirty-two years older than she, isn't enough for her, so once he's asleep, she dons a blond wig and a veil, gilds her nipples, and goes to the local brothel, where she offers her services for the regular fee. She challenges one of the better-known prostitutes to see who can service the most men in one day. Messalina wins hands down with twenty-five clients in twenty-four hours. Whether Claudius is aware of her escapades is unknown, but she takes advantage of his absence to marry a young man in a public ceremony and then consummates the marriage in front of the wedding guests. When Claudius returns, he has Messalina assassinated.

c. 520 The beautiful Theodora, an actress from Constantinople, has a talent for mime and a type of burlesque where she lifts her skirts and performs lewdly. While performing on her back, she meets Justinian and becomes his mistress. When he's crowned emperor, he makes her his empress. Doing a complete 180, Theodora becomes an exemplar of morality, even building a small palace for reformed prostitutes. Unfortunately, a good number of the captured prostitutes are so bored with their new lifestyle that they throw themselves out of the windows.

c. 800 Yü Hsüan-chi is beautiful and talented. She's a poet with a student following. Although she's not registered as a prostitute, she's on her back long enough to make a living. Love is not for poor Yü Hsüan-chi. Twice she is taken as concubine. The wife of her first lover doesn't like her. Out she goes. The second lover is a wandering poet who wanders away one night and never comes back. Her talent, beauty, and popularity keep her afloat, at least for a while. As she ages, she loses her influential patrons and gets in trouble with police officials. Yü Hsüan-chi is finally set up. She's put to death for supposedly beating a maidservant to death.

Great Moments in Sex

c. 1130 At fifteen Eleanor of Aquitaine is beautiful, tempestuous, and energetic, the richest and most powerful woman in Europe. Known for her flirtatious ways and love for men, at sixteen she marries Louis VII, king of France, known for his chastity. The marriage doesn't work. Eleanor's busy with lovers, one of whom—Henry II, king of England—changes her life. She secures a divorce and marries him. Henry is lascivious by comparison to her first husband, which pleases her immensely. Eleanor never tires of romance or of trying to find it; she helps formulate the rules for courtly love, sets fashion trends, attempts to civilize the knights, tries to overthrow Henry, outlives him, reigns as unofficial queen after securing the throne for her favorite son, and dies at the extremely old age of eighty-two.

c. 1385 Isabeau of Bavaria, wife of Charles VI of France, is stunning and takes extreme measures to preserve her beauty, bathing in asses' milk and applying boars' brains, crocodile glands, and wolves' blood to her skin. These treatments must do some good—she's known for her beauty and for setting the fashion of wearing low-cut dresses to expose her breasts. Though she is vehemently warned from the pulpit to "cover up your provocative flesh," Isabeau and her décolletage are the stars of the court.

1444 Agnès Sorel, the first woman to hold the semiofficial position of mistress of a king, begins her romance with Charles VII of France. Agnès has three things going for her: her beautiful face, which she accentuates by shaving the hair on her forehead farther back, and her firm, round breasts. Agnès takes pleasure in showing them off by wearing low-cut necklines that expose her left breast completely. The people

love her, especially after she urges the king to get off his backside and recapture Normandy from England. Agnès bears the king three children whom he recognizes as his own. Her position lasts for six years, until Agnès is inflicted with dysentery and dies.

c. 1530 When Francis I of France hears of Françoise de Châteaubriant's beauty he sends a letter to her husband requesting the couple's presence at court. Hubby's too familiar with the king's reputation to fall for it. He shows up alone. The king tries again, but hubby tells Françoise that unless she receives a letter from him with his ring enclosed, she is not to come. The king catches on to the plan, has a duplicate ring made, and sends it to Françoise. She promptly shows up courtside. After three years of persuasion she becomes the king's mistress and enjoys all a king can offer. When the king's interest momentarily shifts to another, he asks for his jewels back to give to the new trollop. Françoise melts 'em down and sends 'em back in a molten lump. The king thinks it's funny, forgives her, and takes her back. After her royal lover dies, Françoise returns to her husband, but he hasn't forgiven her adultery and blames his misfortune on her. Shortly afterward, Françoise is found murdered.

1534 Roxelana achieves the distinction of wedding the first sultan to marry in over one hundred years. A *kadin* (a woman in a harem who has borne the sultan a son) in the harem of Suleiman the Magnificent, she is a Russian captive known as Khurrem, "the Laughing One," who doesn't mind being his captive.

1538 Diane de Poitiers becomes the mistress of Henry II of France. The difference between

**Diane de Poitiers is the older woman
in Henry II's life.**

aging prostitute where it hurts the most, one critic claims she could use her sagging breasts to paddle a gondola.

c. 1560 The daughter of a cardinal, Tuilla is a favored courtesan in Italy. Smart, blond, and beautiful, she refuses to take all comers. Tuilla limits her partners to seven, one for each day of the week. But even her steady customers must take a back seat sometimes. Tuilla's charms attract royalty, for whom she gladly bumps her regulars.

1588 Queen Elizabeth I ascends the throne of England and plays political Ping-Pong with her virginity. Parliament wants her to marry—who wants a lone queen ruling England? She promises herself to suitors in both Spain and France—and Denmark, Sweden, and Austria—who are forced into good behavior for fear of alienating and losing England. Elizabeth imports her basic fashion style from Spain and with a few nips and tucks lowers the necklines to expose the tops of her breasts, reeling those suitors in even closer. Alas, it's not to be. Court gossip suggests the queen has a hymen made of rubber—it won't be broken. Elizabeth dies without being married and without an heir.

c. 1650 Ninon de Lenclos takes Paris by storm. She picks her suitors carefully, charges a premium price, and tenderly ridicules them if they don't perform to her satisfaction. At the age of forty, she opens a school of lovemaking to teach men the correct way to physically please a woman. At sixty she still has suitors. Ninon de Lenclos is ravishing and racks up nearly five thousand lovers in her lifetime. The list does not include Cardinal Richelieu. The cardinal wants her desperately and agrees to pay

Diane and most royal courtesans is her age: she's twenty years older than his royal highness and puts him off for eight years until he's nineteen. Diane's body sets the fashion for the day. Her breasts are small, high, and round, her legs are full, lips and nose are thin, and her forehead high. Her body is used as the quintessential model for the goddess Diana in paintings and statues. Henry's wife, Catherine de Médicis, can't figure out what the attraction is. She drills holes in the king's ceiling and observes them making love but can't see anything that different going on. Many speculate there's a mistress-mother magnetism. Henry stays with Diane until his death.

c. 1540 Veronica Franco not only makes a beautiful call girl but her brain, self-education, and her ability to communicate help her become a respected poet. That's not an easy thing to accomplish in this age when women writers still aren't allowed into literary circles. Veronica's rise is not accepted by everyone. Attacking an

50,000 crowns up front. He delivers. She doesn't. With money in hand, she sends a friend to entertain the man of God.

Nell Gwynn, "the Protestant whore."

1671 The popular English actress Nell Gwynn is one of two mistresses of Charles II. Though Nell has helped to empty the king's purse, she's spent much of it charitably and is accepted by the English people. Mistress number two, aristocratic French Catholic Louise de Kéroualle, remains aloof and distances herself from the people. As Nell is riding down the street in a carriage, the crowd mistakes her for number two and razzes her. Nell, her curly hair flowing around her, sticks her head out the window and yells to the crowd, "Be silent, good people, I am the *Protestant* whore."

c. 1735 After the queen locks Louis XV out of her bedchamber, his advisers search for a mistress to ease his highness's horniness. They find Louise Julie de Mailly, lady-in-waiting to the queen. The first introduction doesn't take, so they have Louise recline on a sofa with her skirts up and her bodice open, and then they shove the king into the room. Voilà! Instant mistress. Louis buys Louise a château so they can spend time together, but when Louise's sister, Comtesse de Vintimille du Luc, visits, the king switches teams. He later takes up with Louise's younger sister, Marquise de la Tournelle, and is also visited by yet another sister. Four out of five ain't bad. The only reason the king doesn't complete the set is that the fifth's jealous husband swears he'll spill royal blood. What some families won't give for their country.

1738 Irish actress Peg Woffington is tall and voluptuous, with long black hair, dark eyes, and a rakishly teasing personality that captivates audiences as well as lovers. Described by one theater manager as a "fascinating daughter of Eve," she plays breeches parts (male roles), and she does them so well that one lady proposes marriage to her, refusing to believe Peg is a woman. Peg's love life is full and well known. Returning backstage after playing a breeches role, Peg compliments herself by announcing, "In my conscience! I believe half the men in the house take me for one of their own sex." Another actress shoots back, "It may be so, but in my conscience! the other half can convince them to the contrary."

1745 Louis XV meets another mistress at a costume ball given for his son. Before she succumbs to the king, Madame de Pompadour insists on being installed as official mistress. Blond, blue-eyed, witty, charming, and full of

TRIVIA

FETCH!

Successful on the battlefield, Napoleon has less luck in bed. On his wedding night, Josephine tells him to learn to share the bed with her pet pooch, Fortuné, or find somewhere else to sleep. Napoleon acquiesces to his wife's demand, but the dog doesn't. During the height of passion, Fortuné has enough of his new owner and bites him in the leg, leaving a scar that the emperor often has to explain. It could have been worse. Consider Attila the Hun who, after a great banquet to celebrate his marriage to Ildico, returns to his marriage bed, has a heart attack, and dies in action.

wiles, she makes friends with the queen and the ministers, supports the arts, introduces her style to France, and amuses the king by finding new ways to satisfy his physical desires. When she realizes that she can't keep up with him, she finds younger women to gratify the "Polish nobleman" they think they're sleeping with. When one of the women stumbles upon Louis's true identity, she's promptly sent to a lunatic asylum. Madame de Pompadour retains her post until her death.

1745 Catherine, soon to become "the Great," marries a wimpy Russian who will one day become Peter III. From the outset the marriage is a no-go. It takes ten years to produce an heir, and then the child's paternity is questioned. It's not Catherine's fault. She contents herself with lovers who happen to be her ministers and advisers. While Peter's mother, Empress Elizabeth, is alive, Catherine plays the game of doting daughter-in-law. Once she dies, Catherine deposes her weakling husband—easy to do, since the head of the guards is her lover— and takes over Russia. She's German, not

Russian, by birth, but she identifies with the people and they return her affection. After Peter dies, she's crowned empress, and she rules Russia for the next thirty-four years. Catherine's lovers are numerous. Before they climb into bed, she has her physician check them out, and sometimes watches them in action before taking them for herself.

c. 1750 Maria Gunning takes London society by storm with her rare beauty, which she enhances with white face makeup and deep red rouge. After a season as the belle of the ball, she marries the Earl of Coventry and retains her following of lovers. Mr. Earl objects to her makeup, even wiping it off in front of dinner guests, but the vain Mrs. Earl keeps primping even though it's known that the white makeup, which contains lead, is poisonous. While lead poisoning destroys her beauty and her health, her scandalous behavior alienates her husband. She spends the last of her young days looking into a mirror trying to conceal blemishes. She dies a victim to cosmetics. Thousands attend her funeral.

Great Moments in Sex

1769 After the death of Madame de Pompadour, Louis XV is without a love interest until a four-year search produces Madame du Barry, a Parisian courtesan who was groomed for the position by her lover. Her beauty is seductive, and once Louis does her, he decides to keep her on indefinitely. By the time her background is checked, Louis is too enamored of her to let her go. Her birth certificate is redone to cleanse the fact that she's illegitimate, and she's married off to Guillaume du Barry to make her respectable. She outlives the king, who dies in 1774, but falls victim to the Revolution. Charged with conspiring against the republic, she's guillotined in 1793.

1796 Josephine Bonaparte is the future empress of France. Married to Napoleon, Josephine has experience, a beautiful face, an exquisite figure, and charm and she knows how to use them. She had been married to a French nobleman who was guillotined during the Revolution. She herself was imprisoned, but she made "friends" with those in power and was set free. Introduced to the future emperor at her salon, she took him as her lover before she agreed to marry him. She's extravagant in her clothes and makeup (a year's supply of rouge costs him 3000 francs) and sets fashion as long as she's married to him. Josephine gets the heave-ho even though Napoleon claims to love her. He replaces her with a younger woman who will produce heirs to the throne.

1855 The French court of Napoleon III is amused by an Italian import, the Countess of Castiglione, said to be one of the most beautiful women in Europe. Sent to France by King Victor Emmanuel II, who had a good time with her, to get French aid for Italy's unification, she scores big with the emperor. When it wears thin, she goes to England where Lord Hertford gives her 40,000 pounds for one night. He gets his money's worth. The countess is laid up in bed for the next three days.

1867 Cora Pearl isn't well bred enough, beautiful enough, or intelligent enough to be a damsel at court. She does have a lively enough spirit, a great body, and flaming red hair, which captures the interest of men who can provide the niceties of life for her. Cora entertains men like Prince Jerome Bonaparte, a cousin of Napoleon III, with dinner parties at which a huge covered dessert tray is brought out. When the lid is lifted, Cora is found lying nude for their enjoyment. She dances nude on a table covered with orchids, and bathes before them in a tub of champagne. When things go awry for her lovers, she's deported and spends the rest of her life trying to recapture her glory days.

1870s Lillie Langtry becomes the top "professional beauty," a beautiful upper-class married woman who, once proclaimed a "PB," sits for portraits and makes the social rounds. Lillie is adored by the most famous artists, who capture her likeness on penny cards sold throughout England, making her a national figure even before she begins her affair with the Prince of Wales. Although they are both married, Lillie becomes his mistress, living in high society until she is ostracized for dumping ice down the prince's back at a costume party. While the prince is taking his time forgiving her, Lillie's artistic friends convince her to take up acting. She does and as "the Jersey Lillie," with her well-endowed body, classical features, alabaster skin, and violet eyes, she sets the world on fire.

understand Isadora Duncan's interpretive dance style. She's a hit in Europe, where she casts aside the formality of ballet and embraces the freedom of Greek and Roman dance. On the stage Isadora wears thin translucent fabrics to enhance her body's movement. Her offstage antics add to her sensuousness. She doesn't believe in marriage and has two illegitimate children to prove it. She does marry eventually, but it ends in divorce. Tragically, she loses both children in a car accident. Isadora herself dies in a freak accident when her trademark long red scarf gets caught in the spokes of an automobile tire and breaks her neck.

1905 Margaretha Geertruida Zelle divorces her husband, takes a lover, changes her name to Mata Hari, and begins a dance career under the guise of being half Indian. The dance, she says, is of Hindu origin. It may be, but she adds a striptease to it and becomes one of the first performers in Europe to take off her clothes onstage. She's also a courtesan and has one lover after another. Her list of men includes crown princes, barons, diplomats, and bankers. When her popularity wanes with the beginning of World War I, she takes a German lover who is the chief of intelligence in Spain. England and France regard her as a spy, though there is never any conclusive proof. She's arrested in Paris, tried, and, on a foggy, damp morning in October 1917, shot for spying.

1874 Initially her acting career takes off with a flying thud, but Sarah Bernhardt perseveres. Her thin frame, gaunt face, intense blue eyes, messy blond hair, and spirited acting style bring her fame, fortune, and lovers—said to number over a thousand. Men fight duels for this woman who is reported to sleep in a satin-lined rosewood coffin filled with love letters. Oscar Wilde dubs her "the divine Sarah." Her fame is international. In Copenhagen the throng of people running to meet her confuses the authorities into thinking the government is being toppled. England falls for her. In 1880 the widow of Abraham Lincoln goes unnoticed as Sarah disembarks from a ship upon her arrival in America. Tickets to her play are scalped for $40. Despite the amputation of her leg, Bernhardt's fame continues up to her death in 1923.

c. 1900 She's from San Francisco, but American audiences are too prudish to accept or

1906 Evelyn Nesbit is "the most exquisitely lovely human being" who becomes an artist's model at the age of fourteen and then a Floradora girl. She becomes famous when her husband, millionaire Harry Thaw, kills Stanford White, a renowned architect and Evelyn's ex-boyfriend. During the ensuing murder trial

Evelyn testifies about her illicit relationship with White. She becomes "the girl in the red velvet swing" after admitting that White made her swing naked on a velvet swing while he watched her. Thaw is found not guilty on grounds of insanity and is committed to an asylum. Evelyn's reputation and career never recover.

1915 Theda Bara tantalizes the American public by silently hissing, "Kiss me, my fool!" in her first motion picture, *A Fool There Was.* Billed as the woman with "the wickedest face in the world," she was supposedly "born on the banks of the Nile," the result of a tryst between an Arab princess and a passionate Italian artist. Actually she's Theodosia Goodman from Cincinnati, Ohio. After appearing in *The Vampire* she becomes "The Vamp," setting a trend for painted faces, writhing, and lustily

nibbling a string of pearls. Bara's star fades quickly. She ends her film career parodying herself in a Mack Sennett comedy in 1926.

1916 Mae Murray makes her movie debut in *To Have and to Hold* and becomes "the Girl with the Bee-Stung Lips." Her platinum blond hair frames a perfect face that men love. But perhaps the peroxide used to lighten her hair seeped into her brain. Mae really believes she's always been Mae Murray rather than Marie Adrienne Koenig from Portsmouth, Virginia, and doesn't think she's totally from this world. She's prone to forgetting everyday things like putting on clothes when running after actor John Gilbert, who walks off a movie set after an argument with the director. Married four times, she receives bad business advice from her last husband, and she leaves MGM only to be forgotten by the American public.

1918 Gloria Swanson becomes Hollywood's number one box office draw and keeps the title for the next seven years. She's the true movie queen, obliging newsreels and reporters at every opportunity with the same emoting she uses on-screen. Her designer clothes are the envy of American housewives. Her sultry looks ignite passion in her male fans, including the father of a future president of the United States, Joseph Kennedy, whose mistress she becomes. She achieves fame in the silent era but she's best remembered for her role as an aging beauty queen in *Sunset Boulevard.*

1925 Josephine Baker takes Paris by storm with the opening of *La Revue Nègre.* Her beauty is unquestionable. But what she does with that body! Carried in upside down, she wears one bright pink flamingo feather between her legs. Her singing is impeccable, her writhing dance erotic. In another revue, she is lowered from the ceiling in a globe, which cracks open to reveal Josephine clad only in a skirt of bananas and dancing on a mirror that is slightly tipped to the audience's advantage. Parisians go crazy. They love her, as does the rest of Europe. She receives two thousand marriage proposals in two years. America shuns this homegrown talent. Baker never catches on in a racist society.

1927 Clara Bow becomes the "It Girl"—"It" meaning sex appeal—with the opening of her movie, *It*. Her flapper-style bobbed hair and bow-shaped scarlet lips are copied by "It" wanna-bes. Adding to her film persona are her offscreen antics. Her lovers include Eddie Cantor, Gary Cooper, Buddy Rogers, Gilbert Roland, Victor Fleming, Fredric March, Bela Lugosi, and, once, the entire 1927 University of Southern California football team. Bow's lifestyle is her downfall. The American public has little sympathy for the woman who is named as co-respondent in a divorce case. A tell-all exposé by a former employee nails the lid shut. Bow suffers a series of nervous breakdowns while attempting to jump-start her career and calls it quits in 1933.

1929 Marlene Dietrich's international film career is launched in *The Blue Angel*. Cast as a tawdry cabaret singer, Dietrich seduces a self-indulgent professor with raw sexiness and a neurotic earthiness. She comes to the screen in black stockings with garters stretched down her white thighs, her crotch highlighted with heavy lace. It's "gutter sex," lust with a purpose, a way to obtain this man and then dominate him. The audience loves her. She agrees to come to

Dietrich: A raw sexiness.

America, where she films *Morocco*. Already known for dressing in trousers (she starts a fad, and women quickly deplete the limited supply of pants), she appears in a white tuxedo for a musical number that ends with her kissing a woman. Dietrich keeps hitting high notes. In *Destry Rides Again* her performance and her throaty rendition of "See What [or "Vat," as she pronounces it] the Boys in the Back Room Will Have" establish her as a major star. Her refusal to obey Hitler's order to return to Germany endears her to the public. During World War II, Dietrich earns the U.S. Medal of Freedom and the French Legion of Honor for entertaining the troops.

1930 Silver screen sirens can be readily identified. Dark hair and dark eyes equals vamp. Blond hair, blue eyes equals good girl. But here comes Jean Harlow in *Hell's Angels*. She's a blue-eyed platinum blonde, and of her body one critic says, "nobody ever starved possessing what she's got." Men flip and fantasize over this woman who loves sex AND enjoys it. Women curl their lips at her, but they bleach their hair, pluck their eyebrows, and try to walk like her. Harlow's the Blonde Bombshell. She dies suddenly in 1937 at the age of twenty-six.

1930 "Garbo talks!" And the public flocks to see her in *Anna Christie*. They flocked to see her when she didn't talk. Garbo smoothly makes the transition from silents to talkies; her face—with those sad, ethereal eyes gazing out from beneath thin half moon eyebrows, her delicately sculptured features and lips that never smile but promise passion—is enough to draw in a crowd. She may "vant to be alone," but the public won't allow that. While other actresses vie for publicity, Garbo shuns it, making herself into the mystery woman of the century. Rumors that she and her leading man, John Gilbert, heat up more than the silver screen make their love scenes more bristling. The public can't get enough.

1932 Already famous as a femme fatale on the stage, Mae West brings her swinging hips and husky Brooklyn accent to the silver screen in *Night After Night*. She's not the star of the film, but no one would know that as she struts into a speakeasy dripping in jewels. The hat-check girl gives West the setup line: "Goodness, what diamonds!" To which West purrs back, "Goodness had nothing to do with it." George Raft, the star of the film, says, "She stole everything but the camera."

1933 The artistic Czech film *Ecstasy,* featuring Hedwig Kiesler, premieres. The beautiful sixteen-year-old girl, soon to be known as Hedy Lamarr, failed to read the fine print on the movie contract which calls for her to do a scene in which she romps through the woods in the nude and skinny-dips in a pond. Another scene features passionate lovemaking, the camera catching a close-up of her face in the moments of ecstasy. Prudish moviegoers are shocked by the film, and it's almost the end of Lamarr's career. MGM reluctantly offers her a contract in 1937 to make the film *Algiers*. When it is released a year later, Lamarr becomes a bona fide sex symbol.

Hedy Lamarr's nude scene almost ruins her career.

1934 Claudette Colbert has already achieved sex-symbol status with her milk bath in Cecil B. DeMille's *Cleopatra,* but it took *It Happened One Night* to display her comedic ability. Her throaty, sexy voice, big brown eyes, and great acting win her an Academy Award for the flick that teaches hitchhikers that the fastest way to get picked up is to show some leg.

TRIVIA

The legendary Amazons are warrior women who inhabit northern Anatolia. They have only one use for men: sex. They mate with males from neighboring villages or with prisoners of war. POWs often have one of their legs broken—but not to keep them from escaping. Amazons believe the penis is strengthened if a limb is broken. Baby girls are raised to become warriors. Male infants are abandoned or crippled and used as slaves. Although Amazons are depicted as superwomen, some of them are disfigured: their right breast is removed to improve their ability as archers.

1934 Queen of the screwball comedies is Carole Lombard, a vibrant, fun-loving, foul-mouthed, full-fledged star who happens to be ravishingly beautiful with a body that won't quit. Her good-natured personality is beloved off and on screen while her marriage to male sex symbol Clark Gable makes them Hollywood royalty. She's known for her practical jokes and forthrightness. When director Ernst Lubitsch hems and haws about directing a film because he doubts its success, Carole tells him do it and if it flops he can have his way with her. But she warns, grabbing the fat cigar from his mouth, if it's a hit, "I'll shove this black thing up your ass." In 1941, at the height of her popularity, Lombard dies in a plane crash while on a war bond drive.

1937 Sixteen-year-old Lana Turner makes a brief appearance clad in high-heeled pumps, a skirt, and a tight blue sweater in her first movie, *They Won't Forget*—and they don't. She becomes Hollywood's Sweater Girl, and sales of sweaters go through the roof. So does the sale of falsies. Not every woman is as well endowed as Lana.

1941 *I Wanted Wings* is one more World War II propaganda film, except for the young, dishy blonde who walks into a scene with a waterfall of hair seductively falling down her back and across one eye. And it's not even a bedroom scene! Veronica Lake looks like this all the time! American women want to, too. If they can't grow their regular tresses cyclopicly, they buy hair pieces. Veronica's hair continues to fall in her eyes throughout the 1940s.

1943 After a three-year fight with the Hollywood censors *The Outlaw* is released, bringing the talents of Jane Russell to the public's attention. Russell is cast in the role by Howard Hughes, who painstakingly builds a bra to uplift his new starlet and achieve the look he wants (Russell claims she never wore it). The resulting cleavage and a scene where Jane crawls into bed to keep costar Jack Buetel warm—the man's dying for God's sake—keep the censors busy for three years.

1943 The sultry, velvet-voiced Lena Horne appears in *Cabin in the Sky,* the first all-black movie musical. Lena is cast as Georgia Brown, a reincarnation of Eve herself, sent by Lucifer to seduce leading man Eddie Anderson. Horne is known for her singing voice, having made her mark at the Cotton Club in Harlem and having been the first black female vocalist to sing with

Seductive Lena Horne can also sing up a storm.

a white dance band. She's talented enough to break barriers and become the first black actress signed to a Hollywood studio contract.

1944 "If you want anything, just whistle. You know how to whistle, don't you?" a lean, sultry Lauren Bacall shoots to leading man Humphrey Bogart in *To Have and Have Not*. "You just put your lips together and blow." The only person in the movie with a voice lower than Bacall's is Bogart, who falls madly in love with her despite their twenty-five-year age difference. Her almond-shaped eyes that peer out from arched eyebrows and a shock of heavy tresses get her dubbed "the Look." She's it and

she's hot. Bogart knows it, too. They marry a year later and make three more movies together.

1946 Rita Hayworth starts men salivating in the thriller *Gilda*. The audience has to wait almost an hour before she appears on screen. They first hear her singing; then in answer to the knock on the door and the question "Are you decent, Gilda?" she teases, "Me? Sure, I'm decent." The visual is Hayworth flipping back a mane of long, wavy red hair that shudders down a half-draped shoulder—a sight worth the price of admission alone. The movie is studded with innuendos. "If I'd been a ranch," she tells costar Glenn Ford, "they'd name me the Bar Nothing."

She peels off her long, black gloves in a bump and grind dance number that's numbing. The movie is panned, but she's not. Hayworth, who is one of the top pinups of World War II, has her picture plastered onto the first atomic bomb tested after World War II.

1946 Until this time Ava Gardner has owed her success primarily to the studio publicity department, which issues sexy pinup photos of the starlet. One MGM executive critiques a screen test of her with "She can't act; she didn't talk; she's sensational." With her appearance in *The Killers,* the audience sees a smolderingly sexy actress who has just begun to tantalize and titillate. Gardner's full lips and heavy-featured face complement a well-rounded body. American audiences regard her as the only rival of Marilyn Monroe. Her affair and troubled marriage to Frank Sinatra keep her in the public eye for years to come.

1951 Elizabeth Taylor takes her place in the adult acting world with *A Place in the Sun,* which showcases the star's mixture of vulnerability and soft sensuousness. Taylor's been in the public's eye since *National Velvet* in 1944. Moviegoers watch her grow up. Her soft violet eyes help her play socialite-debutante roles but the way she fills out a silk slip in *Cat on a Hot Tin Roof* makes everyone wonder how Paul Newman's character can be impotent. She's dubbed the most beautiful woman in the world. The public has a love-hate relationship with the real-life Taylor. Her husband-stealing of Eddie Fisher from good girl Debbie Reynolds is shocking. She dumps him to take up with Richard Burton. The swinging 1960s make Liz's sex life more acceptable, and she's internationally acclaimed for her talents on-screen and offscreen. During the filming of *Cleopatra,* hundreds of extras are brought in for one scene in which the queen enters Rome. The extras are supposed to yell, "Cleopatra!" Instead, awed by the star, they chant, "Liz! Liz!"

1951 She's famous in Italy already, but Gina Lollobrigida's gorgeous face and voluptuous body are destined for international fame. Known as La Lollo in Italy, it's her appearance in *Fan-Fan la Tulipe* that brings her worldwide attention. She's hamstrung by a contract with RKO, which makes little use of her, but the American public loves what it sees. La Lollo goes one better by educating herself and becoming an unofficial ambassador for Italian films guaranteeing her sexpot status.

1954 Marilyn Monroe stands atop a subway grate on a street in Manhattan clad in an ecru-colored halter-top dress with a sunburst pleated skirt. The scene is from *The Seven Year Itch,* and though it's unusually chilly this early morning, the scenario is a blistering hot night from which Marilyn is trying to find relief. As a subway train passes, a burst of cool air swirls Marilyn's skirts over her thighs, up to her waist, exposing her panties. The scene is watched by thousands of fans. Photographers have a field day snapping away at what columnist Irving Hoffman dubs "the shot seen round the world." This filming, done for the sake of publicity—the entire scene is reshot at a Hollywood studio—continues with countless retakes much to the onlookers' pleasure.

1956 Jayne Mansfield doesn't have Marilyn Monroe's talent or looks, but what a body! With tits measuring anywhere from 40 to 46 inches,

an 18-inch waist, and a 35-inch ass, Mansfield personifies the dumb blonde of the 1950s. She achieves some success on Broadway in *Will Success Spoil Rock Hunter?* clad only in a towel in the opening act. In this year's movie, *The Girl Can't Help It,* she sashays down the street, her swiveling hips registering a solid 8 on the Richter scale. Mansfield is a shark at publicity. When Howard Hughes arranges a photo session for Jane Russell, Mansfield is one of the background bathing beauties. Before Russell can even show up, Jayne falls into the pool and the top of her bikini *accidentally* falls off. By the time Russell shows up, the photogs have used up all their film. The feminism of the 1960s and the style switch to a more boyish-looking female body make Mansfield's type passé. While trying to revive her career in nightclub acts, Mansfield is killed in a car accident in 1967.

*The only gal who came near
to me in the sex appeal department
was pretty little Marilyn Monroe.
All the others had were big boobs.*

Mae West

1956 In a world of mutts, Grace Kelly is a thoroughbred. She's cool, elegant, sophisticated, almost icy. But underneath there's something smoldering in her eyes, her lips, that face, the way she walks. Grace is class—she refuses to tell the studio her measurements so they can publicize them. She's the top female box office star in the world when she films *To Catch a Thief*. While on location in Monaco, she meets Prince Rainier and agrees to marry him. Hollywood mourns the loss of its leading lady but Americans are proud of their fairy-tale princess. Her Serene Highness is killed in a car crash in 1982.

1957 Mom and Dad run to see Brigitte Bardot in *. . . And God Created Woman,* but when their teenage daughter piles her hair on top of her head, dons a bikini, and practices Bardot's famous pout in front of the mirror, they go spastic. Bardot's husband, director Roger Vadim, stars his sexy wife in the racy role of the child-woman who shows more skin and sex appeal than American eyeballs can take in. The movie starts an interest in foreign flicks and in Bardot, whose bare-bottom scenes make American films look juvenile. The film is condemned by the Catholic League of Decency but since it racks up $12 million in one year, who's listening?

1957 Dorothy Dandridge's beauty and the plot of *Island in the Sun* raise eyebrows. Dorothy's gorgeous, outspoken, and saucy. It's no wonder any man would fall in love with her. But the film character who does is a white man.

There's another interracial relationship in this movie, between Harry Belafonte and Joan Fontaine. Neither of the couples make love or even kiss. Dandridge comes the closest when she touches cheeks with costar John Justin. Southern states go a little crazy. Memphis, Tennessee, bans the film. New Orleans tries to stop it from being shown, but fails. A cross is burned at a drive-in theater in North Carolina. The movie is panned with Dandridge getting the best reviews. Personal problems overtake her, and she dies of a drug overdose.

1958 When Sophia Loren arrives in the United States, she's already a star in foreign films, but she is eager to share her sensuality with American audiences. She handles dramatic and comedic roles with equal deftness. Unlike sex kittens who tease, Loren's sexuality is innate. She's the woman who delivers quid pro quo on an international scale. Unlike that of other sex symbols, Loren's acting gets better as she matures, earning her an Academy Award for her work in *Two Women.*

1962 Marilyn Monroe is sex. She proves it by singing "Happy Birthday" to President Kennedy in a dress that boggles male hormones. It's little more than a transparent designer body stocking that has been sculpted to fit the general shape of her body, along with her breasts, nipples, and buttocks. To this transparency are hand sewn 6,000 rhinestones. Monroe makes the dress more dramatic by wearing, as *Life* magazine reports, "nothing, absolutely nothing, underneath." Monroe is sewn into the dress. When the lights hit the rhinestones, Monroe's body becomes a filter of light as she breathlessly sings "Happy Birthday" to the man she secretly makes love to. Fifteen thousand people at

Madison Square Garden cheer wildly as a six-foot cake is wheeled out. No doubt the forty-five candles on the cake have self-ignited.

1964 Ann-Margret is known for her roles in *Pocketful of Miracles* and *Bye Bye Birdie*. She's played with Elvis—figuratively and literally—in *Viva Las Vegas*. This year in *The Pleasure Seekers* and *Kitten with a Whip,* she plays more sophisticated womanly roles, making critics take note of her acting ability. But that face and body won't go away. Movie critic Pauline Kael writes that "she comes through dirty, no matter what she plays." And *Carnal Knowledge,* which features a nude scene, hasn't even been filmed yet.

1965 How do you make a fetish fashionable? Put Diana Rigg in a tight black leather cat suit and star her in TV's *Avengers*. Powerful, sexy, able to karate-kick and judo-chop her way out of any situation while maintaining an air of kinkiness, her character, Emma Peel, is the closest thing TV has to a dominatrix.

1966 She's the pinup girl of the 1960s, exuding a wild animal magnetism in a fur bikini in her role in *One Million Years B.C.* Raquel Welch has only two lines—actually just two words, "akita" (help) and "serron" (giant bird)—in the movie. Who cares? If womankind looked like that a million years ago, mankind would never have evolved. Welch takes her acting seriously but the studio promotes her body and face. Though she never achieves the stature of serious actress, her beauty and figure never fade.

1968 Director Roger Vadim accomplishes with Jane Fonda what he did with Brigitte Bardot. He marries her and turns her into a sex kitten. Fonda appears in *Circle of Love, The Game Is Over,* and *Barbarella,* three French films that show off Jane's natural talents. An eight-story billboard promoting *Circle of Love* shows Jane lying on her stomach with her behind exposed. She bares all in *The Game Is Over* and sues *Playboy* when they run stolen still photos from the movie. *Barbarella* makes her an international sex goddess. Fonda dumps Vadim at about the same time she decides to uncover her brain. She becomes an Academy Award–winning actress and an outspoken militant.

1976 Farrah Fawcett-Majors bursts onto the scene in TV's first T&A (tits and ass) show, *Charlie's Angels.* Farrah plays one of three women detectives who solve crimes bralessly every Wednesday night. Sharing equal billing with Kate Jackson and Jaclyn Smith, it's Fawcett-Majors, with her huge mane of shaggy blond hair and a mouthful of perfect white teeth, who grabs the spotlight. She inspires a line of T-shirts, lunch pails, dolls, and a shampoo, but none do as well as the poster of her that adorns 8 million bedroom walls. When asked to explain the success of his client's poster, manager Jay Bernstein sums it up in one word: "Nipples."

1979 Hugh Hefner says she's "the first sex star of the eighties." She's a perfect 10, which happens to be the title of the picture Bo Derek stars in with Dudley Moore. The vision of her running down the beach in slow motion puts male hormones aflutter. She sets a silly hairstyle of cornrows for white women. Mostly, though, Ravel's *Bolero* can never again be listened to the same way. Bo's stardom is fleeting. Though she makes more movies, none come close to the success of *10.*

Sharon Stone: Possessor of the "most famous pubis aureus."

Sex—128 pages of nude photos and text that *Vanity Fair* calls "perhaps the dirtiest coffee table book ever published." The book explores her sexual fantasies, which include whips, chains, knives, leashes, and gags. She's shown nude at gas stations, hitchhiking in stiletto heels, and eating pizza at a restaurant. She bites nipples, exposes herself in windows, and explores herself. The book is wrapped in Mylar, which is penetrable only with a sharp object, and it's sold only to those over eighteen.

1986 Kim Basinger breaks barriers in the sadomasochistic film *9½ Weeks*. Until this time, Basinger was known mostly as a James Bond girl. Mickey Rourke and Basinger portray a yuppie couple engaged in kinky sex that includes her being whipped, handcuffed to a bed, blindfolded, and crawling on all fours. The ice cube scene inspires more than a few folks to run to their freezers for a sex toy they didn't know they had.

1992 She's a singer, songwriter, dancer, and actress but Madonna excels most at pushing the envelope to find out how far she can go and how much the public will tolerate. She's appeared in *Penthouse* and *Playboy* and in soft-porn films. Her lovers are numerous and of both sexes. Her costumes raise eyebrows and chuckles—who can forget breast cones? But whatever Madonna does, she does to standing room only. This year she takes one more step when she publishes

1992 Sharon Stone rises to stardom when she plays the "fuck of the century" in *Basic Instinct*. Graphic sex scenes, including oral sex with her leading man, Michael Douglas, heat up the screen, but Stone, who plays an aggressive, I-love-to-fuck bisexual, steals the movie. In one scene, Stone, playing a murder suspect, is brought to police headquarters for interrogation. She's wearing a microminidress, and it's been established that she's not wearing any underwear. While she's telling the detectives that she never tied up her now dead lover because he liked to use his hands too much and she likes hands and fingers, she uncrosses her legs, parts them, and gives the cops a crotch shot, which *Playboy* says makes her the "proprietor of the most famous pubis aureus on the planet." The movie bolts to number one and causes a run on $195 white silk Hermès scarves like the one she used to tie up her lovers.

Great Moments in Sex

Chapter Five
SEX SYMBOLS: THE MEN

B.C.

c. 1272 Ramses II is the pharaoh during the Exodus. To the Egyptians, he's not only their brave leader, he's good-looking and romantic. His 150 sons and daughters from several hundred wives prove he's not just hanging around the pyramids at night. He marries a few of his own daughters so they can have eugenically superior kids. So numerous are his offspring that they constitute their own class within Egypt that's tapped for rulers.

c. 435 Alcibiades is on the sexual wish list of every Athenian man and woman. Endowed with great beauty, a sharp wit, self-confidence, and a dollop of derring-do, he's seen in the company of Socrates, groups of male lovers, and consorting with consorts who think he's dandy. He punches out one of the most powerful men in Athens but returns the next day and lies prostrate, naked, and begs to be whipped. The victim is so impressed that he gives Alcibiades his daughter in marriage, along with

a handsome dowry. Marriage doesn't affect his sex life. When his wife tries to divorce him, he goes to court, sweeps her up in his arms, and takes her home. Dashing? Romantic? If the divorce went through, he'd have to give back the dowry. Alcibiades is assassinated by a political enemy. Greece remembers him with a monument on which an ox is sacrificed every year.

c. 80 The young Pompey is so strikingly handsome that he wins the affection of women easily. Rome's noted courtesan, Flora, is agog over him, remarking that he never leaves her without putting teeth marks on her flesh. After a couple of marriages, he finally weds Julia, the daughter of Julius Caesar. He's fifty-nine. She's twenty-two. They're so smitten with each other that Pompey becomes the idol of women again, this time for being faithful to his wife.

c. 78 Julius Caesar is Rome's most famous rake. Not content with multiple marriages, Caesar has multiple mistresses. He beds the wives of powerful politicians and uses the women to influence their husbands in his favor. On campaigns he enjoys Cleopatra and Queen Eunoe of Numidia, earning himself the nickname "the bald adulterer" (Caesar worries about losing his hair). Women aren't the only objects of his affection. Teased about having lost his virginity to King Nicomedes of Bithynia, Caesar is called "the husband of every woman and the wife of every man."

c. 50 Mark Antony is remembered for his liaison with Cleopatra. But before his marriage to the Queen of the Nile, Antony does enough romping to earn a reputation. His sex drive is so strong that he outdoes and scandalizes Caesar by keeping a harem of both sexes in Rome and by traveling with a Greek courtesan. Then he meets Cleo. He's captivated by her, but he marries Octavia for political reasons. Political reasons also prompt him to divorce her and marry Cleopatra. The rest is history.

c. 21 Pylades of Cilicia and Bathyllus of Alexandria bring the art of pantomime to Rome. It's not enough that the two actors capture the hearts of all the ladies; they divide the men into separate camps, too. Street fights and bloody brawls throughout the city and arguing over who is the better actor overshadow political concerns even in the Senate. When Pylades is banished from the city, a near insurrection by the masses forces his recall.

A.D.

c. 117 The rumor is that Hadrian becomes emperor of Rome only because he's having an affair with the late emperor's wife. Hadrian is tall, curly-haired, good-looking, and so influential that when he grows a beard to cover his facial blemishes, other men do likewise. Though he's married, the love of his life is Antinoüs, a young beautiful Greek with curly hair, soft eyes, and a penis. When Antinoüs drowns in the Nile, the emperor weeps "like a woman," and builds a temple to the lad on the shore.

180 At age nineteen, Commodus takes over as emperor of Rome. His bloodlust is satiated by living and performing with gladiators. His sexual lust is taken care of by a harem of three hundred women and three hundred young boys plus a mistress he's particularly fond of. In order to have more time to spend on sex, he hands over the operation of Rome first to one prefect, then to another. When his mistress and one of the prefects find their names on his assassination list, they poison him and have him strangled in his bath at the age of thirty-one.

But, Honey, I Just Did What You Told Me to Do

c. 558 Clotaire, king of Gaul, is married to Ingund and loves her so much he wants to please her. She tells him she wants him to find her sister a husband as good as he is. He obeys. When Clotaire visits the sister, he's so enamored of her that *he* marries her. His explanation to Ingund: "I found none better than myself."

Great Moments in Sex

771 At six feet four inches, the Holy Roman Emperor cuts a dashing figure with his blond hair, animated eyes, and clean-shaven face, except for his mustache. He loves the ladies and they love him. It's said that women prefer sharing Charlemagne's attentions to having the complete attention of any other man. He has four wives in succession, five mistresses, and fathers eighteen children. At a time when the church adamantly insists on self-control, it turns a blind eye to the emperor's lifestyle.

Charlemagne, Holy Roman Emperor and king of hearts.

1095 Oh, those crusaders! Off to capture the Holy Land, these knights and adventurers often cut dashing figures. Godfrey of Bouillon, Duke of Lower Lorraine, is a tall, muscular, "broad shouldered and narrow hipped" soldier whose piety is well known. Tancred of Hauteville's fearlessness is matched only by his handsome features. And Count Bohemund of Taranto, that tall, curly-haired, clean-shaven hunk, has blue eyes that can inspire fear as well as awe. In contrast to the eastern men who are decked out in effeminate luxury, the crusaders from the West appear ruggedly barbaric.

1117 Cofounder of the University of Paris, Pierre Abelard is handsome, charming, witty, intelligent, with a zest for life. His lectures attract a student following from all over the known world. Abelard's famous love affair and subsequent marriage to Héloïse, a young woman he's paid to tutor, ends with her uncle castrating the young philosopher. Pierre becomes a monk, Héloïse a nun, but their letters to each other remain as a testimony to their love.

1154 The passionate energy of Henry II, king of England, shows in his countenance. His gray eyes hold the attention of those he looks upon, especially the ladies. At eighteen, he exudes a rugged manliness that attracts his future wife, Eleanor of Aquitaine, eleven years his senior. Henry's good looks make it easier for him to go whoring within and outside of the castle both before and after his marriage. He can't keep his hands off Eleanor's maids, and when he travels, men lock up their wives and daughters until the king is safely on his way.

1220 Holy Roman Emperor Frederick II is raised by the pope after his parents' death. His first wife dies. His second retires into the background because she doesn't understand his morality. His numerous mistresses are only one thing the pope has a problem with. Besides

WHAT'S GOOD FOR THE GOOSE . . .

TRIVIA The fifteen-year-old Chinese Emperor Liu Tzû-yeh is a sadist who indulges in orgies with women and eunuchs. But he is a good brother. When his sister complains that he has six palaces and more than ten thousand concubines while she has only one husband, he immediately assigns thirty men to be her consorts.

being charged with sodomy and keeping a harem—the eunuchs are a dead giveaway—Frederick has to explain that all the extra ladies and boys are at court to entertain the king. Honest, Pope, they're dancers and acrobats.

1349 King Edward III of England tries to seduce the lovely Countess of Salisbury. In order to see her, he stages a tournament where, while dancing, the countess drops her garter. The king retrieves the leg band saying, "Shame to him who evil thinks of it." Edward forms the Order of the Garter, the highest order of knighthood, and "Shame to him . . ." becomes its motto. When his queen dies, Edward gives her jewelry to his most noted mistress, Alice Perrers. But turnabout is fair play. When Edward dies, Alice sheds a few tears and then removes the rings from his fingers and makes off with them.

1509 Henry VIII is everything the English dream of. He's handsome, almost feminine, with auburn hair, a golden beard, great taste in clothes, and an "extremely fine calf." He's well-mannered, has a sense of humor, is interested in tennis, hunting, philosophy, the arts, music, and the ladies. Commoners love him. So do intellectuals. So do the ladies; he marries six women, two of whom he beheads. But a chronic illness—probably syphilis—takes its toll on his appearance and his mind. From well-loved he descends to well-feared and dies at the age of fifty-five.

1515 If there's any truth to the myth that the length of a man's nose is an indicator of his penis size, then King Francis I of France is a well-endowed man. His long nose spoils his features but not his eye for women. Mistresses abound in his life. Famous is the story that a lawyer whose wife is selected by the king purposely gives her syphilis so she'll pass it on to her royal lover. The king's mother says he was punished where he had sinned. Francis believes all noblemen should have at least one mistress.

A "gift" from a mistress may have shortened Francis I's life.

Great Moments in Sex

101

Those who don't he looks upon as tasteless men. The *grande vérole* shortens his life. He dies at fifty-three.

1572 He's a man's man and a lady's man, able to swagger with the males and provide lusty entertainment for the females. It is said that as a babe he sucked eight nurses dry. Henry IV of France attracts female attention at the age of thirteen with his reddish hair, polished manners, and love of life. He's married twice but takes more than fifty-six mistresses. One of his last alliances, when he's well into his fifties, is with a fifteen-year-old girl whom Henry allows to dress him like a fop. He's assassinated by a religious fanatic in 1610.

1582 Sir Walter Raleigh brings chivalry back to the Elizabethan court. It's doubtful he threw his cloak over a mud puddle for the queen to walk on or that he scribbled verses on a pane of glass to catch her eye. What is true is that Raleigh is a handsome, dashing adventurer who catches the heart of Elizabeth if only momentarily. His secret marriage to the queen's maid gets them both thrown into the Tower of London but Raleigh sweet-talks his way out. He'll outlive the monarch but not her successor, James I, who has him beheaded in 1618.

1660 King Charles II of England wins the Most Scandalous Leader of the Time award. But he's a lazy Lothario. He relies on his intimates at court to find femmes fatales for command performances. Thirteen of his mistresses are known by name, but they're just the tip of the iceberg. He recognizes fourteen illegitimate children, but that's a short list, too. As Charles explains to his wife, adultery is a royal privilege, as is having a wig made from the pubic hairs of his mistresses.

Charles II makes the most of his "royal privileges."

1660 At age twenty, France's Louis XIV loves and wants to marry Marie Mancini but it's beaten into his head that kings don't wed for love. The diminutive king (he's five feet five) does as he's told and marries his cousin, Maria Theresa, then decides to take his pleasure where he may. Indiscriminately, he beds noblewomen, peasants, and chambermaids, never failing to be utterly charming. But the king has a cruel streak, too. He demands cheerfulness even if it means causing emotional pain to others. He makes his soon-to-be ex-mistress guard the bedroom door while he tries out her successor. He falls in love with his final mistress and marries her after the queen dies.

c. 1670 The English court has its own cast of characters. The Duke of York (the future James II) has so many women in his life that the king says the priests give him mistresses for penance. Then there's George Villiers, the second Duke of Buckingham. He kills the husband of one of his mistresses in a duel and is embraced by the new widow on the scene. John Wilmot, Earl of Rochester, who is loved for his sense of humor, disguises himself as a German physician and actually cures people. Women chase after him and he is all too willing to be caught. There is an equality at court: wives are as unfaithful as their husbands.

c. 1715 Lord Chesterfield sets the tone of etiquette in England, though Samuel Johnson notes that he teaches "the morals of a whore and the manners of a dancing teacher." He has a child by his mistress and doesn't marry until he's thirty-nine, and then he chooses a different woman. He deplores lechery. Chesterfield writes a book of helpful hints on how to be a gentleman and handle women. The book is composed of the letters he regularly sends to his son in the hope of making him a candidate for a government position. When his son dies prematurely, Chesterfield discovers that the boy was married to an unattractive woman and content with an ordinary life.

c. 1730 Described as "the handsomest lad in his domain," King Louis XV of France is compared to Eros, the god of love, and women swoon over him accordingly. His marriage awakens his sexual appetite, and the queen begs for his continence at least on the feast days of major saints. Louis obliges her by taking his first four mistresses from one family. The most noted of his mistresses is Madame de Pompadour who tires also and equips a house with young women to entertain the king.

c. 1740 Giovanni Jacopo Casanova is romancing all the ladies of Europe. Being

thrown out of a Venetian seminary at age sixteen for scandalous and immoral behavior sets the tone for the events of his life, which, as an old man, he records in his twelve-volume work, *Memoirs*. He falls in love at the drop of a hat. Then he romances, cajoles, promises, and romances again until, ah, yes, the lady is his. Then he leaves. Women are his cuisine, and he wants to taste them all: from age eleven to over fifty (he admits getting turned on by a nine-year-old), married, unmarried, virgins, vixens, titled, commonplace, nuns. He's a rogue, a bounder, a cad, but always a romantic. Pleasuring the woman is as important to him as the conquest. His fastest time, he confesses, is fifteen minutes with a luxurious all-women-only-dream-of seven hours at the max. He boasts of the night he went the distance twelve times, how he ate fifty oysters for breakfast with a companion in a bathtub for two, and admits to bouts of premature ejaculation, not being able to get it up, at least eleven encounters with venereal disease, and finally becoming too old to do anything but remember.

SACRE BLEU!

In 1899, French President François Félix Faure dies in the throes of passion with a woman other than his wife. Rumor is the prostitute he is with grows so hysterical when he dies while inside her, that her vaginal muscles clamp around the dead man's penis. Doctors surgically separate them.

TRIVIA

1777 By the time he's fifteen years old, England's future George IV's tutor says of him that he will become "either the most polished gentleman or the most accomplished black-guard in Europe—possibly both." At first he's amusing, lavishing large sums of money on entertainment, amusing the ladies, and marrying his mistress. When his debts become unmanageable, he has the marriage annulled and marries his cousin for her money. He's blamed in part for the insanity of his father, George III. He's driving the rest of England nuts, too. The people learn to hate him, hissing and pelting his carriage with whatever is handy. He's crowned king in 1820, but England suffers him only for ten years. He dies in 1830.

1784 Talk about sleeping your way to the top! Don Manuel de Godoy is a seventeen-year-old royal bodyguard. Tall, dark, handsome, and charming, he's makes it with a few of the ladies at court when the future wife of the king of Spain takes him as her lover. King Carlos IV isn't exactly Einstein in the brains department. Not only does he not catch on to his wife's affair, but he befriends the boy toy. Every month Godoy is promoted. By age twenty-one he heads the Spanish armed forces, and by twenty-five he's prime minister. Politics is his downfall. When France overtakes Spain and forces Carlos out, Godoy is sent into exile.

c. 1800 It's not the women who flock after Beau Brummel; it's the men, including the Prince of Wales. Brummel's a snob, but a well-dressed one. He's the trendsetter par excellence. He has tailors for each part of his body, and he takes two hours to prepare to be seen in public. It's too bad he doesn't groom his mouth. Brummel's sarcastic remarks are amusing until

Lord Byron is a dashing poet to everyone but his wife.

he aims one at the Prince of Wales: "Who's your fat friend?" he asks the prince's companion. Soon Brummel's creditors, who were being held at bay, show no mercy. He flees to France, where he lives in poverty, a world away from the life he knew. He dies penniless at the age of sixty-two in a French lunatic asylum.

1812 With the publication of *Childe Harold's Pilgrimage,* Lord Byron becomes famous overnight, arousing the curiosity of women. When they see what he looks like, he arouses something else. But Byron isn't your run-of-the-mill good-looking poet. He's vain, with a quick mind and a quick temper, and he doesn't

The brother of Abraham Lincoln's assassin, Edwin Booth is an early American matinee idol.

1851 America's finest stage actor appears in his signature role of Hamlet for the first time. Edwin Booth's acting is understated, unlike his mop of curly hair and his expressive eyes. His fans are vocal about matching his talents with those of other performers. They are quieted only when his brother, John Wilkes Booth, assassinates Abraham Lincoln. Edwin Booth retires from the stage for a few years but returns to the praise of his admirers.

1853 Louis Moreau Gottschalk's Creole roots influence his music and his looks. He's a major draw in the United States, where his dark, handsome features pack in the ladies. When the pianist returns to San Francisco after a five-year stay in Cuba, he's treated like royalty. Then he's called a "bawdy miscreant" when he's caught in a scandal with a young woman. Gottschalk flees to Latin America, leaving more than one woman brokenhearted.

1860 The Prince of Wales, Edward VII, is the leader of La Belle Époque. He's a dandy who loves partying, horses, yachting, and pretty women. His wife, Alexandra, is beautiful, but that doesn't stop him from forming friendships with professional beauty Lillie Langtry, actress Margot Tennant, and Winston Churchill's mother, Jennie. Queen Victoria won't relinquish the throne to him until her death in 1901, which gives him plenty of time to travel and play.

1861 The world's first trapeze artist captures the hearts and widens the eyes of women. French aerialist Jules Léotard is almost as handsome as he thinks he is. It's his invention of the leotard, a skintight one-piece elastic body suit that he's proud of. Says he, "Do you want to be adored by the ladies? [Then] put on

live by the usual standards of morality. He admits having been involved with over two hundred women. The loudest whispers concern his incestuous relationship with his half sister, Augusta Leigh. He marries Anne Isabella Milbanke and, after boffing her on the sofa before dinner on their wedding day, dedicates himself to making her miserable. He tells her he hates her, fires guns in her bedroom, informs her, while she's delivering their child, that he hopes she and the baby both die in childbirth, and torments her with innuendo about his relationship with his sister. Needless to say, they separate. He leaves England and leads a life that culminates in death at age thirty-six.

more natural garb that does not hide your best features."

1905 Rasputin is a smelly Russian peasant who isn't much to look at but he gains popularity as a faith healer. He draws women in with his hypnotic eyes and sensuous voice and then impresses them with his 13-incher in his "holy of holies," a.k.a. his bedroom. He's brought to the czarina's attention because her young son is a hemophiliac whom doctors can't cure. But Rasputin does. He's accepted by the czar but not by other noble husbands. Prince Felix Yusupov sets up his assassination. Enough potassium cyanide to kill four men doesn't faze Rasputin. He's shot, raped, castrated, tied up, and thrown into a freezing river. An autopsy reveals that the mad monk died of drowning.

1912 "The handsomest man in the world" is Francis X. Bushman, sculptor's model turned actor. Bushman plays romantic roles and is loved by female fans until they find out that he secretly married. How could he! They take their hearts back but Bushman retains his reputation as a good actor, hitting his zenith in the role of Messala in the 1926 version of *Ben-Hur*.

1916 John Barrymore excels in the legitimate theater and on the silver screen, beating out Gloria Swanson *and* Rin-Tin-Tin in one of the first box office polls. In 1926 "the Great Profile" falls in love with his leading lady, Dolores Costello. Their love scenes are particularly intense, since this is the only time he can get his hands on her. Mama Costello chaperons her nineteen-year-old daughter on dates with forty-three-year-old Barrymore. He has no problem crossing over into talking pictures. He does have a drinking problem, though, which results in memory lapses that make it difficult for him to work.

John Barrymore beats out even Rin-Tin-Tin.

1920 Starting with *The Mark of Zorro*, Douglas Fairbanks stars in a series of swashbuckling films that make full use of his athletic and gymnastic ability. Women swoon at his cheeky, impish grin, not to mention his good-looking face and great body. But unlike other heartthrobs, Fairbanks has male fans, too. His adventurousness and daredevil feats make him a man's man, while adolescent boys are breaking body parts trying to emulate his on-screen acrobatics. Fairbanks retires from the screen in 1936 and dies of a heart attack three years later.

1920 Warren Harding is one of the worst U.S. presidents. He's also one of the hand-somest. Over six feet tall and weighing 200 pounds, his imposing figure is dashingly complemented by his silver hair, distinguished looks, and strong charisma. It isn't until after his death in office in 1923 that the public hears rumors of his philandering, including a love affair with the twenty-three-year-old daughter of a friend (when he's fifty-four), which results in the birth of a baby girl. Tales of political corruption in his administration are also brought to the public's attention.

1921 Rudolph Valentino is *The Sheik*. He's the ultimate lover, a passionate animal in human form. He redefines the word "erotic" when he tangos in *The Four Horsemen of the Apocalypse*. Women chase after him, ripping at his clothes, exposing their bodies to him, and sneak into his bed. He doesn't fare well in his real-life relationships with women. His first wife divorces him saying the marriage was never consummated. He prefers the company of men to women. Ironically, men don't like him. They only see his bulging eyes, flaring nostrils, and bared teeth, his modus operandi on the silver screen. The *Chicago Tribune* calls him a "Pink Powder Puff." Critics claim that Valentino would never have succeeded in talking pictures. But it's a moot point. In 1926, at the height of his fame, he dies of peritonitis. Across the nation women sob hysterically. Several commit suicide, and rioting breaks out at his funeral as women try to say one last good-bye.

1921 In the age of Latin lovers, John Gilbert can hold his own with his dark, passionate looks. Unlike the domineering he-man type, "the Great Lover" is sensitive, smiling, yet

Heartthrob Rudolph Valentino does not like "women who know too much."

intense enough to get his point across on screen. His leading ladies are the brightest stars in Hollywood, including Greta Garbo, whom he romances in real life. But when he utters, "I love you, I love you, I love you" in his first talkie in 1929, audiences howl at his high-pitched voice. Gilbert becomes the symbol of movie stars whose careers go down the tube when sound is added to film. His confidence shattered, Gilbert drinks himself into an early grave in 1936.

1922 Ramon Novarro's dark Latin looks make him a perfect choice for the type of leading man Valentino popularized. He gets his break in *Prisoner of Zenda* but his performance in the title role of *Ben-Hur* in 1926 ensures his stardom, at least until talkies debut. Novarro is romantically linked with leading ladies but squelches the rumors himself. Novarro is gay, which is implied by some, but not confirmed until 1969, when his brutal murder reveals that he frequents male prostitutes. Novarro is beaten to death by two gay-hating men.

1923 Hearts throb for Ronald Colman when he appears in *The White Sister*. A bona fide sex symbol of the silent era, when talkies come in, he's got it made. Not wanting a John Gilbert repeat, studio heads cast him in roles that match his voice, which is distinctively reserved and British. Now that he can talk, women know for sure he's what they dreamed of. Voted the top male star in 1928, 1929, and 1932, Colman remains a sex symbol for nearly thirty years.

c. 1930 Charles Atlas is determined to rid the world of 97-pound weaklings through his Dynamic Tension course. Twice voted America's Most Perfectly Developed Man, Angelo Siciliano is the weakling who got sand kicked in his face by a bully, lost the girl, and vowed never to let it happen again. He builds his body through isometrics, changes his name to Charles Atlas, becomes a sculptor's model (that's his body under Alexander Hamilton's head in front of the U.S. Treasury Building), and designs the exercise and

lifestyle program that makes him a wealthy man. Even Arnold Schwarzenegger holds him as a childhood idol. And women don't mind looking at Atlas and wishing their boyfriends would pump up a little, too.

1933 When Mae West spots Cary Grant on the Paramount lot, she has the same reaction that millions of other women have when they get their first eyeful. He's dashing. He's suave. He's charming. He's funny. And he's so damn good-looking. His Bristol accent doesn't hurt, either. West puts him in her movie *She Done Him Wrong,* but she does him right. An immediate star, Grant's still sexy when he stars in *Walk, Don't Run* in 1966 when he's seventy years old.

Truly, madam, nobody is.

Cary Grant, to a female fan
who asks if he's Cary Grant.

Cary Grant, a star with perennial sex appeal.

Sex Symbols: The Men

1933 Women don't necessarily want to go to bed with Fred Astaire. They just want to dance and be romanced by him. When he teams up with Ginger Rogers, every woman in the audience wants to trade places with her. Astaire establishes himself as the best dancer in the world. Not bad for a guy whose screen test report read, "Can't act. Can't sing. Can dance a little."

1934 Clark Gable takes off his shirt in *It Happened One Night*, and lo and behold, he's not wearing an undershirt. Women sigh. Men ditch their T's. Undershirt sales plummet. In 1939, Gable comes back even sexier in *Gone With the Wind*.

1935 Animal magnetism and charm ooze from the silver screen when Errol Flynn appears in *Captain Blood*. The swashbuckler to end all swashbuckling is as large as life offscreen as he is on. Born in Tasmania, Flynn spent his teens and early twenties crocodile hunting, gold mining, dodging headhunters in New Guinea, fighting the Japanese in China, gambling, and smoking opium in Macao. He is described by Jack Warner of Warner Brothers as "handsomer than hell," and women agree he's the best-looking guy they've ever seen in a pair of tights. In 1942, Flynn is charged with statutory rape, which takes him down a notch in the public's eye. He's acquitted, but the swashbuckling genre that brought him fame is passé. Years of hard drinking and drugs take an incredible toll on his once beautiful face. At age fifty, old beyond his years, Flynn dies of a heart attack.

1938 If there's a male equivalent to Greta Garbo, it's Charles Boyer. The foreign film star comes to America from France where's he's already an idol, makes a few films and steals hearts in *Algiers*. Boyer's sad, expressive eyes, his deep, accented voice, and pent-up manner make him the perfect Continental lover. Offscreen he wants to be left alone, never seeks publicity, and refuses to do interviews. He's short, stout, and prematurely bald, but not after Hollywood makeup artists get done with him. Boyer's personal life is tragic: his son commits suicide, his wife dies, and Boyer later takes his own life in 1978.

1939 Clark Gable could give virility lessons after appearing in *Gone With the Wind*. American women knew he was perfect for the role of Rhett Butler, but even that can't prepare them for the heart-pounding moment when the King scoops up his unyielding Scarlett O'Hara (Vivien Leigh) and carries her up the grand staircase. The scene fades out, but imaginations don't. Women love him for his tough, unflinching earthiness. Men like him for the same reason. That relationship continues unbroken up to his death in 1960.

1942 Alan Ladd plays a psychotic killer in *This Gun for Hire*, and something strange happens. When police move in on him, audiences start to boo and hiss. Ladd is a good bad guy, and women let the studio know they want to see more of him. Thirty thousand fan letters pour in after the movie's release. Ladd is terse, unsmiling, and short, only five-six. With most leading ladies, he has to stand on a box to make him look taller. Ladd's insecurities are his undoing. He dies from a lethal combination of alcohol and sedatives.

1942 Humphrey Bogart's sex appeal lies not with his physique. He's on the short, scrawny side. It's not with his looks. Put big, floppy ears on him and a bloodhound starts to emerge. What

Bogey has is himself. He knows the world stinks, and he copes by making his own code of conduct. He's righteous. He's loyal. He'll do the right thing. Bogart proves that this year in *Casablanca, the* movie of World War II. Millions of women want to be in Ingrid Bergman's shoes, even if it means a broken heart at the end.

1944 Already a heartthrob with the bobby-sox crowd, Frank Sinatra causes the Columbus Day riot when he appears at New York's Paramount Theater. Over 25,000 panting young women wait to see him, blocking streets, holding up traffic and running wild through Times Square. Police reserves are brought in to control the crowd of adoring fans who are swooning, fainting, and screaming, "Frankie! Frankie!" Frank wows them at the concert that night and is greeted by similar outbursts in Boston, Chicago, and Philadelphia.

1945 The ladies start to notice Robert Mitchum's half-asleep eyes and that distinct loner act when he stars in *The Story of G.I. Joe.* Hollywood considers him pure beefcake. Even Katharine Hepburn tells him in a pique, "You know you can't act and if you hadn't been good-looking you would never have gotten a picture." But either his fans don't agree with her or they don't care. When he's arrested for possession of marijuana—a sure career killer for most people—they don't bat an eye. Mitchum answers his critics in *The Night of the Hunter,* a 1955 movie in which he excels as a sadistic preacher-murderer who's just too sexy to stop watching.

1948 Montgomery Clift makes his film debut in *The Search.* Women are impressed by his dark good looks. Hollywood's impressed by his ability and gives him a Best Actor nomination. Later, in *A Place in the Sun,* he's as handsome as leading lady Elizabeth Taylor is beautiful. In real life Clift is tormented. His homosexuality in an unaccepting society is just one problem that drives him to drugs and drink. Marilyn Monroe says he's "the only person I know who's in worse shape than I am." A car accident in 1956 disfigures and partially paralyzes his lovely face. His abuses take their toll. Clift dies of a heart attack at the age of forty-five.

1951 There's something earthy and vulnerable in Marlon Brando's portrayal of Stanley Kowalski in *A Streetcar Named Desire.* He originates the role on Broadway in 1947 and it catapults him into stardom. Brando reaches hearts with raw, macho nonconformity. Unlike other sex symbols, there's no quibbling over his acting ability. He's the first successful American actor to use the Stanislavsky method, and it brings him an Academy Award for his next movie, *On the Waterfront.* Always one to push the envelope, Brando will be the first major star to appear in a sexually explicit movie, *Last Tango in Paris,* in 1972.

1953 Hugh Hefner touts a hedonistic lifestyle and then puts it into practice, making him the envy of men. The founder of *Playboy* magazine runs his empire from his bed, clad in his signature purple silk pajamas and smoking jacket. He's surrounded by buxom bunnies and able to take his pick of the hutch, the idealized American harem. Celebrities flock to him and Hef comes and goes on his Playboy jet. Divorced, he clings to bachelorhood for thirty-six years until, at the age of sixty-three, he marries 1989's Playmate of the Year. That marriage ends in divorce, too.

1954 There's no inner turmoil with Rock Hudson. He's as homogenized as the decade in which he emerges. Known as Roy Fitzgerald, his agent takes his new first name from the Rock of Gibraltar, his last from the Hudson River. Hudson makes his presence known in *Magnificent Obsession,* but is best known for chasing after Doris Day's virginity in romantic comedies. Women fall in love with his impish wolf-in-sheep's-clothing characters. Hudson's private life is spotlighted in the 1980s when his homosexuality is revealed. He becomes the first major star to die of AIDS.

1955 The angst of an entire generation is contained in one human being: James Dean. He broods. He aches. He has a lonesomeness a world of people can't fill. He's a star in *East of Eden.* He's an idol in *Rebel Without a Cause.* He makes one more picture, *Giant,* and then crashes his Porsche, ending his life at the age of twenty-four. But Dean's fame doesn't die. His fans won't let it. Fan clubs spring up across the country, and everyone wears the Jimmy Dean look—blue jeans, short-sleeved shirts, and partially zipped jackets. Dean maintains a cult following even today.

1956 Elvis Presley makes his first appearance on *The Ed Sullivan Show.* Over 54 million people watch as Presley's smoldering sexiness drips through the airwaves when he sings *Love Me Tender.* Conservative groups are shocked when Elvis's pelvis thrusts through *Don't Be Cruel, Ready Teddy,* and *Hound Dog.* Presley makes two more appearances on the Sullivan show. It isn't until the last performance that cameramen receive orders to shoot Presley only from the waist up.

1958 He's got the face of an angel, but somewhere along the line it got a big kiss from the devil. You don't get a smile like that by being a Boy Scout. And those eyes. Even the sky isn't that blue. Paul Newman's made a couple of films before, but this year he appears in *The Long Hot Summer* and *Cat on a Hot Tin Roof.* The sizzling sound heard in movie theaters isn't coming from melted butter on the popcorn. It's women's blood reacting to Newman on film. He plays bad boy parts but there's always redemption. Guys like him, too. He's his own man. There's no such thing as age to him. He's a cross between Adonis and the Energizer Bunny—the sex appeal just keeps going and going and going. . . .

1959 Clint Eastwood plays ramrod Rowdy Yates on television's *Rawhide.* His chiseled face and steely eyes make women watch the western.

More important, director Sergio Leone tunes in, too, and offers him a part in the spaghetti western he's filming in Italy. *A Fistful of Dollars* is released in Europe in 1964 and Eastwood becomes their superstar. Americans wait two years to see their homegrown boy, and when they do, hearts start pounding. Eastwood plays an unkempt, cold-blooded cowboy. That dangerous edge adds to his allure while the years only add more ruggedness to a brutally handsome face.

1960 John Kennedy is not a stuffy politician. The young, athletic war hero has a shock of hair, twinkling eyes, a square jaw, and a smile that would warm a mother's heart. His message captures the minds of the young and he's considered a leader in every respect. It's time that puts Kennedy into perspective as his amours spill out and dim the Camelot legend. An affair with Marilyn Monroe is long rumored. But skinny-dipping in the White House pool with female assistants, an affair with mobster Sam Giancana's girlfriend Judith Exner, a string of prostitutes, and a tryst with a suspected East German spy give the president a continuous stream of venereal diseases. JFK has everything, but he's taking penicillin for half of it.

1963 He's Bond . . . James Bond. And he's hot . . . very hot. Sean Connery is virtually unknown until he plays .007 in *Dr. No*. He's adept with guns, real and phallic. A bit of a Scottish burr, penetrating eyes, a well-toned body, and the sophistication of never taking himself too seriously make him an ultimate fantasy.

1963 Sidney Poitier emerges as the first African-American actor to achieve leading man status in *Lilies of the Field*. What's more, his handsome features, intensity, and innate mas-culinity fill the screen. If there's any doubt about his sensuality, his role in *Guess Who's Coming to Dinner* in 1967 puts it to rest. Poitier transcends color barriers in an age of civil unrest.

1964 When the Beatles arrive in America they're met by thousands of love-struck girls. John, Paul, George, and Ringo are the darlings of the British invasion. While teenage girls argue over who's the cutest, the fab four evolve into serious musicians and songwriters and revolutionize pop culture as well as rock 'n' roll. The Beatles are a cornerstone of the sexual revolution and are on the top ten list of crushes of every baby boomer woman.

1964 Mick Jagger of the Rolling Stones emerges as hell's bad boy. He's not handsome. His features are overpowering. But he's sex on two legs, strutting across the stage in a kinetic, impassioned energy. Leather pants are molded onto his body, and Jagger does his own netherworld bump and grind. The songs he sings are as lurid and dark as he is. He revels in it. And so does everyone else. Ed Sullivan books the Stones, but after near rioting in the audience, he vows to book only wholesome groups. That's one word never used to describe Jagger.

1965 When Tom Jones sings, his vocal chords don't gyrate half as much as his pelvis. His Qiana shirt strains against a muscular chest even though it's unbuttoned. Women respond by throwing their panties on stage, and he uses them to mop his brow. The Welsh singer reigns for the next six years with seventeen Top 40 hits.

1967 Warren Beatty was gorgeous in 1961 in *Splendor in the Grass*. Women couldn't understand how Natalie Wood could hold out on him (she didn't in real life). When Beatty teams up with Faye Dunaway in *Bonnie and Clyde,* sex is fused with violence, and flames ignite. Beatty is dashing on the screen, but it's his real-life romances that keep fans interested. His affairs with Leslie Caron, Michelle Phillips, Joan Collins, Cher, Mamie Van Doren, Julie Christie, Britt Ekland, and Diane Keaton are widely publicized. Even the news world isn't immune. He plays anchorman to Diane Sawyer and Connie Chung. Beatty loves 'em and leaves 'em until Annette Bening comes along. In 1991, at the age of fifty-four, he makes her his permanent leading lady.

If I come back in another life, I want to be Warren Beatty's fingertips.

Woody Allen

1969 A woman could suffer whiplash looking back and forth between Paul Newman and Robert Redford in *Butch Cassidy and the Sundance Kid.* The film catapults Redford into superstardom. That tousled blond hair, that perfect face, and that hold-back-nothing smile have women falling in love en masse. Redford lends an elegant earthiness to whatever role he plays. The millionaire Gatsby, the romantic Hubbell Gardiner in *The Way We Were,* and mountain man *Jeremiah Johnson* would all get a lady's telephone number for the asking. By 1974 he's the number one box office star in America.

1972 Women get their choice of fantasies this year. Enjoy Burt Reynolds in his *Cosmopolitan* layout and as a hairy-chested macho man supreme in *Deliverance.* Prefer smoldering and dangerous? There's Al Pacino as Michael Corleone in *The Godfather.* Feminists aren't left out. For them it's ultrasensitive Alan Alda in TV's *M*A*S*H** who instinctively knows what a woman needs. Most women are greedy. They want all three.

1973 A bald guy sucking on a lollipop—a sex symbol? You bet. Telly Savalas shaves his head for the role of Pontius Pilate in *The Greatest Story Ever Told* and keeps his pate bald for this year's title role in *Kojak.* He's gruff and rugged with a tag line thousands of women want whispered in their ears: "Who loves ya, baby?"

1980 Being a damsel in distress is worth it if Tom Selleck, as *Magnum, P.I.,* bails you out. The tall, gorgeous hunk of hairy-chested manhood is elegant, sympathetic, funny, charming, and has a laugh that's more infectious than the common cold. Millions of women tune in weekly to watch Tom in a bathing suit, Tom in a tuxedo, or Tom in jeans, and then go to sleep thinking about Tom in bed.

1981 He's unpredictable at best, slightly mad at worst, and his blue eyes make female hormones moan every time. Mel Gibson emerges in *Mad Max,* but this year's *Gallipoli* and *The Road Warrior* bring him stardom and lots of attention from women. A string of movies follows, some good, some bad. But even when they're bad, well, there's still Mel to look at.

1986 Three years ago Tom Cruise raised curious eyebrows when he danced in his underwear in *Risky Business.* In this year's *Top Gun,*

Great Moments in Sex

his charm seems to have grown exponentially to the brightness of his smile. Once they get past his devilish good looks, critics notice he can act. He's a regular on *People*'s Most Beautiful People in the World list, and as the roles he plays get meatier, Tom keeps getting sexier.

1988 *People*'s Sexiest Man Alive is John Kennedy Jr., the son of the late president. Cameras have captured him growing from toddler to a gawky teenager into a well-defined mass of muscles. Deemed America's Most Eligible Bachelor, he has the best possible combination of looks from mom, Jackie, and JFK Senior. Add a social conscience, a healthy helping of the Kennedy mystique, and a tender, compassionate quality, and he's on the top of everyone's list. He gives up his free-agent status in 1996 with his marriage to Carolyn Bessette.

1989 One of life's biggest conundrums for women is deciding if they would rather watch Denzel Washington walking toward them or walking away. He gives a breakthrough performance in this year's *Glory*. Washington defines his own sex appeal: it's dignified, subdued, a second skin that he's not even aware of. It oozes. And being extremely talented doesn't hurt, either. The preacher's son is in full command of his career during the 1990s, choosing roles that magnify his ability and keep women on the edge of their seats.

Denzel Washington wears his sexiness like a second skin.

I regret nothing.

Giacomo Girolamo Casanova,
Chevalier de Seingalt

> The most virtuous woman,
> far from being offended at a declaration
> of love, is flattered by it, if it is made
> in a polite and agreeable manner. . . .
> If she listens, and allows you to repeat
> your declaration, be persuaded
> that if you do not dare all the rest, she
> will laugh at you. . . . If you are not
> listened to the first time, try a second, a
> third, and a fourth. If the place
> is not already taken, depend upon it,
> it may be conquered.
>
> Lord Chesterfield

1994 In 1991 Brad Pitt is on screen for fifteen minutes in *Thelma and Louise,* playing a one-night stand who gives Geena Davis her first orgasm. Three years later in *Legends of the Fall,* he's holding the heartstrings of women who want him to give them an orgasm, first one or not. Pitt's got a basic sensuality. It's not just a great face, expressive eyes, and a smile that can warm the cockles of your heart, among other things. It's the way he moves and the way he's so comfortable with himself. Female fans get a sneak peek at Pitt when *Playgirl* prints nude photos of him sunbathing. An injunction halts more copies from being printed but those on the stands quickly become keepsakes.

1995 Hugh Grant is as cute as a little boy with his hand caught in the cookie jar. It's a sexy cookie jar he's playing with when the heartthrob English star of *Four Weddings and a Funeral* is caught in Hollywood with a hooker. His regular squeeze is model Elizabeth Hurley, but apparently Grant is in the mood for a little noncommittal oral sex. Years ago the incident would have marked the end of an actor's career, but Grant does a public mea culpa on the talk shows, admitting, "I did a bad thing." Fans forgive him.

1997 Leonardo DiCaprio reaches bona fide hunkdom in *Titanic,* the most successful movie ever made, thanks, in no small part, to teenage girls worldwide who see the movie more often than they see their dermatologists. The 6-foot-tall blue-eyed twenty-two-year-old actor started capturing hearts in 1996 when he appeared in *Romeo and Juliet* but with the release of *Titanic* Leo-mania explodes. Over 150 Web pages are devoted to the charmer with one page receiving nearly three million hits. Four Leo biographies make the *New York Times* best-seller list. Hysterical teenagers hoard any fan magazines in which his face appears. *Teen* magazine votes him the "all-time favorite movie babe." Whether DiCaprio's sex symbol status will survive depends on whether teenage girls' crushes clear up when their skin does.

Great Moments in Sex

Chapter Six

SELLING SEX, SEX SELLS

B.C.

c. 1200 Assyrian prostitutes are easy to identify. You can see them. Unlike nonworking women, who are veiled, loose women are forbidden to cover their faces, lest the veil lend them respectability. The price of wearing a veil when you're not supposed to is immediate arrest and flogging.

c. 400 Run-of-the-mill prostitutes in Greece don't lead the glamorous life of the hetairai. Residing near the waterfront where boatloads of sailors and foreigners make up their clientele,

the *deikteriades* veil themselves in whisper-thin fabrics that allow customers a glimpse of the merchandise. The younger the woman the greater the chance that she'll do without clothing altogether.

An Epitaph of a Different Sort

c. 400 Long before voice mail there are cemeteries. The tombstones of Greek warriors serve as bulletin boards where admirers write messages and propositions to the sought-after hetairai, a chancy prospect, since a woman is under no obligation to accept every advance. Until she responds, his message is there for everyone to read. If an offer is suitable, the hetaira returns in the evening and further negotiations take place.

c. 300 The common whores of Greece loiter in doorways wearing little and calling out to passersby. But ingenious prostitutes don't miss a trick when they wear the right shoes. Embossed in reverse on the soles of their sandals are the words "Follow me," which leave a continuous calling card and convenient, error-proof directions.

c. 200 Rome has its own classifications of prostitutes. The *dorides* and the *alicariae* stand out in their attempts to promote themselves. The dorides have youth and beauty on their side and use their doorways to show off their nude bodies as if they are nymphs. In the buy-one-get-me-free category are the alicariae who bake unleavened bread for offerings on the altars of Venus and Priapus. Buy the loaf, get the girl. Other courtesans who roam the streets are identified by their bright blue robes. If young boys wear their robes girded about them much like the ladies, there's good reason. They're for sale, too.

TRIVIA

To guard yourself from shame or fear,
Votaries to Venus, hasten here;
None in my wares e'er found a flaw,
Self-preservation's nature's law.

—Mrs. Philips's handbill

of the night's activities. Others resort to the poor waif look, camping out near churches until some "good-hearted" soul takes them under his wing.

c. 1300 European prostitutes are forced to advertise with their clothes. Selling their services isn't the object. Distinguishing them from respectable women is. In different cities, different frills are used. A whore's left shoulder of her dress is trimmed in red or a garter decorates her upper arm. Shoes have bows. Short cloaks and caps are also employed. In Strasbourg some prostitutes inhabit cathedral towers. They can be distinguished from the churchgoers by their white-and-black caps topped with a white veil.

A.D.

Medieval prostitutes rely on the kindness of strangers.

c. 1000 Medieval prostitutes are clever in their methods of attracting customers. By acting mad, a harlot can expose the tantalizing parts of her body, giving knowing passersby a preview

c. 1350 The Virgin's Bridge on the banks of the Spree serves as a landmark leading to Berlin's red-light district. The city fathers set up the pay-and-play area, thus controlling the spread of prostitution and lascivious acts of citizens. Anyone caught hanky-pankying outside the district is severely punished and can be put to death.

c. 1500 The female breast is so popular in Renaissance Italy that Venetian courtesans show theirs off to the max on the Bridge of Breasts. The bridge is a living billboard where prostitutes stand with their breasts exposed and solicit customers. Since a firm bosom is mandatory in this age of youth glorification, a whore's career sags with her breasts. Eventually a law is passed that mandates prostitutes uncover their breasts, since many have taken to cross-dressing in order to lure homosexual men.

c. 1580 The "blue gowns" of Elizabethan England are prostitutes. And that's how you find them. Look for the ladies in the blue dresses. The color blue becomes associated with things lascivious and later signifies anything pornographic.

c. 1750 The area surrounding the Palais-Royal in Paris boasts a wide array of eateries, shops, theaters, and brothels. Over 1,500 prostitutes sell their services here each day. Those outside the more famous districts are left with the problem of promotion, which they solve by posting men on street corners to pass out cards with the names of "seamstresses" and "laundresses," along with their specialties. Directories are also distributed that include addresses and descriptions of the working ladies, some as blunt as "she has crabs."

c. 1750 Lonely hearts in America advertise in the colonies' weekly newspapers to search for the person of their dreams. Men look for wives and sweethearts. Women look for husbands and protectors. By the 1800s the lack of

censorship of ads in the personal columns allows prostitutes to advertise as well, making many a newspaper a handy guide to a city's nightlife.

1776 In England Mrs. Philips uses handbills to advertise her handmade specialty—condoms. Doing a banner business, the good lady takes her profit, sells her store in the Strand, and retires. Ten years later she returns. Apparently her successor, Mrs. Perkins, isn't up to Mrs. Philips's standards, and the war of the handbills begins. Mrs. Perkins tells everyone that Mrs. Philips has died. Mrs. Philips counters that Mrs. Perkins's store has closed. While Mrs. Perkins augments her line with perfumes, soaps, waters, oils, and essences, Mrs. Philips boasts of new foreign shipments and reminds captains of ships and those going abroad to stock up.

c. 1790 London directories that list Covent Garden harlots give way to monthly publications like the *Rangers' Magazine,* which are meant to keep patrons of the ladies up-to-date on new arrivals and their specialties. Magazines of this sort remain a viable source until the mid-nineteenth century.

1823 Reformer Francis Place writes *To the Married of Both Sexes,* a handbill calling for the use of contraceptives. Place's sympathies go to the poor who cannot afford to feed unplanned children and to women and infants who often die during childbirth. Place speaks from experience. He's the father of fifteen. The handbill also sympathizes with young men forced into a life of debauchery because the cost of raising a family prohibits marriage.

c. 1870 An ad for Cadbury's Cocoa reflects the quest for a zaftig figure. The well-proportioned woman, by modern standards, seeks help from her understanding doctor, who just happens to have a Cadbury's Cocoa poster hanging in his office. The ad promises "FLESH FORMING INGREDIENTS" that will, no doubt, increase the size of her scant bosom and every other part of her body.

1875 The derangement of the female organs will ruin your life. So drink Lydia E. Pinkham's Vegetable Compound, a sure cure for female weaknesses. It even relieves labor pain. Its success continues well into the twentieth century when it's advertised to give energy to wives who tell their husbands, "I'm sorry. Not tonight." Does it really work? Well, no. But

with an 18 percent alcohol content, you don't really care.

1893 Artist Paul Thurmann's *Psyche at Nature's Mirror* becomes the new logo for White Rock Mineral Springs water. A nubile young girl turning into a goddess kneels on a rock, gazes into a reflecting pool and watches delicate wings sprout from her back. Psyche, her knees spread apart for balance, wears only a diaphanous skirt; her exposed breasts are as rounded as the rest of her body. The White Rock name is emblazoned on the rock she kneels on. The lovely Psyche is well accepted, and as the years pass, she is updated for the times. Her hair is cut in a chic marcel in the 1920s, and by 1944 she has dropped 28 pounds and become svelte. Her skirt becomes even more transparent, though any undue immodesty is corrected by putting her knees together.

c. 1897 Fashion dictates a flat stomach and a heaving full bosom. Don't have one? Don't worry. There are plenty of bust developers for sale. The Sears, Roebuck and Company catalog offers the Princess Bust Developer and Bust

Cream or Food, which enlarges "any lady's bust from 2 to 3 inches." The Bust Cream or Food is applied as a massage. The bust developer is a pump that exercises the "muscles of the bust," and comes in two sizes, 4- and 5-inch. The Aurum Medicine Company promises a 6-inch enlargement "no matter how flat the chest may be," so "unattractive women are quickly developed into commanding figures." As late as 1975, the quest for the breast continues. Beauti-Breast, a combination of cream and hydrotherapy massage, builds bosoms an additional 3 inches.

1897 Quaker Oats uses Ceres, the goddess of grain and agriculture, to show off its oats— "The Easy Food—Easy to Buy, Easy to Cook, Easy to Digest." Quaker uses the topless goddess at a time when most Victorians deny the existence of breasts. If the fair maiden doesn't get men to buy their oats, she sure gets them thinking about sowing them.

1900 Phoebe Snow is created to advertise the benefits of riding on the Lackawanna Railroad, which uses cleaner-burning anthracite on its New York–Buffalo passenger line. Dressed in pristine white, the innocent, beautiful young woman is adored by college men who clip the ads and hang them in their dorm rooms. The rhyming ads describe how clean she stays during her railroad adventures. Phoebe meets the crew (they're polite), gazes at the mountain scenery (a wondrous sight), meets the love of her life (also dressed in white), and is married by a traveling bishop all "upon the Road of Anthracite."

1900 Picture cards of foreign lands and such are often included in cigarette packs. Want the entire series? Keep buying the cigarettes. But Buck Duke of the American Tobacco Company

twists the idea. He issues premium certificates. Collect 75 of them and you can redeem them for a set of "Sporting Girls" cards featuring the beguiling, belly-button-showing French actress Madame Rhea.

1902 *The Blue Book*, a Yellow Pages of the brothels, madams, and prostitutes of the Storyville district of New Orleans, is published. Having originated in 1895 as *The Green Book, or Gentleman's Guide to New Orleans, The Blue Book* is best known and has the longest run in print. Sold for a quarter at hotels, railroad stations, steamboat landings, and saloons, it lists the locations of houses, the status of madams, the types of girls, and the services offered. A typical entry: "Diane and Norma, 213–215 North Basin. Their names have become known on both continents, because everything goes as it will, and those that cannot be satisfied there must surely be of a queer nature."

TRIVIA Dr. John Harvey Kellogg invents cornflakes, and his brother, Will, promotes them. One week, early in the 1900s, advertisements instruct housewives that "next Wednesday is Wink Day in New York! Give the Grocer a wink and see what you get!" Any woman who dares to be so flirtatious receives a free sample of Kellogg's cornflakes. And a questionable reputation.

1904 Short men, take heart. The Cartilage Company of Rochester, New York, wants to relieve "the unpleasant and humiliating position" felt by the man in their ad. Two gorgeous women dine with two men. One is tall and suave and receives the attention of the ladies, while the other man, well, needs the Cartilage System on "How To Grow Tall." Just write for more details and soon, you too will enjoy the "advantage of proper height."

1916 Wherever America goes, Ivory soap goes. Our doughboys are preparing to fight in World War I. But, hey, soldier! You're completely out of uniform. The Ivory ad shows soldiers by a stream cleaning up after a hard day of defending, and the noncom in the foreground is relaxing au naturel. The nude male is permitted long before the nude woman and is used in ads that sell products primarily to women.

1919 A woman's arm "should be the daintiest, sweetest thing in the world." But not if her pits stink. After all, the ad informs us, the body's chemicals cause odor and even if you can't smell it, others can—especially that good-looking guy in the ad. Fortunately, there's physician-formulated Odorono for "women who want to be sure of their daintiness." When the ad appears in the *Ladies' Home Journal* hundreds cancel their subscriptions. How dare they suggest a woman stinks? Deodorant sales soar 112 percent.

c. 1920 Trying to unseat Camels as the leading cigarette, George Washington Hill, president of the American Tobacco Company, introduces Lucky Strike. Hill hires adman Albert J. Lasker, who targets women smokers by using celebrities to endorse their product. Their next volley is aimed at men with a thinly disguised sexual message: "So round, so firm, so fully packed, so free and easy on the draw."

c. 1920 The forerunner of the pinup girl is created by artist Coles Phillips who draws sensuous, leggy women for Holeproof hosiery. The distinctive ads showcase his females in geometric settings that frame the woman and highlight the product. The young woman who sits on a table and reaches down to stroke her silken leg, a movement that causes her sleeveless dress to shift and expose her upper chest, is considered quite risqué.

1922 An upper-class woman dressed for the evening is caressed by her adoring tuxedoed husband. She's beautiful, confident. Of course, she has "A skin you love to touch." By using Woodbury's Facial Soap you, too, can have skin that will keep your husband interested. During the Depression, Woodbury is one of the first to use nude women in its ads. Caught from a three-quarter back view, the model's lean bare body, clad only in sandals, sprawls down an outside staircase getting the benefits of a sun bath, the same benefits that can now be gained by using Woodbury's Facial Soap.

1922 Palmolive soap ads stress the need for women to remain youthful. A bride—the career goal of every woman—vows "to keep that schoolgirl complexion" by religiously following the Palmolive cleansing routine. During World War II, it's the soldier, the pilot, and the sailor the model thinks of when she says, "I pledge myself to guard every bit of Beauty that he cherishes in me," because moments with him are "fleeting, rare, and . . . infinitely precious."

Q: Whatever happened to the girl in the black stockings?
A: Nothing.

Vaudeville joke when silk stockings become the fad for flappers who love to expose their gams, 1920s

1923 Beautiful stage actresses have a secret for maintaining their "perpetual loveliness" and clear complexion. It's being able to defecate every morning. Yes, "She who prizes beauty must obey Nature's law!" Eat Post Bran Flakes and say good-bye to "shallow skin, dull and listless eyes." Those whistle-clean intestines make you radiant to all men.

1924 Poor Edna! Poor Dunbar! All of Edna's friends are getting married but she's "often a bridesmaid never a bride." And Dunbar's madly in love with his wife who won't even kiss him. What could be the reason no one wants to come

In 1534 Anthony Fitzherbert writes about buying a horse: "If he be tame and have ben rydden upon, then caveat emptor." The age of "let the buyer beware" begins.

near these two? Listerine knows. Two years ago they gave it the name *halitosis*. If these two would just gargle, their sex lives would improve.

1925 Why don't they just show her genitals? The print ad for Allan A hosiery is considered over the line. A pair of black silk stockings adorn the legs pictured, but the legs are shown from the back. That's not done. Displaying the back of the knee and a bit of the thigh is equivalent to showing the pubic area. Needless to say, the stockings are well remembered by consumers.

1925> The dearth of birth-control information has women desperate to try anything. Lysol is a disinfectant, but ads in women's magazines promote it as a female douche as well. A French woman gynecologist urges women to rid themselves of the "FEARS" that can ruin "the beauty of the marriage relation" with Lysol that reaches "into every fold and crevice." Other disinfectants make the same claims. Doctors warn against their use.

c. 1927 Artist J. C. Leyendecker brings his talents to advertising for Cluett and Peabody's Arrow shirts and collars and creates the Arrow Man. Tall, suave, and devastatingly handsome,

How to Make an Extra Buck

"WHY PUSH with a paddle when you can lay alongside a SPRINGMAID® sheet?" asks Minnehaha as she sails past the bow-oar Buck who is panting from prodding propulsion.

Hereafter this Buck will be ballast for Minnehaha, who knows that one SPRINGMAID sheet to the wind is better than two paddles in the pond. She has proved that SPRINGMAIDS are strong enough to give smooth sailing in rough going. They can't be split by sudden squalls, torn by jibing, or frayed by luffing; and you can tack about as often as you wish when making a buoy or laying a mark. Make SPRINGMAIDS your main sheet," and they will make those extra bucks for you.

"Whether sail or sheet, SPRINGMAID will take the strain. They stand up so well to wear and washings and yet are soft and beautiful; any number of bucks couldn't get you a better sheet value. We sent them to an independent testing laboratory and, honest Injun, what happened to them would make Custer's Last Stand look like a Vassar Daisy Chain. First, they were washed 400 times—abraded 100 times warpwise and 100 times fillingwise. That was equal to a whole generation of constant use! And those sheets came out looking like—you guessed it—a million bucks, with a lot more wear left in them too!

SPRINGS MILLS, Inc.

Now by popular demand—a revised 25¢ pocket edition of ELLIOTT WHITE SPRINGS' hand-whirling book "CLOTHES MAKE THE MAN." It has the possible solution to three of New York's most famous unsolved murder mysteries and even more of his sizzling letters and short stories, plus how to lose friends, write advertisements and build cotton mills. Available now at better newsstands. If yours can't supply you, order from us.

He has designed a brand new sport shirt in the SPRINGMAID Harem print . . . featuring the famous SPRINGMAID girls in a colorful Oriental setting. Sizes: small, medium, medium-large and large. On sale at better retail stores for $3.95. Also SPRINGMAID Sports Cap for men or women—Sizes: 6⅝ through 7½—$1.00.

©1951, The Springs Cotton Mills

he has the sophistication and savoir faire that middle-class women dream of. The Arrow Man is the personification of Fitzgerald's *Great Gatsby* and probably sells more shirts to women than to men.

1937 Simoniz car wax features a full frontal nude, though shadows obscure everything but the outline of her left breast, hip, and softly reveals facial features. What's the connection to the wax? "Your car's no nudist." Protect it with Simoniz. Though most guys would probably opt for spending Saturday afternoon waxing the model.

1948 Elliott White Springs, president of Spring Mills, introduces "the tease" in advertising. His cartoons are naughty, offering readers a peek at something they shouldn't see. The wind blows a skirt too high, slightly revealing the panties (made of Springmaid fabric) of a long-legged woman. His slogans are catchy. "We Love To Catch Them On A Springmaid Sheet" say the firemen who catch a billowing-skirted, garter-showing woman who is saved from a burning house by jumping into a firemen-held Springmaid sheet. Magazines refuse to carry the print ads at first but acquiesce as readers show their approval. Brand-name recognition soars and sales mount steadily for the next decade.

1949 Maidenform begins its "I dreamed I was . . ." campaign, and suddenly women are no longer just submissive housewives. They're confident professionals and adventuresses, as long as they're wearing a Maidenform bra. The ads show a woman acting out her fantasy—I dreamed I took the bull by the horns, swayed a

A buck well spent on a Springmaid Sheet

THIS buck may look more like 47¢—which is what *most* bucks are worth these days. But not *this* "dearslayer." Any buck spent on a SPRINGMAID sheet gets you value of *100 cents* on the dollar— as any two smart squaws know.

Because they stand up so well to wear and washings and yet are soft and beautiful, any number of bucks couldn't get you a better sheet value. We sent them to an independent testing laboratory and, honest Injun, what happened to them would make Custer's Last Stand look like a Vassar Daisy Chain. First, they were washed 400 times—abraded 100 times warpwise and 100 times fillingwise. That was equal to a whole generation of constant use! And those sheets came out looking like—you guessed it—a million bucks, with a lot more wear left in them, too! But don't take our word for it! See for yourself their luster and even yarns. And compare the "washability" of SPRINGMAID sheets and pillowcases with any other sheet on the market. We're betting plenty of wampum every time that you'll put your buck on a SPRINGMAID sheet—*and it'll be a buck well spent!*

SPRINGS MILLS, Inc.

PROTECT YOUR ASSETS

SPRINGMAID FABRICS

SPRINGS MILLS, Inc.

izes it. The company redesigns the package and finds nonprofessional, tough, rugged he-men to be the Marlboro Man. One of the images is a cowboy who becomes the ultimate masculine image of the 1960s. "Come to Marlboro Country" where independence and rebellion is status quo. The Marlboro Man becomes *the* sex symbol—virile and aloof enough for men, yet so attractive to women. By 1976, Marlboro is the best-selling cigarette in America.

1956 "Does she . . . or doesn't she?" The double entendre isn't wasted on men but the tag line, "Hair color so natural only her hairdresser knows for sure!" leads women to the product. At the time of the first Clairol ad only 7 percent of women dye their hair. A decade later that figure has skyrocketed to 70 percent, and the rise

jury, barged down the Nile—fully dressed from the waist down but wearing nothing but a bra waist up. The Maidenform woman is aggressive, assertive, but always feminine. The campaign runs for twenty years, until women become more concerned about burning bras than dreaming about wearing one.

1954 The problem with seamless nylons is unsightly sagging around the ankles. When heat-shaping is introduced, Hanes raises a leg—actually two—to announce form-fitting hose. A happy model lies on her back, butt to the readers, her legs lifted in a wide *V* to show how well they fit, of course, while her skirt obeys gravity and reveals a stocking top. "I've fallen for seamless stockings by Hanes," she says. And a few guys have fallen for her.

1955 Smoking filtered cigarettes is something only women do until Marlboro masculin-

Beware the Goose!

During the war, The Springs Cotton Mills was called upon to develop a crease-proof cotton fabric. It was used with great success as a backing for maps, photographs, and other valuable assets. This fabric has been further perfected and made available to the hem hamper and hug lug trade.

Whether you are on Capitol Hill for business or

pleasure bent, you need not eat off the mantel if you have your foundation covered with SPRINGMAID POKER, woven of combed yarns 37" wide, 152 x 68 count, in tearose, white, nude, and black, light and medium gauge.

If you bruise easily, you can face the future confidently with the SPRINGMAID trademark.

SPRINGS MILLS, Inc.

is attributed to the commercial. In 1965, Clairol poses another landmark question: "Is it true blondes have more fun?"

1960 Sometimes a cigar is just a cigar. But not when Edie Adams sings about Muriel Coronas. The first sexy lady of ads is a voluptuous blond songstress with a throaty voice who temptingly bumps and grinds as she sings, "Hey, big spender, spend a little dime on me."

1962 What happens when you twist off the cap on a tube of Brylcreem? Saxophones moan in the background while a sultry woman squeeeeezes out, rubs up against Mr. Brylcreem user, removes his glasses, loosens his tie, runs her hands through his hair, and lays a kiss on him that smokes up the screen. When the smoke clears, she sexily challenges, "Brylcreem. Are you man enough to try it?"

1962 Harper's Bazaar leads the way in nude fashion advertising when it features a Richard Avedon photograph of model Christina Paolozzi in the altogether.

1965> "Was it him . . . or his Piping Rock?" asks the woman lying in bed—referring, no doubt, to her lover's cologne. As the popularity of men's fragrances increases, ads promote the message that the way a man smells affects his love life. Three photos of a couple in a suggestive pose are labeled "Before," "During," and "After," instructions on when to wear Aztec cologne. Then there's the beautiful model stroking a pool cue, who reminds everyone, "I like my men in English Leather, or nothing at all."

1966 Gunilla Knutson, a former Miss Sweden, tells men to "Take it off. Take it all

Pretty Teeth

You will always be ready to smile if every night and morning you beautify your teeth with the toothpaste that has a guaranteed measured, germ-killing power. If you do not yet know what a delicious clean feeling Euthymol gives to the mouth, send for the seven-day free trial sample and booklet or buy a large 1/3d. tube with the convenient spring-cap from your chemist, and observe the Golden Rule of Dental Health—Visit the dentist twice a year and twice a day, night and morning, use

Euthymol
TOOTH/PASTE

KILLS DENTAL DECAY GERMS IN 30 SECONDS.

TRIAL OFFER Send to Dept. 86/49, Euthymol, 50 Beak St., London, W.I. for a free trial sample tube.

off!" "The Stripper" music grinds as a shaving-creamed-faced man strips his beard off with rhythmical strokes, interrupted by shots of Knutson biting a string of pearls, mugging for the camera with bedroom eyes, and caressing a can of Noxzema shaving cream. The ad runs for years with sport celebrities taking it all off. One spokeswoman asks, "Ladies, want to see Joe Namath get *creamed?*" Of course we do! The ads are teasingly cute but not to Senator John Pastore who calls for the Code Review Board to stop such "egregious sex" on television.

1966 Twiggy, the first fashion model to achieve international celebrity, drastically changes the ideal female body type. Gone are the curves of Marilyn Monroe. The five-foot-six-inch, 91-pound teenager's 31-22-32-inch frame sends women scrambling for diets. Lesley Hornby (her real name) is dubbed "The Face of '66." There's not a fashion magazine that doesn't carry her picture or a mannequin that doesn't mimic her physically. *Newsweek* calls her "four straight limbs in search of a woman's body." Her fame diminishes, but the reedlike body image stays put.

1968 Is the Dodge Charger symbolic of the male organ? A youthful model raises her miniskirt slightly higher while caressing the car. "Mother warned me that there would be men like you driving cars like that," says the ad copy. "A girl with real values" wouldn't be impressed with "a 440 Magnum, whatever that is." Or would she? Why else would she be raising her skirt?

1968 "Should a gentleman offer a Tiparillo to a dental hygienist?" The dewy-eyed blonde holding a dental mirror to her parted lips and showing her braless cleavage through her unbuttoned blouse would cause any red-blooded man to salivate more than a dentist could suction out. The ad admits that "she's the best thing to hit dentistry since Novocaine." If you offer her a Tiparillo cigar it "would be cleverly psychological." The ad's unabashed sexiness urges further, "and who knows? Your next visit may be a house call."

c. 1970 The sultry blonde in a backless black velvet gown languidly relaxes horizontally on a billboard near you. A glass of the product over ice sits before her. She's looking at you and tempting you with the slogan, "Feel the Black Velvet." The liquor or her? You choose the fantasy.

How to Piss Off a Feminist: Lesson One

c. 1971 "I'm Judy. Fly me." National Airlines wants your business. They use the stewardess—a career that's been the butt of sexual jokes and fantasies—to lure customers. "Everything they say about Miami girls is true. We're always on the move . . . And I adore to fly." Then the stewardess strips down to a bikini and walks off into the Florida sunset. Feminists are outraged. National tries to defend itself. It names its planes after stewardesses: "And soon you'll be able to fly Barbara." Subsequent spokeswomen admit, "We were born to fly," and promise, "I'm going to fly you like you've never been flown before." Continental Airlines isn't much better. They boast, "We really move our tail for you."

1974 "Beautymist Pantyhose can make any legs look like a million dollars." The camera caresses a pair of legs beginning with toes, then moving over the shapely ankles, past full calves, smooth knees, rounded thighs, up to a pair of satin boxers? Then to a football jersey? And finally to Joe Namath's face! "If Beautymist can make my legs look good, think what they'll do for yours." Point taken. Football's sex symbol not only boosts Hanes Beautymist's name recognition, Joe Willy becomes such a hot commercial actor, he makes more money off the field than on.

1975 Underalls are innovative panty hose that combine panties and hose in one. The model teases, "I don't wear panties anymore," a statement that's sure to give men whiplash as they do a double-take to see who said that. As the model informs women that Underalls get rid of panty lines, men are treated to close-ups of her butt in various outfits, sans panty line.

1976 When Bic introduces disposable lighters it advertises, "Flick Your Bic." Everyone but the censors catches on and the line soon becomes a common invitation during the age of free love.

1977 A hip bearded man in a bell-bottomed leisure jumpsuit stands next to a bed. Seated on it is a naked woman, shot from an angle to expose a breast and nipple. She's pulling down the chest-to-crotch zipper of his suit. The leisure suit advertised is from The Fifth Season in Dallas, Texas. The ad's heading reads "One Easy Piece." You decide who or what it's referring to.

1978 She can "bring home the bacon, fry it up in a pan, and never let you forget you're a man." She's the Enjoli woman, the new woman who does it all from boardroom to bedroom with the aid of Enjoli perfume. SQUIRT. The Enjoli woman appears in a gray flannel business suit. SQUIRT. Then casual clothes for serving dinner. SQUIRT. Finally a plunging neckline

IMPORTANT: Mate-Herb is not a harmful Aphrodisiac, nor does it require a doctor's prescription. It is not a pill, capsule or any type of vitamin formula. Mate-Herb is a concentrated powder unlike most anything you ever tried . . . you can be sure ! ! !

Great Moments in Sex

gown and she's ready to seduce and be seduced. The emancipated woman isn't a threat to men after all. And Enjoli becomes the third best selling perfume in America.

1978 A long-haired blond temptress is mounted on a horse. Blue jean short-shorts and an open shirt reveal every curve of her immensely feminine body. "Come With Me" suggests the ad copy for Rough Rider condoms. They're studded from head to shaft to "unleash the sexual animal inside me." It's only a print ad. Condoms aren't allowed to advertise on TV.

1980 Designer jeans are *the* fashion. Calvin Klein kicks off the craze with Brooke Shields poured into a pair of CKs, asking viewers, "Know what comes between me and my Calvins? Nothing." A follow-up ad has Shields confessing, "If my jeans could talk, I'd be ruined." Gloria Vanderbilt lines her models up and bends them over, her jeans doing more lifting and separating than an eighteen-hour bra. Her slogan: "The *Ends* Justify the Jeans." Bon Jour jeans are "built to look like you're moving even when you're idle." Some television stations refuse to run the ads. The message gets across anyway. "Jeans are about sex," Calvin Klein says and sells a quarter million pairs a week.

1980 Chanel No. 5 invites you to "Share the Fantasy," in a phallic-filled thirty-second TV spot. Director Ridley Scott sells the perfume with a surreal vision of a woman lying pool side, the elongated shadow of a plane passing over her, foot to head. Suddenly a man appears at the other end of the pool, swims the length, emerges between her legs, then disappears. She lies on her side, now relaxed. More shadows overhead. At $120 an ounce, you deserve multiple shadows.

1981 Paco Rabanne cologne features French actor-hunk François Marie Bernard waking to a ringing telephone. The bed is mussed, a note lies on the pillow. His new lover is on the phone. "You snore," she teases. "And you steal the covers," he bandies back in the nude, though only shown from the waist up. The cologne helped him get what he wanted. Women's groups approve of the ad because it depicts a working woman now off on a business trip, which proves she's on an equal footing, sexually and economically.

If your wares bee not vendible, why do you open your shoppes?

Thomas Nashe

1981 When Baltimore Oriole Jim Palmer pitches for Jockey underwear, his coterie of female fans grows by leaps and bounds. The three-time Cy Young Award winner, his all-American body clad only in Jockeys, graces magazine pages for years. When Jockey decides to revamp its campaign to include a number of "Real Men," Palmer heads the list.

1982 Calvin Klein proves that men have balls. And penises. He erects a billboard over Times Square in New York to promote his designer underwear. The gorgeous, well-muscled model is nude except for his Calvin Klein briefs, which show a well-defined bulge. Men as sex objects. Hmm. Women and gay men approve not only of the ad but of sexy male underwear. It isn't long before other designers create their own labeled underwear.

1984 American Medical Systems advertises penile prostheses directly to the public in print ads. Rather than waiting for the patient to seek help, the company reaches out to consumers who want to improve their lives. Showing a middle-aged couple hand in hand, readers are informed by the man, "I'm enjoying a full life again." By 1987 mainstream magazines such as *Newsweek* and *Time* are accepting the ads.

1985 Calvin Klein introduces Obsession cologne and uses black-and-white or sepia-tinted ads that feature the human body in all its artistic form. Nude bodies are entwined, bare-breasted women sprawl, and couples come close to coupling to sell the cologne. Three years later his Eternity ads feature married lovers. By 1991 Escape perfume ads focus on taut thigh muscles breaking through the water, or a biceps that hauls up the sail on a boat. Klein sells not only perfume but his own brand of sensuality.

1987 Playtex becomes the first bra maker to feature a real live woman wearing only a brassiere in a television commercial. Up until this time, bras were shown on dress dummies, floating through the air, or being held up while the pitch tried to convince viewers of a proper fit.

1988 Charlie perfume has used the independent woman to advertise its fragrance since 1973. This year's print ad proves she's sexually aggressive as well. A man and a woman, both in business attire and briefcased, walk away from the camera. She's barely, but noticeably, taller than he is and she's giving him a pat on the butt. The *New York Times* refuses to run the ad because of its reverse sexism. Women's magazines see its humor. They run it.

How to Piss Off a Feminist: Lesson Two

1989 Miller beer helps college guys enjoy their spring break. They issue a sixteen-page insert for college newspapers titled *Beachin' Times,* touting "the three Bs of spring break . . . beer, beach, & babes." Bikinied blondes fill the supplement. In one photo, cheerleaders hold up an oversize long-necked bottle of Miller Lite, which is captioned, "Way Big Fun." What can you dink, bump, and poke? "Hint—it's not a Babe." It's a volleyball. The cover sports a pig in a bikini with the tip, "Lose weight, Lots of it." There are no complaints until the ad hits the University of Wisconsin. Miller then pulls the supplement from the remaining ten campus papers it's supposed to appear in. A month later Camel cigarettes does its version of Neanderthal man. The "Old Joe" camel mascot pops up with "smooth moves" for college guys at the beach: "Run into the water, grab someone and drag her back to the shore, as if you'll save her from drowning. The more she kicks and screams, the better." After receiving complaints, R. J. Reynolds pulls the ad.

1991 For years Old Milwaukee beer advertises, "It doesn't get any better than this." The guys are sitting around a campfire but when one of the actors gives the signature line, a voice-over stops him. He's wrong. It does get better. A band appears, lobsters fall from planes and the Swedish Bikini team parachutes in. The overstuffed bikinis in platinum wigs are the ultimate sex object fantasy. They're a team. We just don't know what they play. Or do we? The ad prompts a sexual harassment lawsuit by five women workers at the Stroh Brewery Company, the makers of Old Milwaukee. Stroh refuses to pull the ads but does put the kibosh on their ad for Augsburger beer, where the bikinied behinds of three women are headlined with the statement, "Why the average beer commercial has more cans than bottles." The copy explains that pretty girls sell beer.

1992 Kate Moss introduces the waif look and decimates the female form. Appearing in *Harper's Bazaar* and, more notably, in Calvin Klein ads, Moss's childlike face and 105-pound anorexic-looking body earn her fans who struggle to copy her emaciated look, and foes who scribble "Feed me" across her outdoor ads. In Klein's jeans and perfume ads she flirts with hints of masturbation, S&M, and bestiality. Because of her adolescent androgynous appearance, detractors say, her ads cater to pedophiles.

In a couple of years, she transcends submissiveness and begins domination. Her new, heavily made-up look includes stiletto heels, fishnet stockings, and fake fur.

1992 Rapper Marky Mark, with his chiseled body, becomes the poster boy for Calvin Klein underwear (his third nipple is airbrushed out). Throwing away the script written for him, Mark wings a pitch about his favorite button-fly boxers: "They just fit good and they hold me snug, so if I'm about to go out and get some skins, I'm not about to put on no silk underwear . . ." Cute enough for mothers to love, sexy enough to be the heartthrob of teenage girls, his well-pumped body is also appreciated by the gay community. CK Jeans and underwear sales soar.

1994 Diet Coke® shows us what women have known all along: that women enjoy looking at men as much as men enjoy looking at

Diet Coke shows that women appreciate a sweet sight just as much as men.

women. An office full of women scurry to the window. Why? It's break time for the construction crew outside and one of them takes his break from the heat by taking off his shirt—oh that chest!—and downing a can of diet Coke. Dancing hormones are in full display. Nostrils flare. Lips are bitten. Eyes go to half-mast. Breathing becomes less than easy. The commercial receives some backlash from feminist groups for reverse sexism. But most women are too busy watching to complain.

The real hope of the world lies in putting as painstaking thought into the business of mating as we do into other big business.

Margaret Sanger

1995 Calvin Klein's latest jeans ad has the look and feel of 1960s pornography. The setting is a seedy basement where young models are questioned by an offscreen male photographer who cajoles them into removing their clothing and makes comments about their bodies. But the models look too young. The ads are labeled "kiddie porn" by watchdog groups who demand the campaign be stopped. The outcry is so loud that the FBI moves in to investigate whether Klein violated child pornography laws by using

models under eighteen. The U.S. Justice Department reaches its conclusion in November: none of the models are underage.

1995 Ads for Jaipur, a French perfume, feature a nude woman whose wrists are cuffed behind her by the bracelet-shaped bottle of perfume. When the ad appears in London's subways, it's condemned for "peddling bondage and degradation." Ditto in Canada. In France, though, the ad is so popular it's turned into a postcard.

1996 KCPM-TV in Chico, California, and KING-TV in Seattle air condom commercials. The ads for Ansell's Lifestyle condoms promote safe sex using a computer-generated image of a skeleton who died from AIDS giving all of the reasons he never used a condom while he was alive.

1997 A young man in a gray flannel suit lies on the floor and licks the pointed toe of the stiletto-heeled, over-the-knee boot of his dominatrix. A glimpse of her chiseled, pointed fingernails and fishnet stocking are all we see of the mistress. What are they selling? Bass Ale. The brewery is just one of several companies that jump on the S&M trend in advertising. Gucci shows stiletto heels on their runway and can't keep them in stock. How do they advertise them? With the spiked heel poised between the nipples on a bare male chest.

Great Moments in Sex

Chapter Seven
LET ME ENTERTAIN YOU

B.C.

c. 2500 Dancing is first recorded in Egypt with its roots in religious celebrations. The first chorus line is depicted in reliefs with rows of dancers high-kicking in precision, wearing only the sheerest of draped fabrics. Other entertainers opt out of clothing entirely, wearing only G-strings made of pearls and gold to emphasize their hairless bodies. To honor Osiris, a greatly oversize movable phallus is paraded by women who control its movement with strings.

c. 1500 Belly dancing is imported into Egypt via Hindu dancing girls, part of the spoils of war. The gyrating hips and the rolling belly movements are the result of young harem members who must do the work during sex with their old, fat master. As the men get older and their potbellies grow, it's up to the women to provide the rhythmic bump and grind that causes orgasm. Since status in a harem is usually based on the number of sons borne, getting that hootchy-coo going is worthwhile. It's a mere step to incorporating night movements into dance movements that provide coming attractions.

c. 1000 The Greek Dionysian festival, to honor Dionysus, the god of wine and fertility, includes a procession of phalli through the streets, singing, dancing, and an outpouring of devotion that results in free-for-all sex. Women have their own ceremony, Thesmophoria, to honor Persephone and Demeter. Five days of revelry are preceded by a nine-day abstinence from sex that is made up for by the end of the celebration.

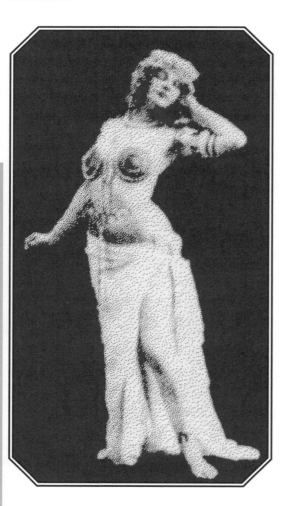

c. 600 Romans celebrate Lupercalia on the spot where Rome was founded. In ancient Rome, morality is taken seriously, though during festivals strictures are set aside. During the rites frenzy builds and results in orgies between priests and the congregation. Sadism is practiced with reason. Priests wield leather straps to beat women they encounter to ensure fertility. Romans also celebrate Bacchanalia, the equivalent of the Greek Dionysian festival. With each succeeding generation the morals of Rome slacken until festivals are just an excuse for another drinking and sex party.

c. 560 Theater grows out of the Greek Dionysian festivals as dances and mime take on plots. Comedies have all of the licentiousness of the phallic parades with a touch more obscenity and always end in marriage and procreation. The traditional garb of the actors includes a goat's tail, a fertility symbol, and a large red leather phallus. That phallus remains part of the clown costume for a thousand years.

Arthur Murray, Take Note

c. 500 Greek men and women both like to dance, but not necessarily with each other. Women dance the *kordax,* an erotic swaying and reeling while removing their clothing until nude. The *rhathapygizein* requires great leg flexibility since the dancer slaps her butt with the soles of her feet until it's pink. The *gymnopaidiai* consists of naked men who perform wrestling-type steps in honor of Apollo as a god of war. Men and women do dance together in an erotic satyr dance in which one man lasciviously moves toward two *maenads,*

**Greek women are among the
original party girls.**

or madwomen, who ceremoniously scratch at the earth in a gesture of fertility.

c. 500 When a harem isn't enough, Chinese princes and high officials turn to their dancing girls. Known as nü-yüeh, these dancers and musicians entertain at dinner parties and private get-togethers and then get together with their master and his guests. Since the women are owned, they can be sold or given away. Some princes like more diversion. They also keep young boys. The boys don't sing or dance, but they're still entertaining.

411 Aristophanes uses sex as a weapon in his satire *Lysistrata*. Tired of a long, drawn-out war between Athens and Sparta, the Athenian women gather and agree to withhold feminine comforts from their husbands until the war is over. The women of Sparta agree to this sex strike, and the fun begins. Lysistrata arranges a meeting of the warring parties, gets them drunk, they sign a treaty, and conjugal bliss is restored.

c. 350 Greek *auletrides* are talented entertainers who happen to be beautiful and physically well-endowed who happen to be prostitutes. Clad in robes so finely woven that many guests think they are nude, they sing phallic songs, dance seductively, and slowly remove what little they wear. Most patrons wait until the show ends to procure their services but there are exceptions. When King Antigonus uses auletrides to entertain dignitaries from Arcadia, the emissaries are overcome with passion. They rush the women and rape them on the spot.

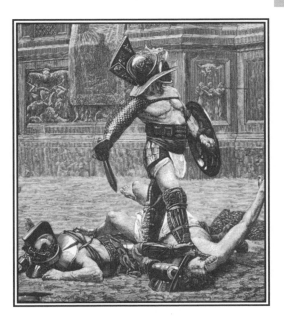

264 Gladiatorial combat begins in Rome. Butchery contests between men and men or men and animals, chariot races, reenactments of wars, and even naval battles in temporary man-made lakes within the Coliseum feed the sadistic tastes of the Romans. While the audience's blood is pumping, Roman prostitutes solicit the men. But Roman women don't let their boiling blood simmer until cool. As gladiators gain popularity, they become stars. Since it's against the law for women to approach men in any lewd manner, they arrange their liaisons with the combatants quietly. More than one upper-class woman flees with her gladiatorial lover to safety for both of them.

c. 25 Rome allows women to participate in mime—but those who do so are branded as prostitutes. Rome has strict conduct rules for women, and only prostitutes are exempt from chastity laws that generally prohibit women from acting anything but dignified with a man. Scores of decent women register as prostitutes to evade the law. Because of the lewdness of the mime, female performers need the legal protection of being marked as working women. Then again, many of them live up to their billing.

A.D.

0> "Houses of singing girls" are established where middle-class Chinese men can go for an evening of entertainment, dinner, conversation, and—oh, yes—sex. Chinese men are allowed to have wives and concubines, but they aren't allowed to socialize with them. They depend on these houses mostly for female companionship.

<50 The sulfur springs at the Roman baths at Baiae near the Bay of Naples are used for curative treatments. And I've got an amphitheater I'd like to sell you. Even the pretense of monogamy is dropped at this resort. Private tête-à-têtes are the appetizer to all-night parties

and orgies. Seneca the philosopher complains about the lascivious atmosphere. But this spa is not for the common man. Aristocrats and anybody who pretends to be anyone build villas nearby and monopolize the spring.

WHAT HE DID FOR LOVE

TRIVIA Germany's most renowned thirteenth-century troubadour is Ulrich von Lichtenstein. Smitten with a married princess when a page at court, he waits until he's knighted to declare his love but is rebuffed and rebuked by the repulsed princess. Ulrich has his harelip surgically repaired but still no luck. For fifteen years he courts, woos, and writes songs for the princess, drinks her bathwater, and declares his love. He has clumps of hair pulled out by his lady love, cuts off his little finger for her, jousts with over three hundred opponents without being thrown, and stands in line with lepers to win her love. He swims a moat and scales a wall to reach her window, and just when the princess is about to kiss him, she lets go of the rope, dumping him into the water. Ulrich finally wins his lady love, but history doesn't disclose if his prize is a kiss, a naked embrace, or a full royal court press. Soon afterward the romance ends. Ulrich continues to write songs, but most of them are not complimentary to women.

Bathing is only one activity at the Roman baths, and the least sexual.

<200 Performing three times daily are the *devadasis,* the Indian temple dancers. These girls of nine or ten are dedicated to the temple and married to heaven. When they are of age their virginity is taken by a stone phallus representing the god Siva. Then the temple priests can avail themselves of their services. The girls provide music for Siva twenty-four hours a day and assist in musical accompaniment for religious services. They're not well paid. To supplement their earnings, they sell their services to the man-on-the-street. The best-known temples, at Samanatha and Tanjore, have at least four hundred dancers each.

c. 500 The Byzantine Empire is fond of beauty pageants. One of the lucky contestants is none other than Theodora who meets Justinian,

her future husband and the future emperor, while appearing in a pageant. (She's also selling her services on the side.) That the contests continue is undisputed. In 900, Empress Theodosia hosts twelve of the loveliest lovelies so her son, Leo, can pick out his future bride.

c. 1056 During festivals the emperor of China and the ladies of his harem walk to the gate of the capital to watch the acrobats and the naked women wrestlers. There are voices of opposition to the bouts, but the emperor approves. He hands out prizes of silver and silk to the winners. Now if they had only added a little mud . . .

c. 1150 The songs of the troubadours begin to fill southern France. The first troubadour is

c. 1150 The Feast of Fools may have begun as early as the ninth century as a festival for subdeacons to blow off a little steam. Held after Christmas, it gives the clergy a chance to ridicule the hierarchy and church routine. Over the years the festival takes on burlesque overtones with ribald songs and priests dressing like women. Throw in the townsfolk (they love this feast), some wine, and soon there are drunkards in the church and lascivious behavior in the cathedral. Three centuries will pass before the church fathers make Feast of Fools a memory.

c. 1250 Chinese wine houses are restaurants that provide escorts for the men while they eat and may have special compartments where the diner and his lady can later retire. Services are first rate. The women are beautiful and finely attired. The food is good. Wine is served in silver cups. These houses can easily be spotted by the bamboo and red silk lamps outside their doors and may well be the first red-light district. Houses of singing girls are later updated to teahouses, a term the Japanese adopt and still use. For the lower class there are mere brothels serviced by untalented women who are criminals or relatives of criminals and serve for sexual purposes only.

1501 Cesare Borgia, son of Pope Alexander VI, hosts the Chestnut Ballet at his Vatican apartment. He invites fifty beautiful prostitutes for drinks and dinner. Once their appetites are sated, the lights are lowered, the women strip and crawl around on the floor in search of chestnuts that have been scattered there. As the excitement mounts and the women start shoving and pushing each other, lights are brought in so that observers, including the pope, can watch.

William IX of Aquitaine, duke of the most powerful duchy in France, who is more of a ladies' man than soldier. Unsuccessful in the Crusades, he's influenced by Arab love songs and begins to pen his own. During the age of courtly love, the love song catches on quickly and spreads fast. Troubadours range in social class from foundlings to royalty, with the lower-class singer trying to win not only the attention and body of his lady but also food, shelter, clothing, and a little pelf. What the troubadours have in common is their song. The *chanson* begins with a reminder to look for true love and the singer sees his lady love, so distant and so unattainable. He sings of her beauty, her charms, and her flawlessness. If she puts up too much of a struggle, his songs turn to a hymn of insult: she's perfection with a deceptive nature. If the lady grants him her charms, the affair is often short-lived and the troubadour moves on to entertain again. The granddaughter of William IX, Eleanor of Aquitaine, imports the songs to England. In Germany, the *minnesinger* warbles his tale of love. During the twelfth and thirteenth centuries, as long as the troubadour sings, romance is in the air.

c. 1580 Even Queen Elizabeth dances the volta. After two hopping steps, the woman leaps into the air aided by her partner who supports her on his hip and thigh, with his arm holding her firmly around the midriff. A kiss from the woman completes the dance. Men not only like to dance it, wallflowers can get into a little voyeurism. As the skirts fly, "something pleasing to the sight" is always revealed.

c. 1600 Japanese men have sex with their wives for procreation and sex with *yujo* for recreation. Yujo are prostitutes trained in the ways to please a man, how to bring him to a quick climax, and how to fake an orgasm. The primary service *yujo* offer is an evening of dining and entertainment. Into this atmosphere the geisha appears. Originally, the geisha is a man who offers comic entertainment and plays an instrument. By 1780, most geishas are women with expertise in entertaining, organizing parties, and setting fashion standards. The geisha is not a prostitute. She may choose to grant her comforts, but she does so at the risk of incurring official disapproval. Geishas are not legally allowed to sell their bodies. That's the *yujo*'s province. Geishas reach the peak of their popularity in the 1860s when they have the last word on everything socially stylish.

1603 Japanese entertainer O-Kuni originates Kabuki, popular theater. Coached by her actor-lover to sing more popular songs and loosen up her dance, O-Kuni enlarges her troupe and is immensely successful. Copycat versions composed of male and female prostitutes cause such a scandal that by 1629, Kabuki is prohibited. It reemerges with a cast of men and young boys, but sex problems are said to undermine the warrior class, and it, too, is banned. Different forms of Kabuki are performed with women allowed back on stage in the mid-nineteenth century and with male mimics performing the female roles offstage as well as on.

c. 1750 Madame Riedl's first brothel in Russia is for men. She opens a second on the island of Vassily Ostrov and builds an aquarium to attract well-to-do ladies. But it's not fish they're watching. Male bathers swim in the huge wooden pool with windows on the sides, allowing women to peer in from their own separate attached rooms, each equipped with a divan should the lady request the services of a visitor. The aquarium is successful (even Catherine II is said to visit). Madame abandons her first brothel and concentrates primarily on her female clientele.

c. 1780 *Tableaux vivants* are living pictures. In a classical setting, a young woman, barely clothed and sometimes covered with chalky powder to simulate a statue, strikes a pose. One creator of these tableaux is England's Dr. James Graham, a charlatan health adviser who uses Emma Hart, the future Lady Hamilton, to hawk his wares. He opens a Temple of Health and she's his goddess, her comely face and perfect body illustrating the benefits of Graham's goodies. In the mid-1800s the tableaux move to New York, where Palmo's Opera House offers *Eve in the Garden of Eden, Esther in the Persian Bath,* and others, slowly reducing the amount of clothing until nude women are covered only by a drape of sheer gauze. When an outraged community has enough, police ban the shows.

"correctly." Contemporary artists know better than to include the nude figure, male or female. As for the old masters, exposure is limited by the addition of fig leaves and draperies.

1789 The law forbidding theatrical performances in Philadelphia is repealed. The theater has long been connected with immorality, since the acting profession does harbor and attract some undesirables. In New York, prostitutes take over the third tier of at least one theater. Performers evade the law by staging shows under the guise of lectures or by slipping in acts during concert intermissions. The righteous will have their day. In 1792 theaters are closed when a yellow fever epidemic hits the city.

1806 Curators at the Pennsylvania Academy of Fine Arts schedule separate visiting days for ladies so they may view the old masters without embarrassment. Throughout the Victorian era, efforts are made to show art

1827 Ballet is introduced to America by Madame Francisquay Hutin at New York City's Bowery Theater. Clad in a transparent costume that barely covers her calves, her three-minute performance of *The Flirtatious Shepherdess,* full of pirouettes, divides the audience. There are those who applaud approvingly and call for an encore, which she obliges. But the ladies seated in the lower tier of box seats file out of the theater en masse.

1830s The can-can begins as a dance of the working class of Paris. Its boisterous leaps and high kicks make it unsuitable for proper ladies. But that doesn't stop the common folk and the cocodettes (middle-class prostitutes) from showing off their charms. Professional dancers make the can-can their own, lifting their skirts to show frilly petticoats, lacy panties, and shapely legs in black net stockings. Men love the dance. They're also taken aback by the outright sexual assertiveness of the dancers. If Frenchmen feel that way, how do American males feel about the New Orleans waiter-girls who dance the can-can without underpants?

1848> When gold miners in California take a break they make their way to the tenderloin districts of the nearest cities for a little sinning. An early form of burlesque provides comedy and ladies to look at. For twenty-five cents, dance hall girls reel around the floor, flirt, and get the guys to buy more drinks than they might normally buy. (Dime-a-dance girls and taxi dancers become popular later on, during the Great Depression. Men purchase ten-cent tickets allowing them to dance with a hostess, whose duty is to relieve the gent of his tickets before he knows what's happening.) Most women who follow the men out west are looking to make their own fortunes. The general rule is all can be "had for a price." Decent God-fearing townsfolk tolerate the wild nightlife for the revenue it brings, but the entertainment establishments are restricted to the edge of town.

1850s> Vaudeville begins as entertainment for men, with raffish songs, dances, comedy, and dramatic presentations. In 1881, New York's Tony Pastor cleans it up to provide wholesome entertainment for the entire family. Sex still sells, so there's always a Lillian Russell, Mae West, or Eva Tanguay ready to tease on stage. Other vaudeville houses present tableaux. Vaudeville actresses break new ground in sexual relationships. Their careers, not a husband, take center stage, and they use stage-door Johnnies and burly stagehands for

stud service with no apologies. Vaudeville dies a slow death in the 1920s as radio and moving pictures become popular.

1860s Adah Isaacs Menken tours the United States in *Mazeppa,* the story of a Tartar prince who is stripped naked and tied to a horse as punishment for falling in love with a married woman. Menken plays two roles, including that of the prince. The actress is tied to a real horse, which she rides up and down simulated hills, a feat never before attempted by a woman on stage. Menken wears flesh-colored tights but the audience believes she's nude. She and the play are denounced, but the theater is always full.

c. 1865 Yanks dance the kiss quadrille, the American version of a square dance that's been the rage in Europe. The colonists speed it up and add a touch of intimacy. The *Rocky Mountain News* reports that "when it comes to 'swinging corners,' each gentleman kisses his partner, and very delightful it must be."

1866 *The Black Crook,* the biggest stage extravaganza New York has ever seen, opens at Niblo's Garden. The drama, critics contend, is "rubbish." But opulent sets, a ballet, risqué songs, and over one hundred beautiful girls in scanty costumes make sitting in the theater from 7:45 P.M. to 1:15 A.M. worthwhile. Clergymen warn their congregations that seeing the play is a sin, but ticket sales never flag. Grossing over $1 million during its two-year run, *The Black Crook* is the precursor of the Ziegfeld *Follies* and the *Earl Carroll Vanities.*

1870s> Burlesque is patterned after minstrel shows. But while minstrel shows are composed of all male casts, burlesque adds girls and plenty of them. The women are sandwiched in between acts, showing a shapely leg or appearing in union suits. Gradually costumes become flamboyant and show more skin. The ladies tease, removing a piece of clothing here and there, flashing a bit of flesh, and their acts are more or less comedic. Many theaters install warning systems between the box office and backstage to alert performers of potential police raids so they can switch to the cleaner "Boston version" of the show. It doesn't take long before the ladies get top billing over the male performers. By the mid-1920s, the theatrical striptease is in its infancy, but the baby has already taken over the show.

1893 What sets most tongues wagging about Chicago's World's Columbian Exposition is that "Darling of the Nile," Little Egypt. Fahreda Mahzar, a beautiful dancer from the Middle East, shakes, vibrates, undulates and manipulates her hips, making eyeballs bulge from their sockets. Her scandalous coochee-coochee belly dance, done in a semitransparent skirt, starts a belly dancing fad and inspires Sol Bloom to write "The

Hootchy Kootchy Dance." Not everyone is delighted with Little Egypt. Bluenoses click their tongues and pronounce her "hardly a lady."

1893 Mona, an artist's model attending the Four Arts Ball at the Moulin Rouge in Paris, performs the first striptease for attending students. The spontaneous event gets Mona notoriety, the devotion of the students, and a 100-franc fine. The first theatrical striptease is performed a year later at the Divan Fayouau Music Hall, in Paris, by a young woman who removes her dress, petticoats, knickers, chemise, and black net stockings and slips into a bed. Other ladies peel in various settings: undressing for a doctor, a bath, during a heat wave, and to look for a flea. Americans wait until 1907 for their first take-it-off performance. A dancer named Odell strips at the American Theatre in New York City.

1893 Oscar Wilde starts a show business trend when his play *Salomé* is performed in France and includes the dance of the seven veils. Salomés pop up everywhere complete with the necessary veils and Saint John's head on a platter. Within twenty years the dance begins to be satirized as people become Saloméd out.

1894 The first Kinetoscopes are presented in New York with other cities soon following. For a nickel, patrons can view short films or view celebrities like Annie Oakley and Buffalo Bill. New Jersey shows *Carmencita in Her Famous Butterfly Dance,* at least for a while. The parlor featuring the film is ordered to get rid of the movie or shut down. Carmencita has the audacity to show her bare ankle. Thomas Edison puts sex on the screen in 1896 when he records *The*

Kiss. Actor John C. Rice plants one on actress May Irwin in the thirty-second short.

1897 New Orleans finds a solution to its prostitution problem. Sidney Story proposes putting the nighttime business in one place where it can be carried on legally. To his chagrin the area adopts his name. Every kind of experience with every kind of woman is offered in Storyville, a thirty-eight-square-block shopping mall of sex. Houses specialize in every type of woman and entertainment. "Circuses" provide voyeurs with the defloration of virgins, ménages à trois, lesbian acts, bisexual acts (although homosexuality is frowned upon), and talented ladies who use their vaginal lips to pick up coins set on end and other objects off tables. Over two thousand prostitutes work in well-appointed houses that are advertised in *The Blue Book.* The musical entertainment provided in Storyville provides a place for jazz to develop.

1907 Florenz Ziegfeld glorifies "the American Girl" in his yearly *Follies.* Top-rated comedians—Will Rogers, W. C. Fields, Fanny Brice, Eddie Cantor—are only breathers between appearances of Ziegfeld's obsession: beautiful women. His ideal woman is 5 feet 5 inches tall, weighs 117 pounds, and measures 36-26-38, with the emphasis on the 38. He swathes them in chiffon, feathers, rhinestones, and outrageous headdresses; some of the costumes cost nearly $20,000. They liltingly parade, each having her turn in the spotlight, flashing a momentary smile before turning. He puts them in tableaux—men, too, but they wear oversize fig leaves—drapes them on curtains, swings them from chandeliers, and sets them on papier mâché horses. Ziegfeld auditions 15,000 Ziegfeld girl wanna-bes a year. Being a

Ziegfeld girl is hard work, but it guarantees $75 a week, glamour, dates with millionaires, and being in the spotlight even when you're off-stage. Men come to the *Follies* to see the girls. Women come to see the latest scandal-causer in person. The *Follies* continue until 1931. Ziegfeld dies in 1932.

1910 The tango, created in Argentina in the mid-nineteenth century, mutates by the time it gets to Europe and the United States, where it catches on and spreads like wildfire. It's so lusty, the way he holds her. It's so indelicate, the way she bends. It's so immoral, with the halting, erotic steps. How do you do it? Dance

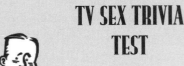

TV SEX TRIVIA TEST

1. Who was the first TV couple to share a double bed?
2. What prime-time miniseries first showed bare breasts?
3. What sitcom featured the first gay character?
4. What miniseries showed a cowboy's penis (for a split second) in the opening credits?
5. What show featured the first pregnant man?

1. Darrin and Samantha Stevens on *Bewitched*. 2. *Roots*. 3. *Soap*. 4. *Lonesome Dove*. 5. *Alien Nation*.

Great Moments in Sex

teachers charge up to $25 an hour, and there's no shortage of pupils. Or, pick up a few steps from Valentino in *The Four Horsemen of the Apocalypse*. Ministers rail against it. By the time the new version makes it back to its birth country, an Argentine ambassador says that any woman dancing the tango would be "suspect."

1914 The dance craze in America hits a peak. For wives who can't wait until their husbands come home to cut a rug, there are *tea* dances. Ladies while away the hours with men who wait for the women to buy them a drink or hand out a bit of cash in exchange for a few dances and a little romance. Husbands are outraged when it's publicized that many a lady removes her corset in the powder room so that dancing cheek to cheek becomes even more familiarizing. The end comes when the gigolos resort to blackmail. Wives and sisters are ordered not to attend any matinees.

1916 Nudity comes to the screen in Herbert Brenon's *A Daughter of the Gods* starring former professional swimmer Annette Kellermann. The movie is panned by critics. One says that Kellermann "wanders disconsolately . . . through the film, all undressed and nowhere to go." This is Kellermann's second first. In 1915 she also caused a sensation by wearing the first one-piece bathing suit.

1921 Atlantic City suspends its ban on the display of nude limbs and tight bathing suits to allow the first Miss America pageant to take place. The beauty contest is a brainstorm to lengthen the tourist season after Labor Day. Eight young ladies roll down their stockings so that King Neptune—actually Hudson Maxim, of the armaments-inventing Maxims—can judge their knees. The idea pays off as thousands of onlookers applaud each girl and cheer when Margaret Gorman, a five-one-inch-tall, 16-year-old blue-eyed blonde with measurements of 30-25-32 (oh, but what knees!) wins the crown. The pageant helps to make the one-piece swimsuit de rigueur.

1923 The Charleston appears in the black touring show *Runnin' Wild*. A few modifications are made to allow ordinary folks to master it (the original dance has over four hundred steps), and soon the country's youth are knocking knees and kicking up their heels. Of course, it's vulgar, degenerate, even "reminiscent of negro orgies," but that doesn't stop the dancing hordes even when it does prove tragic. The dance floor at Boston's Pickwick Club collapses under the stress of a thousand dancers; forty-four people are killed.

1925> The striptease begins its domination of burlesque. Sure to make them well-paid stars, the girls begin by flashing a little skin. Eventually they develop gimmicks—fans, animals, furs, feather boas. Their acts can be slow and seductive, like that of Gypsy Rose Lee, or they can choose the dynamic, pump-it-out, bump-and-grind action of Georgia Sothern. Basically the bit remains the same. The tease begins slowly. The stripper parades seductively, flirting and winking, and removes extraneous gloves, hat, jewelry. A zipper unzips, a button unbuttons. The dress is removed but still covers her while she flashes body parts and grinds to the music. When she's down to a G-string and pasties (nipples and pubic areas are never shown), the show is over. During the Depression, women flock to burlesque in search of jobs. But the producers can't afford full orchestras, and the theaters grow old. It's a downward spiral as the customers get a little seedier, the theaters shabbier, and the acts less inspired until it's a bump-and-grind show in a dim theater filled with blue smoke sprinkled with customers sitting with newspapers over their laps. New York Mayor Fiorello La Guardia pulls the operating licenses on some clubs in 1932. By the end of the 1930s, burlesque and its striptease shows fade into memory.

1925 The top burlesque star is Carrie Finnell, who introduces the wearing of tassels on her nipples. Carrie's main claim to fame is being able to rotate her enormous breasts clockwise and counterclockwise, singly or in tandem.

1926 The Black Bottom is only one of many ragtime dances that have fannies wiggling and tongues wagging. The grizzly bear, bunny hug, Boston dip, hug-me-close, and shiver dance are slower than the now acceptable waltz and give couples a chance to hold each other in "lingering close contact." The new dances are so easy to learn—only variations on the one step—that everyone's doing them except the people who are chastising others for dancing them. Critics say that people aren't dancing for entertainment; they're taking "advantage of the dances to embrace."

1933 Chicago's Century of Progress Exposition shows how far man has come. The

Fred and Ginger cut a rug doing dances that many deemed "degenerate."

midway's Streets of Paris review shows how far one woman will go. There Sally Rand, freshly patted down with white powder, dances nude to the strains of *Clair de Lune* with the help of two ostrich plumes. Who wants to see neon tubing when they can watch a naked lady dance? Practically no one. Exhibition halls are virtually empty when Rand performs, one reason why her $125 weekly salary skyrockets to $3,000. Fair organizers credit her for the financial success of the exposition, and every dancer picks up a feather and hulas away after that. Rand copyrights her next act, a bubble dance, which she does behind a transparent screen to keep pricks from bursting her bubbles.

1936 If the world needs proof of America's move toward sexual freedom, then the jitterbug is what they need to see. A perfect dance to accompany the swing music of the 1930s, the jitterbug shakes every part of the body. For the first time since the seventeenth century men get to show their stuff by breaking away from their partner and doing a solo dance that's athletic, vigorous, and at times, dangerous to them and others. The air step begins when both of the woman's feet leave the floor in a variety of gymnastic maneuvers that are great for showing off legs and getting into suggestive poses. During World War II the GIs take the dance to Europe while their girlfriends keep it heated up at home. The jitterbug survives until the 1950s.

1950 Belgian Gerald Blitz develops his idea of a perfect vacation into an international business. Club Med opens resorts from Bora-Bora to Copper Mountain, Colorado, all offering a relaxed atmosphere, plenty of food and entertainment, and no worry about tipping. In the mid-1970s Club Med becomes a mecca for swinging singles in search of a torrid romance, at least for the duration of their stay. The "summer camp for adults" hits its peak in 1989 but struggles in the 1990s to change its hedonistic image to a family-oriented one.

1959 Russ Meyer begins his career in big-tit movies with the premiere of *The Immoral Mr. Teas,* a story Meyer himself sums up as "three naked women, sixty minutes." The movie can't be shown in mainstream theaters; nevertheless, it grosses more than $1 million—not bad, considering it cost $25,000 to make. Meyer is mammary-obsessed, so all of his leading ladies are cantilevered and gravity-defying. Ensuring his position as king of the breast movies are his later productions, *Faster, Pussycat! Kill! Kill!, Beyond the Valley of the Dolls,* and *Mondo Topless,* his 1965 documentary.

1960 With your upper body pretend you're drying your back with a towel. With your feet, smash out an imaginary cigarette. Your butt wiggles back and forth. That's how you do the Twist. All those pelvises gyrating everywhere is considered lewd by some. By the time mom and dad decide to be hip, the kids have moved on to something else.

1960 Hugh Hefner opens the first Playboy Club in Chicago. Hefner designs the club to be a place where upscale men can retreat for a drink, entertainment, and a dinner of basic fare served by a not-so-basic waitress. The Bunny is your physically above-average girl-next-door fantasy who is poured and squeezed into a high thigh–cut satin swimsuit, with a fluffy ball on her butt, rabbit ears on her head, a detached collar and bow around her neck, and cuffs around her wrists. She's given demerits for wearing

Chicago is host to the first Playboy Club.

heels less than three inches high. She's not allowed to chew gum, smoke, or drink (even water) while on the job. Bunnies don't sit, they "perch." And they are taught the Bunny Dip, the approved way of serving drinks and dinner to customers. For $25 to $50 clients buy a key allowing them into the club where they can look but not touch. Exceptions to that rule are the special key holders—Hefner and celebrities—with whom the Bunnies are allowed to mingle. Husbands and boyfriends aren't allowed within two blocks of the club in order to preserve the image of the fantasy Bunny. The clubs spring up in all major cities. With the advent of topless bars, they lose business and eventually close.

1963 *Beach Party* is the first of five beach movies filmed during the next two years. Combining three things teenagers love most—the beach, music, and the opposite sex—the movies are remarkably innocent. The female star is one reason for the wholesomeness. Annette Funicello is on loan from Disney with one stipulation: she can't show her navel. The other beach girls wear the standard bikini while Frankie Avalon, the male lead, has to be content with the only girl on the beach in a respectable two-piece swimsuit. Until the mores of the 1960s are

thrown topsy-turvy, *Beach Party, Muscle Beach Party, Bikini Beach, Beach Blanket Bingo,* and *How to Stuff a Wild Bikini* pack 'em in.

1964 The topless-dancer craze develops in San Francisco when cocktail waitress Carol Doda, wearing a Rudi Gernreich topless bathing suit, dances to the music at the Condor Club. Sure, men can see nearly naked women at strip joints, but Doda ushers in no-pasties boobs. Nipples are the rage. After a few months, Doda gets silicone injections that push her from a 36 to a 44DD cup. Customers respond even more. Topless bars pop up across the nation with the entertainment form constantly evolving. From the go-go dancers of the 1960s, platforms are added with poles for the girls to wrap their bodies around and perform other seductive gymnastic feats. Private table dances emerge where a dancer performs on your table for one song for an additional $5 to $20. Couch dances, usually in a secluded area, are privately offered for a fee. And lap dances, outlawed in many states, where dancers bump and grind while sitting on the customer's lap bring the evolution up to date. The money keeps the girls flocking in; a good performer at a top-rated club can earn as much as $1,500 a night.

1964 The first glimpse of a man's bare ass on stage occurs during Peter Weiss's play *The Persecution and Assassination of Marat as Performed by the Inmates of the Asylum of Charenton under the Direction of the Marquis de Sade,* otherwise known as *Marat/Sade.* It's only for an instant but it's a start.

Sexual deviations are the theme of the Jerry Springer Show.

1967 Phil Donahue launches the daytime talk show. The audience-participation format highlights current affairs and alternative lifestyles. Although Phil does his share of sex-related shows (lesbian nuns, male strippers, unfaithful spouses) the sleaze factor rises in the late 1980s. Oprah Winfrey's the first to mimic Donahue, but she's tame compared to the likes of Geraldo Rivera, Jenny Jones, Sally Jessy Raphael, Ricki Lake, and Jerry Springer. One hundred variations on the theme of sexual deviation are presented daily, the weirder and wilder, the better. Most wanted are guests with multiple adjectives modifying who they are: bisexual, thrill-seeking, cheating, dominatrix moms or impotent, controlling, abusive homosexual secret lovers. A hue and cry arises in 1996 that talk shows have gone too far. Though some shows try to rein in the sleaze, it continues. Apparently there's no dearth of sexually aberrant, willing-to-talk-about-it-on-national-TV guests and people who want to watch them.

1967 The off-Broadway production of *Hair* is different from the version that opens a year later on Broadway. The story is watered down for the Broadway run, the songs are highlighted, homosexual overtones are added, and there's a group nude scene. Actors don't have to appear in the buff. The no-costume option is left up to them. Some critics use words like "vulgar," "offensive," and "dirty" to describe the play, which comments on current concerns such as drugs, sex, and war. Most critics hail the musical but that doesn't stop it from being banned in Boston, South Africa, and Mexico or from having trouble opening in Indianapolis, South Bend, Saint Paul, San Antonio, and even Los Angeles. In Paris the Salvation Army objects to it. *Hair* does set a trend. Producers are just beginning to experiment with on-stage nudity.

1969 Sweden invades America via two sexually explicit films, *I Am Curious—Yellow* and *The Language of Love. Yellow,* the story of a woman who experiments with politics, religion, and sex, is seized when it enters the United States in 1967. When a U.S. Court of Appeals reverses the obscenity judgment, people line up to satisfy their curiosity. *The Language of Love* is an "educational" film. Experts discuss sex and couples act out their suggestions, a to and fro that ends with less to and more fro. The acceptance of the films liberates Hollywood whose producers are itching to make their own statements. Among the first is *Midnight Cowboy,* the first X-rated film to win an Academy Award.

1969 A political satire entitled *Che!* opens off Broadway. The play includes nudity and twenty-three sex acts, plus the characters of a nymphomaniac nun, the president of the United

States, and Che Guevara. Critics say the play is boring—even without clothes. The cast, crew, and producers are arrested for obscenity and public lewdness, and when the play reopens, it's at much higher ticket prices. Opening on the heels of *Che!* and billed as "the hottest show in town," *Oh! Calcutta!* is an erotic revue composed of bawdy one-act plays in which the entire cast appears mostly in the nude. Tickets for the first two rows sell for $25. The rest of the seats are $15.

1969 The defining moments of the baby boom generation come in Bethel, New York, where the Woodstock Festival is held. Billed as "3 Days of Peace and Music," at $18 a head, the concert is supposed to attract 100,000. Half a million show up. They live for three days on a 600-acre dairy farm, sharing food, drugs, and each other while listening to the best rock bands music has to offer. Sex and nudity are commonplace, overlooked and treated as natural by fellow attendees, but viewed derisively by those on the other side of the generation gap. Woodstock spawns other concerts across the country and England, but none come close in content or atmosphere.

1972 The sixty-two-minute movie *Deep Throat,* starring Linda Lovelace, becomes a cause célèbre when it's temporarily banned in New York. Men and women from all walks of life, people who normally wouldn't be caught dead seeing a porno movie, flock to it. The story is simple: Linda's clitoris is located deep in her throat. The only way she can achieve orgasm is through oral sex with exceptionally well-hung men. It's the first publicly shown film to show full erections. There's also anal intercourse and cunnilingus. *Deep Throat* is on everyone's lips.

President Nixon and his first lady, Pat, are the butt of *Deep Throat* jokes. A one-liner elicits sniggers: "Nixon's seen *Deep Throat* twice, and he still can't get it down pat." The movie's title also becomes the code name of the informant who leads reporters to uncover the Watergate conspiracy.

1973 PBS enters risqué territory when it presents *Steambath,* a play by Bruce Jay Friedman, which features frontal nudity. Heaven is a steambath and God is the Puerto Rican attendant. Bill Bixby takes the role of Tandy, the hip single guy. But it's Valerie Perrine who shows off her talent as Meredith, the sweet, sexy soul.

1977 Studio 54 opens its doors and becomes the country's hottest nightclub. Truman Capote writes in his diary of the sex and drugs available at the club, marveling at "boys with boys, girls with girls, girls with boys, blacks and whites, capitalists and Marxists, Chinese and everything else, all one big mix." Regulars include Liza Minnelli, Andy Warhol, Bianca Jagger, Halston, Calvin Klein, Cher, and Michael Jackson. But even big-name celebrities aren't guaranteed entry. Warren Beatty, Michael Douglas, John Kennedy Jr., and the President of Cyprus are all turned away at least once.

1978 Plato's Retreat in New York City epitomizes the sexual revolution. It's a swinging couples-only club (you don't have to be married but you do have to come in twos) with private rooms, a clothing-optional disco, hot tubs, a swimming pool, and a steam room. It's the best-known club of its type but certainly not the only one. California is the home of the Sandstone Club and nearly a quarter of the sex clubs in the United States.

1979 Why should men have all the fun? They don't anymore. Chippendales, a Hollywood nightclub, is a women's only domain where gorgeous young studs bump and grind and strip down to their G-strings. Bachelorette parties replace bridal showers and girls' nights out will never be the same. Performers are the all-American male type with chiseled bodies and well-stuffed thongs. Women are just as raucous as men are in strip clubs and delight in shoving tips in the dancers' G-strings. Chippendales is so successful that branches open in major cities, and the club is copied by look-alikes.

These Really Are the Moments of Your Life

1980s Most folks use their camcorders to record baby's first steps, graduations, or vacations. But behind closed doors the cameras get turned on by couples who get turned on by seeing themselves in action. Other folks want to see what they're doing, too.

Professional porn flicks disenchant some people who can't relate to silicone-laden women's bodies and guys with unbelievably large penises or fake orgasms and passion. Amateur videos provide the complete voyeuristic fantasy, real people doing real things with real emotions and real bodies. They won't put the pros out of business, but amateur porn movies account for nearly 60 percent of all the adult VCR movie trade.

1980 A Strip-A-Gram is a human greeting card who arrives fully clothed and strips down to a G-string (a male stripper) or lace panties and a bra (female stripper) and produces a written greeting from the sender. A six-minute strip from the New York–based company costs under $100—a perfect gift for the person who has everything.

Great Moments in Sex

Ziegfeld took Michelangelo's statues, took some of the fat off them with a diet of lamb chops and pineapples, then he and Ben Ali Haggin brought the statues to life, only with better figures, and the only marble about them was from the ears north.

Will Rogers

1981 MTV premieres with 125 music videos and a new television concept. The videos amount to advertising for photogenic rock bands and are soon met with charges of sexism over the use and perceived abuse of scantily clad, hosed-down, dog-collared women. The National Coalition on Television Violence complains that 40 percent of the videos contain acts of aggression, 39 percent of which are sexual. Tantalizing male bods decorate the videos, too. Or you can watch Madonna and Michael Jackson grab their crotches.

1983 Hooters opens in Clearwater, Florida. The restaurant boasts about its chicken wings and hamburgers, but the best dishes aren't the food. They're serving it. Waitresses are perky college-age cheerleader types wearing the traditional Hooters garb: orange running shorts and a Hooters T-shirt, tied or cut to expose the midriff and accentuate the server's figure. Emblazoned on the T-shirt is Hooters' motto: "More than a mouthful," which refers to the size of the hamburgers, of course. The main crowd is thirty- to fifty-year-old guys who drop in for a beer and a leer. Hooters catches on quickly. Franchising nationwide, it also gives rise to a new type of eatery that wants to cash in on the fad. Hooters-type "breastaurants" spring up nationwide.

1988 The lambada dance craze takes off in France where the sensuous rural Brazilian dance from the 1920s is seen as a form of safe sex. The man holds his partner around her waist and holds her hand in his. But down below is where the action is. The man's thigh separates his partner's legs and locks on to her thigh. He holds her so close at the pelvis that when the bump and grind starts, it's best to be on a first-name basis with your partner. Short lambada skirts and skimpy tops for the ladies and chest-revealing shirts for men add to the dance's sultriness. The hip swivels and floor-sweeping back bends the women do look great, but medical warnings are issued. Broken vertebrae at the back of the neck are called lambada fractures.

Let Me Entertain You

1990 Madonna's Blond Ambition tour takes rock concerts to new sexual heights by combining Broadway razzle-dazzle, performance art, and deviantly suggestive songs. Mimed masturbation, spanking, male dancers in G-strings, pointed brassieres, homosexuality, bisexuality, fishtailed mermen, and coming on to a priest help Madonna achieve her goal of "let's break every rule we can." Gossips talk, fetishists smile, and the Material Girl, who started the trend of wearing underwear as outerwear, rakes it in as her concerts sell out just hours after the tickets go on sale.

1990 Cable television's HBO premieres its irregular documentary series, *Real Sex.* While Playboy TV features perfect-body beauties, *Real Sex* features real people. Women don't have breast implants. Men aren't equipped like porn stars. In fact, you won't see the sex act. Segments include treats such as a nude bungee-jumper, a seventy-six-year-old man who has sex ten times daily, transvestites, masturbation techniques, a Mr. Nude Universe contest, a home striptease class, dominatrices, prostitutes, and kinky grandmothers. Fortunately, the emphasis is on real sex and not real people.

1991 TV's first bisexual kiss gets planted on *L.A. Law* when attorney C. J. Lamb (Amanda Donohoe) puckers up with Abby Perkins (Michele Greene).

1997 *Ellen* becomes the first prime-time TV show to have a gay main character when Ellen DeGeneres outs her character in a much-hyped episode. For four years Ellen Morgan was a heterosexual who had no luck with men. The story line is simultaneously played out with DeGeneres's real-life public announcement that she's a lesbian.

Great Moments in Sex

Chapter Eight
A LITTLE HELP

B.C.

c. 2700 Want sex? Get married. See your local Egyptian jeweler for the ring. The placing of the band on any finger represents the act of sex, the ring being the woman and the finger being the man. In the East the same tradition holds true. During the ceremony the ring is often shifted from finger to finger symbolizing the in-and-out of intercourse.

c. 2000 The scents of jasmine, cinnamon, and myrrh are used to help turn heads but none has the persuasiveness of musk. Tracked down by hunters aroused by the heady fragrance in forests, musk is found in a small pod located near the abdomen of the musk deer of western China. This aromatic, considered the most powerful scent aphrodisiac, is used by nearly all cultures. So long-lasting and so potent (essential musk oil can be detected in amounts as little as 0.000,000,000,000,032 ounce) is its effect that some Islamic mosques are built with musk mixed into the mortar. Its odor lingers for hundreds of years. In the nineteenth century the British East Indies Company prohibits importing musk in the same ship with tea. They can't

get rid of the smell. Musk makes a comeback in the early 1970s when every hip person smells of deer gland secretions.

c. 2000 Perky breasts are a prerequisite for the afterlife in Egypt. They may sag while you're alive, but don't worry: embalmers will round out those knockers with wax and sawdust as soon as you breathe your last breath.

c. 1500 When the Chinese move out of their winter quarters, rural families attend spring festivals where young men and women meet. And sing and dance. Pair up. And have sex. This continues all summer long. In autumn a couple's liaison is "regularized" if the girl is pregnant. If she's not, cheer up. There's always next spring.

c. 400 Can't get it up? Want the woman of your dreams? Be more attractive to the opposite sex? Get a lizard. Mix the penis of a copulating lizard into a potion and secretly give it to the lady you want and she's yours! Don't throw away that lizard yet. Wear the tail as an amulet and you're guaranteed an erection. You can powder the rest of the lizard and drink it as an aphrodisiac. Too squeamish to kill a lizard? Then hold it in your hand. It stimulates love.

c. 400 Flat-chested Greek women adhere to the advice of Hippocrates on how to build up the bustline. They sing at the top of their lungs. When that fails they just bunch up their chitons, creating a precursor to the padded bra.

c. 350 Aristotle ponders the problem of the age difference between a man and his wife. If she's young, she's easy to control; older women have minds of their own. But young women are too sexually demanding for older men. Aristotle's comments apparently hit a nerve: before long, the Greeks make it a law that a wife has a legal right to have sex three times a month.

Orchids enable Hercules to have fifty women in one night.

c. 300 Need help getting aroused? Want to feel like a young buck again? Determine the sex of your child? Ravage fifty women in a single night? Try orchids or a related species. The Greeks, Romans, and Arabs are all aware of the plant's potent properties. The root dissolved in goat's milk arouses excitement and increases stamina: Hercules beds the fifty daughters of Thespius after imbibing. The drink is also given to old men to help them fulfill their conjugal duty to young wives. A plant that may be related to the orchid is Satyrion, whose root can influence the sex of an unborn child. The lower part produces a boy, the upper part a girl. If you want to get your hot intentions across to a woman, present her with a lady slipper orchid. Its similarity to the male genitalia lets her know exactly how you feel.

c. 200 You've been with your wife or concubine for so many years that it's just not that exciting anymore. Tough. The Chinese are specific about a husband's duties. Until a woman is fifty, she's entitled to sex once every five days. She simply has to be clean, neat, and properly attired. Men don't get off the hook until they're sixty years old (some sources say seventy) or in mourning for a close relative, which lasts only three months. Before you say "I do," remember—you will.

c. 150 Hsiao-ching gets the credit for creating erotic wall murals in second-century China. The walls of some private houses are adorned with scenes of couples making love in various positions. One has a woman holding on to a tree limb while sitting on her partner's erection. The bounce of the swaying limb provides the movement.

<100 Couvade is practiced in Europe, China, and South America to name a few countries. It's relatively simple. When a pregnant woman begins having labor pains, her husband goes to bed, moaning and groaning, faking delivery while wifey's doing the real thing. Once the baby's delivered the child lies with him. Mom gets an hour of rest and goes back to her work plus some of hubby's, stopping only to nurse the infant. He stays in bed, being waited on by the women of the village, until the umbilical cord falls off. Holy health care! What's this about? Evil demons are hiding everywhere. Mother and child are vulnerable, so dad acts as a decoy, drawing evil toward himself until mother and child are able to fend off spirits themselves. Or so they claim.

c. 100 The Druids begin the custom of hanging mistletoe, and all guests passing under it are embraced. Mistletoe is also used in a potion to enhance female fertility. Britons and Japanese use it to make their cattle and soil more prolific. Scandinavians kiss under it. Romans use it in their sex orgies during the Saturnalia festival in December. When the Catholic church schedules Christmas for December 25, they ban mistletoe.

THE FOURTEENTH-CENTURY CURE FOR IMPOTENCE

TRIVIA

BURDOCK SEEDS

THE LEFT TESTICLE OF A THREE-YEAR-OLD GOAT

BACK HAIR FROM A WHITE DOG CUT ON THE FIRST NIGHT OF A NEW MOON, BURNED ON THE SEVENTH DAY, AND POWDERED

4 DROPS OF CROCODILE SEMEN

Put the first three ingredients in half a bottle of brandy. Let it sit, uncorked, for twenty-one days. Cook the mixture until it is thick. Add the crocodile semen and apply the mixture to the limp male member. Impotence should be gone forever.

<50 Philters are magic potions that induce love trances. They are composed of all sorts of ingredients, the stranger the better. Frog bones; bird livers; animal genitals, entrails, brains, and kidneys; human fingers and excrement; deer semen and urine; honey; flowers; and camel's milk are a few items on the brewer's shopping list. Well into the Middle Ages philters are used, their popularity growing with witchcraft. Even moss growing on a murdered man's corpse is used, with the reasoning that his unused virility is contained in the green stuff growing on his skull. Some are said to work but others—no surprise, considering their content—are poisonous and sometimes deadly.

33 Agrippa, a Roman soldier and statesman, builds Rome's first public baths to keep his fellow citizens clean and entertained. At first the sexes are separated, but before long, bathing becomes a mixed activity, as do a few other amusements. Entertainment is offered. Business is discussed. People find sexual partners. If you can't find someone to your liking, there are prostitutes to give you the final massage. Promiscuity and scandals are so prevalent that in A.D. 138 Hadrian decrees that the sexes must be separated. The Romans have another problem. Water for the public baths is carried by the aqueducts in lead pipes. The lead poisoning leads to mass sterility.

<0 They won't do much for your breath, but oh! what onions do for the rest of you. Nourishing, strengthening, and cleansing, they add virility and stimulate desire. The Roman poet Martial declares, "If your wife is old and your member is exhausted, eat onions in plenty."

A.D.

<50 Thank Zeus for modern medicine. The poor Roman suffering from impotency has a plethora of remedies. The dirt on which a bull has urinated is made into a paste and applied to the loins of the man. Or he can eat chickpeas, pine nuts, and anise seed. Imbibing drinks mixed with pepper or saffron helps, too. Crocodile feet, dried horse balls, and mare sweat are all considered aphrodisiacs.

c. 70 In *Natural History,* Pliny the Elder tells of a popular aphrodisiac: wearing a bracelet containing the right testis of an ass will enhance your chemistry. Animal and plant parts can also be used in the conquest of love, especially any part that is erotic in shape or function. Donkey balls are at a premium since the donkey is considered a lascivious animal.

Chocolate was once considered an aphrodisiac. Today there's proof that it may be true. The treat contains phenylethyl-amine, a stimulant that is similar to the chemicals released by the body during sex. But chocolate has other traits as well. For a while it was used to cure venereal disease. It has also been used as a laxative. The Aztecs allow only members of the court to drink the liquid because of the power it imparts. But it's given too much credit in some cases. One Frenchwoman claims she gave birth to a black baby because she ate too much chocolate.

Screw Twice and Call Me in the Morning

c. 100 Roman physician Galen says sex is necessary for good health in men and women. Lack of it causes hysteria in women, while a good sex life relieves depression, increases appetite, and frees the mind.

c. 200 For the man who has everything except that virgin bride he's yearning for, the *Kama-sutra* suggests mixing vajnasubhi powder with monkey dung and throwing the mixture over the wanted lady. That should keep her from marrying anyone else. Or getting a table at her favorite restaurant.

c. 590 The Chinese have two aces up their sleeve. For impotency, a mixture of jou-tsung-jung, wu-wei-tzû, t'u-szû-tzû, yüan-chih, and shê-ch'uang-tzû taken three times a day makes you "invincible." In sixty days you'll be able to "copulate with forty women." This cure is known as the Bald Chicken Potion. Seems the prefect of Shu took the potion when he was seventy and sired three sons. He was so feisty his wife couldn't sit or lie down. Being kind, the prefect threw the mixture into the yard, where a rooster ate it. The cock jumped a hen and copulated with her for a few days nonstop all the while pecking at the hen's head. Hence, the Bald Chicken Potion. If size is a problem, they use powdered jou-tsung-jung and hai-tsao mixed with liver extract from a white dog killed during the first moon and applied as an ointment to the penis three times. It's guaranteed to add three inches of length.

800 Hindu temples erected in India between the ninth and thirteenth centuries feature row upon row of erotic sculptures. They are built mainly for the common class who believe in Siva, the god of, among other things, fertility. For the Indians, who accept sex as a natural part of life, the many-position, multi-partner friezes serve as an aspect of worship, a built-in sex manual, and an oversize calling card to attract clients for the *devadasis,* the temple prostitutes.

1288 Scotland passes a law allowing a woman, regardless of class or station, to propose marriage to the man of her choice during leap year. Unless he's engaged and proves it, he must accept the lady's advances or pay her one pound. She has the right to ask as many men as she pleases. While it may not get her a husband, it might get her a bank account.

c. 1400 She's the woman of your dreams and you want her to stay that way. So cut a lock of her hair, burn it, smear the bed with honey, and throw the ashes in. That'll do it. If you're in love with a married woman who won't cheat on her husband, put a magnet under her bed. It will draw her to you. If it fails, it's because her hubby sprinkled the bed with hair ashes.

Let 'Em Hang

c. 1500 A woman's breasts are her pride and joy, especially when the fashion has them nearly totally exposed. Of utmost importance is their firmness. Recipes to help are offered. Bathing boobs with poppy water, ivy, camphor, and rose oil is one way. Or follow the seventeenth-century directions in Nicholas Lémery's *To Preserve the Firmness of the Breast:* "Take Lentil-seeds two handfuls, Red Roses half an ounce, reduce the whole to Pouder, and boil in the Smith's Forgewater, then apply to the Breasts, and let 'em hang Twenty-four Hours; then renew the Application, and continue it for Five days together; repeat this course every month."

c. 1570 Chinese erotic art reaches a pinnacle with the production of printed color albums. Every elegant page is folded in an accordion pleat measuring about ten inches square and is accompanied by a poem to complement the pic-

DREAM LOVER

TRIVIA

Forget aphrodisiacs, love potions, and wishing on a star. If you really want to know whether you'll meet your true love, follow the Valentine's Day advice offered in *Poor Robin's Almanac* in 1729—if you dare: ". . . In the Evening of Valentine's Day, do take two White Oak Leaves, and lay them across your Pillow, when you go to bed, putting on a clean Shift or Shirt, and turning it the wrong Side outwards, lay down and say these Words aloud, Good Valentine be kind to me, in Dreams let me my true Love see. So carefully drawing your right Leg behind you, put it over your left Shoulder. In like manner put your left Leg behind you, laying it across your right Shoulder; and be sure take Care that the Soles of your Feet meet under your Chin. Then go to Sleep as soon as you can. And if you dream you see two Moons touching each other, you will certainly be marry'd very speedily, when you be a young Man, Maid or Widow."

ture. Ranging from partial nudes to complicated positions, the albums are produced until the middle of the seventeenth century.

c. 1585 The great ladies of Goa know how to have a good time. Confined to their homes by their husbands, they mix small quantities of the drug datura into a drink or soup. The husband loses his judgment at least—consciousness at best—and the ladies don't have to leave home to have fun. They invite their lovers in. The husband's memory of the entire evening is lost.

1585 When Protestants sack the town of Embrun in France, they find the phallus of Saint Foutin, red from wine that had been poured over it for years. Saint Foutin is a phallic saint worshiped by women hoping to become fertile. The phallus is made from a piece of wood that women scrape shavings from, steep in water, and drink, or, they pour wine over it, collect the runoff, and drink it to overcome barrenness. As the phallus shrinks from use, it "miraculously" grows back. The wooden phallus is a long piece that passes through the statue. Only a portion of it shows. When it shrinks, the priest hammers the piece farther out.

Nothing Beats Home Cooking

1600s If the way to a man's heart is through his stomach, then cockle bread is the perfect recipe. An Englishwoman prepares a small loaf of bread and, before baking it, impresses it on her vulva. The loaf is offered to the man of her dreams. If he eats it, he falls under her spell. An entire romantic dinner also includes a fish which she inserts into her vagina before preparing. After-dinner mint, anyone?

c. 1600 Elizabethan Brits enjoy their aphrodisiacs as much as the Romans did. Best loved is the prune. Brothel owners offer prunes to their clients on the house. It can be confusing. Between its aphrodisiac properties and the way prunes clean the colon, a customer might not know if he's coming or going.

c. 1625 For the ladies of the seventeenth century makeup is a must. One popular concoction is Aqua Toffana, which contains arsenic. Men who like to kiss a cheek can wind up six feet under. Over six hundred husbands buy the farm after their wives buy the makeup. Arsenic isn't the only poisonous ingredient in makeup. The popular ceruse contains lead. And Soliman's Water, a lotion for those who want to have a perfect complexion, contains mercury, which corrodes the flesh under the outer layer of skin and rots teeth. Many ladies succumb, true victims of vanity.

1634 Parents in Puritan New England who want to hasten the engagement of their daughters allow bundling. The couple remains fully dressed and goes to bed. Either there's a board between them, the girl's dress is sewn shut, or her ankles and legs are bound. A little court and spark ensues and by morning there's a decision to be made: the couple gets engaged or they part forever. By 1756 upper-crust families of New York, Boston, Salem, and Newport cast aside the custom, preferring the sofa for courtship. Country folk see the sofa as more dangerous than the bed and rail against preachers who rail against bundling. By the Revolutionary War bundling becomes a lost tradition.

1700s Sex clubs are formed in England and France for those whose libidos are stuck in overdrive. Initiation is steep. Membership fees can run up to 10,000 pounds for men, half that for women. Initiates "perform" before judges who decide if they're up to club standards before being accepted. It's not unusual for a member's sexual encounters to number into the thousands, and there is a risk of being found out. It's common for a man to have a spouse and a lover, but more than that makes him a scandalous lecher.

c. 1700 Dog or goat wine gets the hormones pumping. This wine is made by fermenting meat from either animal with a few other ingredients for several days before straining the liquid off and serving it. Possibly, because of poor nutrition, the protein has a beneficial effect.

c. 1750 If you're a member of the clergy, a politician, a respectable woman, or anyone of note who wouldn't—shouldn't—be caught dead in a Paris brothel, go to Madame Gourdan's. Most people use the front door, but if you go to the antique dealer on the next street, slip into his closet, and follow a short hallway, you'll find yourself in Madame's closet, and you can come out and enjoy the fun. You can have your pick of beauties dressed in high fashion, in a shepherdess costume, or as a fairy. Or spend the afternoon looking into peepholes and watch the goings on of others, enjoy erotic art, or get into some S&M. Then you can leave the same way you entered.

1774 The first hotel is opened in Covent Garden. David Low opens Low's Grand Hotel, a residence for the traveler as opposed to inns whose primary function is to provide nourishment. Low's idea isn't entirely new. Ancient Greeks had *pandokeia* which provided shelter for travelers but were also used as rendezvous points for sexual liaisons. The Irving House in New York City first serves newlyweds with a bridal suite in 1844.

1828 Feminist and abolitionist Frances Wright establishes Nashoba, a free-love utopian community near Memphis, Tennessee, where

THE NEW-HARMONY AND NASHOBA GAZETTE

SECOND SERIES.
VOL. 1—NO. 1.
Published every Wednesday.

OR

THE FREE ENQUIRER.

WHOLE SERIES.
VOL. 4—NO. 157.
Terms: $3 per ann. in adv

JUST OPINIONS ARE THE RESULT OF JUST KNOWLEDGE.—JUST PRACTICE OF JUST OPINIONS.

NEW-HARMONY, (IND.) WEDNESDAY, OCTOBER 29, 1828.

PROSPECTUS
OF THE
NEW-HARMONY AND NASHOBA GAZETTE,
OR
THE FREE ENQUIRER.
IN CONTINUATION OF
THE NEW-HARMONY GAZETTE.

freed or escaped slaves can live among white socialists and where mixed relationships are encouraged. About ten slaves and a few white folk make up the founding colony. Had Fanny Wright stayed there, the settlement might have worked. While she's off pursuing other interests, one white man announces to the outside world that he is cohabiting with a black woman. A local paper calls the community "one great brothel." By the time its founder returns, Nashoba is out of money and on its last legs. Wright continues to be a free-love advocate but the Nashoba failure damages her reputation.

1836 John Humphrey Noyes founds the Perfectionist Community in Putney, Vermont. Noyes sets up the communist community with a system of "complex marriage," that is, every man and woman in the community is married to each other and may have sex with each other as long as both parties consent. The polygamous arrangement is too much for Vermonters who force Noyes and his band of very merry men and women to move to Oneida, New York, where they flourish. A system of eugenics is established so that no couple may conceive a child unless the governing body decides that the gene-swap will enrich the community. Complex marriage survives until 1879 when Noyes is pressured by neighboring towns to revert to the status quo. During the intervening years, the group becomes proficient and well-known for making silverware.

1842 Fourierism is introduced to America. François Fourier believes people should live in phalanxes of 1,600 people dedicated to communal living and equality of the sexes. Marriage is a no-no. Anyone who is married must renounce their vows. Free love is allowed, as are homosexuality, promiscuity, and chastity. Fourier believes that each person has a sexual appetite that must be sated. There are members whose job is to take care of the basic needs of members who may not be attractive or savvy enough to get some loving on their own. After that your hormones are your own responsibility. Out of the forty or so phalanxes that are founded in the United States, one lasts for eighteen years and then, like Fourierism, fades into history.

A Little Help

1850s London and other European cities are agog over the stereoscope, a viewing device that allows a twin-image photograph to be seen in greater dimension. It's not the Thames or Big Ben they're looking at. In demand are photos of half-clad women exposing at least their breasts. Usually models are set in a classic art scene, reclining in draped surroundings, or occupied in some mundane task, such as ironing. The models exhibit no coyness or alluring modesty. Many gaze directly back at the viewer, adding to their coarseness. But they are nude, and the Victorian pornography is extremely popular.

1869 The bustle is created to give women a stick-out rump that only female Bushmen of South Africa have naturally. The smaller bustle,

TRIVIA

When President Calvin Coolidge and his wife are on tour of a farm, Mrs. Coolidge spots a rooster having his way with a hen. The first lady asks her guide how many times a day the rooster accomplishes this feat. Dozens of times, comes the answer. "Please tell that to the president," she directs. The guide obeys and informs Coolidge of the rooster's accomplishments. "Is it with the same hen?" the president inquires. No, he's told, it's a different hen every time. Coolidge directs the guide, "Please tell that to Mrs. Coolidge."

which is a semi-cage strapped around the waist with the back of the dress draped over it, fades away quickly but comes back with a vengeance in the 1880s in a more exaggerated form, turning women into less a human shape than a Minotaur. By the 1890s the bustle is on its way out in favor of fashions that allow women to be more athletic.

1875 Nevada finds a way to make easy money by providing a solution to unhappy marriages: a quick divorce. While other states make divorce a prolonged, if not impossible, procedure, Nevada requires six months' residency and two agreeable unagreeable partners. Can you spell "alimony"?

1882 The first birth-control clinic in the world is opened in Holland. Besides disseminating information, its founder, Dr. Aletta Jacobs, helps popularize the Dutch Cap, one of the first truly usable diaphragms.

1888 Twenty-three distinguished gentlemen meet in Washington, D.C., and found the National Geographic Society to increase geographical knowledge. That's accomplished through the society's house organ, *National Geographic* magazine. Besides great adventure stories and photographic innovations, the photos of bare-breasted women from primitive tropical locales make this magazine a keeper. Junior is suddenly just as interested in geography as Dad.

1888 Although the Egyptians were the first to combat body odor by shaving underarm hair and perfuming their bodies, the first product to curtail underarm sweating which causes odor is not introduced until Victorian times. Mum antiperspirant uses zinc in a cream base. Men won't become the focus of BO ads (a term coined in advertising by Odo-ro-no deodorant in 1919) until the 1930s. Before you roll on or spray, most sex manuals nix the use of deodorant, opting for the heady aroma of a clean body as a sexual stimulant.

1889 Abbotsholme School in England becomes home to the first sex education class. Headmaster Cecil Reddie wants "to prevent mental illusions due to false ideas from within," and stop the trading of information passed between students. Boys from ten to thirteen are taught the facts of life and "the dangers that surround them." The "During Pubity [*sic*]" group (ages thirteen to sixteen) is taught that it's better not to think about sex right now. Those between sixteen and twenty are taught

"the laws of later life" so they'll be well equipped.

1889 Corset maker Herminie Cadolle designs an undergarment that pushes breasts up and out without deforming the body. The underwear is the *soutien-gorge,* the precursor to the modern soft bra. In silk and tulle, the almost-bra is introduced as a health aid that supports the bosom without constricting the diaphragm. Women can breathe a sigh of relief—until the underwire is invented.

1898 The first advice-to-the-lovelorn column appears in the New York *Evening Journal.* Marie Manning writes the Beatrice Fairfax column after the letters-to-the-editor column receives requests for advice about personal problems. Her modern no-nonsense approach to readers caught in love triangles, unwanted engagements, and unhappy marriages soon nets her 1,400 letters a day from readers looking for help with their love life.

1913 The first nude calendar is adorned with a reproduction of artist Paul Chabas's *September Morn.* The picture of a nude young woman bathing in a lake raises the ire of self-anointed moralist Anthony Comstock who says of the picture, "There's too little morn and too much maid."

1914 Socialite Mary Phelps Jacob invents the modern soft bra. While she's trying to get dressed for a ball her corset keeps peeping out of the top of her dress. In her frustration she and her maid sew together two handkerchiefs and some ribbon to create a bra. Jacob tries to produce them herself but eventually sells the patent for $1,500 to the Warner Brothers Corset

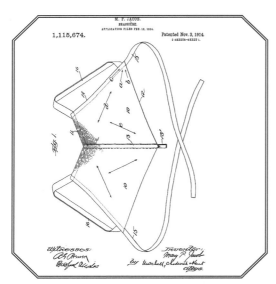

The original modern soft bra.

Company, which becomes a major player in the underwear game.

1920 The automobile is now common and cheap enough to work its way into the dating habits of the young. Although parents still want the over-the-shoulder chaperoning, the car makes privacy available. The automobile is "a bedroom on wheels" and "parking" becomes more than just shifting the car into a gear.

1925 Motorists traveling from San Diego to San Francisco can stay at the Motel Inn, the first motel in America, on the north side of San Luis Obispo. Each cabin has its own bathroom, telephone, and garage. It isn't long before motels get a second use. One study of a Dallas motel reveals that only 6 percent of guests register under their real names.

1933 Richard M. Hollingshead and Willis Smith open "The World's First Automobile Theater." This drive-in movie, situated on ten acres in Camden, New Jersey, has a 40- by 50-foot screen and sound broadcast from huge speakers. About 600 people attend opening night. Hollingshead later updates his idea by installing individual speakers and car heaters. After World War II the boom in the sale of automobiles with roomy back seats adds to the drive-in's allure. Nearly 4,000 of the outdoor movie theaters open, each with its own gimmick: playgrounds, Laundromats, fishing holes, miniature golf courses, or amusement parks. By the end of the evening all drive-ins have one thing in common: foggy car windows.

1935 The company that bought the patent for the modern soft bra from its inventor comes up with the latest innovation in bras: cup sizes. Warner Brothers joins the chest measurement with the fullness of the breast and introduces A, B, C, and D cups so women can have a more natural shape.

1936 If Mother Nature hasn't been kind to you, there's a way out and up. Falsies are marketed. Their popularity soars in the 1950s when large breasts are mandatory. More than one lady has the most embarrassing time of her life when an inflatable falsie deflates or slips out.

1940 They are real only in the sense that they live in the hearts, minds, and hormones of every GI. Beginning this year and continuing until 1946, pictures of Alberto Vargas's Vargas Girls appear in *Esquire* magazine. They are dream women, perfect women, with legs longer than a rush-hour traffic jam, breasts that are full, firm, pointed, and nippled, faces that are sweet and promising. They're wearing translucent lingerie, halter tops that suck the skin, and soooo short short shorts. GIs hang the drawings in billets and bunkers, on bulkheads and bombs. They're re-created by amateurs on airplanes. In 1944 Postmaster General Frank C. Walker bans them from the mails, and servicemen bellow loud and long. Vargas creates more beauties for *Playboy* in the 1950s.

1952 News of the first transsexual operation is announced. George Jorgensen experiments on himself by taking female hormones and contacts doctors in Denmark who are researching the possibility of sex changes. He's accepted, free of charge, as the first transsexual surgical patient. A series of operations and 2,000 hormone injections do the trick. George becomes Christine. News of the operation is received with curiosity and derisiveness. Over 500 other surgical hopefuls contact the Denmark team with pleas for help. The first she-to-he operation takes place in 1977.

1953 Hugh Hefner publishes the first issue of *Playboy* with a fully clothed Marilyn Monroe waving from the cover and a nude centerfold of her stapled inside. Hefner purchases the only previously unpublished one of three nude calendar photos of Monroe, who had posed early in her career. The red velvet backdrop features the voluptuous sex symbol with "nothing on but the radio" and her pink nipples in plain view. At fifty cents, the undated premiere issue sells nearly 54,000 copies. Monroe is the Sweetheart of the Month. The second issue, published in January 1954, is the first to feature a Playmate of the Month. Initially, Playmates are chosen from a job lot of color plates that Hefner has bought, until he comes up with the image of the girl-next-door. Whether blond, brunette, or red-haired, Playmates are large-breasted, red-lipped—and ultimately responsible for making

Hefner a millionaire and a legend. For the next twenty years the breasts of Playmates are the magazine's main feature. *Playboy* doesn't feature a beaver shot until its January 1972 issue.

1957 Men's favorite part of the female anatomy has always been the breasts, and thanks to the influence of Lana Turner and Jane Russell, they can get an eyeful. Women achieve that voluptuous tight-sweater look by wearing torpedo-shaped bras that are stiffened and built to sharp points, wholly defying nature and gravity. The vast majority of buxom beauties need help. The Corset Guild in Great Britain figures three out of four women wear falsies or padding to achieve the perfect look.

1960s A solution for adventurous souls stuck in monogamous relationships comes in the form of mate swapping. More talked about

than practiced, couples meet via personal ads in swinger magazines, in clubs, and by word of mouth. Depending on the number of couples and proximity of homes, "key parties" are held where husbands deposit their house keys in a bowl, wives pick one out and partners for the night are set. Group sex is possible or people choose their own partners. Psychologists reason that mate-swapping eases the guilt of otherwise philandering spouses, careful to note that liaisons are short-lived so as not to ruin the marriage. Another disadvantage is performance anxiety, which leaves some men limp. Once you get past all that, swinging is one way to live out your wildest fantasies.

In general most people do wrong whenever they have the opportunity.

Aristotle

1962 Injections of silicone have been used to enlarge breasts in Japan and Hollywood since the 1940s. This year the silicone gel bag is invented and soon June—and a lot of other women—is busting out all over. By the 1980s some two thousand American women a week have implants implanted. A poll taken of such women shows an increase in self-confidence. Husbands and boyfriends show an increase in eye-bulging. At $4,000 an operation, plastic surgeons are a pretty happy lot, too. But the bubble and the gel bag have to burst sometime. By 1991, complaints of disfigurement, hardening of the breasts, chronic fatigue, and autoimmune diseases allegedly attributed to silicone seeping into the body cause the industry to go bust.

1962 Grossinger's Hotel in the Catskill Mountains in New York plays host to the first singles-only weekend, beginning the use of "singles" as an adjective. Before long there are singles bars, singles cruises, singles resorts, singles tours, singles dances, and, yes, singles apartments—the first one in 1965 in Torrance, California—where singles activities are a 24-7 lifestyle. While some are successful at finding a mate for life, many more find the singles scene produces nothing more than a mate for the night.

1964 When football season ends in January and baseball season hasn't begun, what's a sports magazine to do? *Sports Illustrated* sends a crew complete with a model for the cover to Cozumel, hands Babette (the model) a white leather bikini, and does a travel piece. Then the magazine repeats the feature yearly, using athletic, gorgeous women shot in beautiful tropical settings, in the hottest swimwear. The swimsuit issue soon becomes an event readers look forward to every February. Sure, there are subscribers who cancel their subscriptions because they don't consider swimsuits a legitimate sport. But the million extra copies sold at newsstands make up for it.

1965 Helen Gurley Brown takes over the editorship of *Cosmopolitan*. Fresh from the success of her book *Sex and the Single Girl,* Brown creates the Cosmo woman. While other women's magazines are dishing out articles on cooking and housekeeping, Cosmo tells women how to be sexy, assertive, self-supporting, and how to

Great Moments in Sex

catch a man. Circulation figures rise from 800,000 in 1965 to 2.5 million in 1996.

1966 The first feminine hygiene spray on the market is FDS, designed to be applied to the vulva. Birth control pills and pantyhose add to the proliferation of vaginitis, which does cause an odor. Feminists don't think the sprays are a great idea. They argue that the concept of a deodorant for women's genitals is demeaning. Men don't get off the hook. If you can deodorize one set of genitals, you can deodorize the other. Products are marketed for sweeter smelling penises. Before long total body sprays are for sale, so no orifice has to go unscented.

1967 Extracurricular activities get more interesting as college dormitories begin to go coed and rules governing opposite-sex visitors are lifted. Administrations shrug their shoulders and accept couples living together. Within a few years traditionally all-male and all-female campuses open their doors to both sexes.

1969 Denmark legalizes pornography. As proponents of porn predicted, there's a marked increase in consumption. But once the novelty wears off, the market shrinks. The reaction of most Copenhageners to pornographic stimulation is boredom. What keeps sales high? Foreigners who purchase materials they can't buy at home.

1969 Bob Guccione's *Penthouse* lands on American shores four years after being introduced in England. Determined to undercut *Playboy* at any cost, Guccione's weapon is his willingness to cross obscenity lines. (Hard-core skin magazines feature all sorts of shots and angles, but they aren't "respectable" men's

magazines with national advertisers.) Initially Guccione's Pet of the Month is as tame as the *Playboy*'s Playmate, but in 1970, *Penthouse* shows pubic hair and couples frolicking. Lesbian love scenes follow. In 1974 the Pets start fondling themselves and masturbating for the camera. Threesomes are introduced. Finally, the "pink shot," a get-to-know-the-Pet-as-well-as-her-gynecologist photo, is featured. *Penthouse* is brought up on obscenity charges but ultimately sets standards that even *Playboy* has to follow.

1969 *Screw* magazine begins as an underground publication that lampoons and parodies whatever it wants. Publisher Al Goldstein includes porn pix and lets irreverence run wild in no-holds-barred reviews of "fuckfilms," records, television programs, celebrities, restau-

1972 *Cosmopolitan* magazine makes its readers drool. The April issue features a centerfold of Burt Reynolds lying on a bearskin rug, completely nude, his left arm his only cover-up from the prying camera. The brainstorm of *Cosmo*'s editor, Helen Gurley Brown, the beefcake issue sells 1.6 million copies. The English edition's model is Paul de Feu, recently separated from his feminist wife, Germaine Greer.

1972 The Dallas Cowboys introduce the Dallas Cowboy Cheerleaders, the first professional cheering section in sports history. Where other teams, and formerly the Cowboys, use high school squads, seven very healthy, very beautiful, and very scantily clothed women shake their pompons to cheer the Texas team while fans cheer them on.

1973 *Playgirl* magazine appears on the newsstands, offering enough eye candy to titillate and educate women as to the various shapes, sizes, and colors that males and their members come in. In 1998 the publication is slightly revamped to achieve a more sophisticated look. The centerfold and the boy-next-door finds sent in by their girlfriends are still the centerpiece, but now they're more artistically done. Also, a wider range of features and articles is published in the hope of broadening the reader base, which includes gay men.

rants, and consumer reports, many of which are measured on a "Peter Meter." Nothing is untouchable. Unlike *Playboy* which considers itself a guidebook for the well-sexed man, *Screw* opts for individuality. Obscenity charges are brought against the magazine because of the sexual aids ads and personal classified ads submitted by readers looking for partners for sex acts. The publishers are fined and continue publication.

1970 The Federal Commission on Obscenity and Pornography says pornography does not cause crime, sexual deviancy, or emotional disturbances. Its recommendation: remove all restrictions on pornography available to adults. While the commission is firm in its stand against the sale of porn to minors, it's adamant that the level of communication for adults cannot be lowered to a child's level.

1974 Nevada legalizes prostitution at "sex ranches." Taking the business out of the hands of pimps, brothels are only allowed in towns with populations of less than 200,000. Prostitutes must be over eighteen and are medically checked on a regular basis. Taxes are paid to the state depending on the number of hookers in the house.

Great Moments in Sex

1974 Larry Flynt puts out the first official issue of *Hustler*. Initially *Hustler* was a newsletter aimed at promoting Flynt's strip-joint bars. Flynt, who says he lost his virginity at age eight to a chicken on his grandmother's farm, shows what he believes most men want to see: female genitalia. Along with politically incorrect cartoons, articles, and fake ads—a liquor ad with the Reverend Jerry Falwell claiming that his first sexual encounter was with his mother in an outhouse results in a First Amendment lawsuit—Flynt scores big with the release of nude photos of former first lady Jacqueline Kennedy Onassis. The August 1975 issue sells over a million copies in days.

1977 Embarrassed and frustrated after trying to buy his wife lingerie at department stores, Roy Raymond founds Victoria's Secret, a chain store and catalog service specializing in upscale lingerie. Though the merchandise may be for women, the store's ambience and the catalog's scantily clad, sensuous models definitely attract males. Negligees, demi-bras, thongs, and G-strings clinging to the forms of Claudia Schiffer, Tyra Banks, and Daniela Pestova make the VS catalog as wanted a read as *Playboy*. And you don't have to pretend to read the articles.

1980s If you want to breathe heavy on the phone it's okay. Someone will even breathe heavy back. But it's going to cost you. Usually one to four dollars a minute. That's what phone sex is about—your wildest fantasy with a woman of any shape, color, or form, though it's usually a secretary, a housewife, or a bank teller on the other end moonlighting for extra money. Who cares? She sounds like your fantasy. It's safe sex. It's cheap sex (compared to paying a prostitute). It's available sex. And since phone sex is a billion-dollar-a-year industry a lot of men must have a lot of fantasies.

1980s Surveys of video stores show that some 63 percent of X-rated videos are rented by women or couples. So erotica from the female point of view hits the market. Leading the pack is former porn star Candida Royalle who forms Femme Productions and puts the emphasis on atmosphere, foreplay, and consent. Violence is limited to soft, silky bondage. And men actually stay awake afterward. Women watch—with their partners or alone.

1989 A few artists' models breathe a sigh of relief after an eighteen-day exhibit of nude art at China's Beijing Art Gallery comes to a close. The nude human figure has been excluded from Chinese art since the Cultural Revolution. When the exhibit of 120 works in oil and mixed media opens, record-breaking crowds flock to see them, causing a great deal of consternation for the women who posed for the artists. Two models sue to have their likenesses removed from the exhibit. Other models are ostracized. One marriage ends in divorce. Visitors to the gallery fare a little better. While some find the works titillating, many more respond to the artworks with downcast eyes and gasps of shock.

1990s Personal computers add a new dimension to sex. Cyberporn is available to anyone with a modem who knows how to reach a bulletin-board system. Because there's no going out to seedy bookstores, it's much more available to the average man. Cyberporn differs from the usual pornography. The on-line demand is for deviant material: pedophilia, bondage, sadism, masochism, urination, defecation, and sex with animals. The allure of sex in chat rooms is in its anonymity. It's not real so you can change your persona and experiment at will without suffering any real-life ramifications. "One handed typing" and "busy fingers" messages let cyberpartners know that the homemade erotica is doing the trick. It'll never take the place of real sex. But in the nervous nineties it's a safe alternative.

1992 After looking at airbrushed centerfolds, a woman can develop an inferiority complex. And a man, after watching long-dong porn stars,

The Wonder Bra is an immediate hit with women and men.

may feel his ego waning. As implants help lift a woman's confidence, a man can grow in stature also. And girth and length. To add thickness to the penis—but only to the shaft, the head stays the same—body fat is taken from the abdomen and injected. About four-tenths of an inch is the maximum engorgement. The penis can be elongated by cutting the suspensory ligament that connects the penis to the pubic bone. That little guy can be stretched anywhere from ⅜ inch to 2 inches. Sound good? Well, breast implants have downfalls and so does penis puffing. Fat is absorbed back into the body, leaving you pretty much where you started from. Before it disappears (a word that no man wants to hear in the same sentence with the word penis), the fat can clump up. New injections are required every three to six months. At $2,500 to $5,000 a procedure, that can be costly. Elongating a penis has its own shortcomings. Once the ligament is cut, that's it. Since the ligament supports the penis, when it's cut the penis won't point as high as it did before. Infections are possible with both procedures. Suddenly a magnifying glass seems much cheaper and safer.

1992 Cole of California introduces Top Secret, an inflatable bikini able to increase the bust one cup size. The built-in plastic cushion inflates the bra when the sewn-in pump is pressed. A reverse valve lets the air out. In pressurized situations such as airplanes or scuba diving, it deflates. And at $72 you're going to need an air pump for your wallet.

1993 The Erox Corporation, founded by Dr. David Berliner who pioneered work in pheromones, introduces the

Great Moments in Sex

first perfumes containing synthesized human pheromones. REALM Men and REALM Women do not guarantee a date every Saturday night. But male dabbers report increased sociability and comfortableness while women note a rise in confidence and friendliness.

1994 What Mother Nature has forgotten can always be restored by . . . the Wonder Bra and cookies (its built-in pads). Cleavage is the operative word of the 1990s, and this underwire bra with fifty-four separate pieces of latex, wire, and fabric, pushes in, pushes up, and plunges down. It's not a new invention. Introduced by Gossard in England twenty-five years ago, its reintroduction by Sara Lee generates publicity when bodyguards in an armored car bring the first delivery to Macy's in New York. The bra sells at the rate of one every fifteen seconds. Not only do women buy out the Wonder Bra, which stores can't keep in stock—but its competitors, the Miracle Bra, the Super-Uplift Bra, the It Really Works Bra, and the It Must Be Magic Bra, do almost as well. Although the Wonder Bra starts off as a push-up bra, the line expands to include bras for everyday wear. Perkiness isn't in the eye of the beholder. It's shoved into a pair of cantilevered cups.

A Little Help

Chapter Nine

YOU CAN'T DO THAT!

B.C.

<1275 By the time of Moses, the Jews' ban on masturbation is in place. The emphasis is on multiplying the Chosen People, not getting your rocks off in the desert. This is in contrast to surrounding civilizations, including the Egyptians, who consider it a religious duty to masturbate and offer the semen as a sacrifice. The Egyptians believe their god Aton-Re created the universe through masturbating, making the life-giving rivers like the Nile. To maintain this force, it's only right to give it back. Through the years the ban on masturbation among Jews grows stronger. Some rabbis even call for the death penalty for lawbreakers.

c. 1200 Don't even think about breaking a law in Assyria. Known for their cruelty to their captured enemies, their brutality doesn't stop at home. Abortion is a capital crime. Even if a woman dies from the abortion, she suffers the same punishment as if she were alive: impalement on a stake. If a woman hides a runaway wife, her ears are cut off. There are equally severe punishments for hitting your husband and for infidelity. Men have it easier but there are punishments for them, too. If a man rapes a virgin, then his wife is raped. And to really put the screws to him, if her father wants it, he has to marry her.

c. 625 The city of Catania in Sicily allows divorce. Either husband or wife is allowed to initiate proceedings. There's one prohibition: upon dissolution you may not marry anyone younger than your divorced mate.

500> Chinese men can have wives and concubines aplenty. Visits to the local prostitute? No problem. The only thing they can't do is remain single. That's an affront to their ancestors. Local officials in charge of pairing up unwed men and women make sure that men are nuptialized by age thirty and women by age twenty. Women don't have the sexual freedom men enjoy. Chastity is so strictly attached to a woman's feeling of worth that many commit suicide if they feel they've been compromised by an accidental male touch.

First, the Good News . . .

c. 500 The Persians do not value chastity or bachelors. Status is attained through marriage, children—especially sons—a house, and wealth. Polygamy and concubinage are accepted. Now the bad news: Masturbation gets you flogged. Promiscuity and prostitution bring the death penalty. There's no forgiveness for practicing pederasty, although young boys are said to be popular. Adultery might be forgiven, but aborting a child is considered vile and must result in the woman's death. A member of the king's harem can kiss her sex life good-bye. No woman can share the royal bed twice unless she's extremely beautiful.

443 The censors set the moral tone for Romans and create laws to ensure their guidelines are followed. They see marriage as a foundation, lay into bachelors who enjoy their freedom too long, and deride men who marry too often. Once married, the onus of fidelity is on the woman. Cato, a famous censor, believes it's a husband's right to kill his wife if he catches her cheating. She, however, may not lift

TRIVIA

Coitus interruptus, the act of withdrawing the penis and ejaculating outside the vagina, has been practiced by nearly all cultures from ancient time to the present. The story of Onan, in the Old Testament, is the basis on which Judaism and Christianity condemn the practice. According to custom, when Onan's older brother died, Onan was to marry his brother's widow in a levirate marriage and have children with her. But during sex, Onan kept pulling out and "spilling seed on the ground." This didn't sit too well with the Lord and that was the last time good old Onan pulled out—or did anything else, for that matter. While the Catholic church forbids coitus interruptus on the grounds that it's sex with no procreation and any nonprocreative sex is a sin, the Jewish faith, which once forbade the practice and later condoned it, still gives Onan the thumbs down for refusing to comply with the law. Levirate marriage was practiced to continue the family line in a way that would ensure the dead husband's remembrance, and to keep property within the family. By the eighteenth century, the story of Onan was interpreted as masturbation and helped lay the framework society used to condemn playing with your own toy.

a finger against him if he is unfaithful. Censors aren't fond of the theater; they believe it undermines morals. When Pompey builds a theater, he safeguards it from destruction by building a temple to Venus over it.

<100> A menstruating woman is considered unclean and in some cultures is thought to be possessed by demons. In primitive cultures anything she touches loses its usefulness. Hindu women must stay out of the sunshine because they might get pregnant. They can't touch a man's food or utensils. In British Guiana women can't bathe because they'll poison the waters. In a forest, they will be bitten by turned-on snakes, so the woods are off limits to them. Maori women can't use anything men use, including walkways. If a wife lies on her husband's blanket, he can kill her, though in two weeks, he'll die of terror. In Tanzania young boys are told that lying with a menstruating woman causes the penis to fall off. A menstruating woman has been known to destroy grass, dissolve asphalt, and ruin crops. Getting pregnant doesn't help much. In Egypt as well as Greece, after giving birth or having an abortion a woman cannot enter the temple until she's purified.

c. 100 The barbarians of Germany have an interesting way of dealing with an adulteress. Adultery isn't a major problem, but when it does occur the woman's hair is cut off and she is driven naked through the streets while being flogged.

A.D.

c. 90 Roman emperor Domitian feels that prostitutes have too much influence, so he takes them down a peg. They can no longer be carried in litters through the streets, nor are they, or their offspring, allowed to marry a senator. Domitian does away with one type of prostitute: young boys, who at times outnumber female prostitutes.

198 Tertullian rages against the evils of the Roman theater, which "fans the sparks of carnal lust." The stage is filled with immodesty "wherein nothing is approved save that which elsewhere is disapproved." He warns of fates to befall theatergoers including demonic possession and death. The attack clearly states the church's position against lascivious plays. The Roman stage ceases to exist by the end of the sixth century. The theater won't return for almost a thousand years, at which time only religious plays will be presented and will gradually evolve into morality plays.

c. 300 The frown lines on the face of the Catholic church are deepening. If semen is for making babies, then wasting it is not tolerated. That includes masturbation. As Rome weakens and the church gains strength, the ban on using your penis as a joystick extends even to soldiers. In later centuries penitentials (as mentioned in Chapter Two) lay down guidelines on whacking off. Adolescents get a slap on the wrist, but church elders must atone for up to three years.

c. 300 Dancing is popular with everyone, but Rome's professional dancers earn kudos for their licentious movements. That doesn't please the church. Those who shake their booty or participate in mime are refused baptism. Saint John Chrysostom, the inventor of hymn singing, denounces the dance as devilish. By the end of the century excommunication is threatened for anyone brazen enough to attend the theater on church holy days.

c. 342 Basing his decision on an ancient belief that food which has a sexual shape acts as an aphrodisiac, Saint Jerome forbids nuns to eat beans lest they lose their chastity. Not only do beans have an immodest shape (they're supposed to resemble testicles), it's thought that they secrete a body fluid that arouses passion.

c. 500 The Dark Ages brings its own rules for sexual satisfaction: you don't get any. Outlawed, or at least considered sinful according to Christian teachings, are sex with the man entering the woman from the rear, sex on Sunday, Wednesday, or Friday of *any* week, sex during Lent (the forty days before Easter), sex in the forty days before Christmas, and sex three days before receiving communion. Nix also on masturbation, premarital sex, oral sex, homosexuality, etc. The only sex that *is* allowed is the man-on-top-get-it-over-with-quick position, and it better be with the wife for procreative reasons.

544 King Childebert I puts his foot down and forbids the religious dances that have crept into church services and processions. Once the wiggling starts, it's hard to keep out sexual overtones, especially when some are trying to bring back pagan influence. But keeping people from dancing is like trying to get priests to remain celibate. In 744 Pope Zacharias forbids religious dancing because of its licentiousness. In the 1100s the bishop of Paris again tries to stop it. Clever clergy make a little cash by selling dancing indulgences—that is, paying the church up front so you don't have to do time in purgatory for your sins.

Until Death, and Then We Really Do Part

585 The Second Council of Macon rules that no dead male body can be buried next to a woman's body unless she has been dead long enough to be decomposed.

c. 700 In Japan the father has complete rights over his family including sons- and daughters-in-law. He can kill any family member convicted of a serious crime or unchastity. Wives caught with a paramour also get a ticket to heaven courtesy of the husband. However, if he chooses to kill his wife, he must also kill her lover. Failure to do in one without the other gets the husband executed by the authorities.

c. 1200 The button is invented but you can't use it as a fastener. As a decoration have as many as you wish, but using one to fasten a garment marks you as a loose person. People who want to slip in and out of their clothes that easily must want to for a reason. Morals are judged to be as yielding as your clothes.

1279 With the advent of Mongol rule, the Chinese institute, in the *Table of Merits and Demerits Regarding the Ten Precepts,* a list of guidelines governing behavior in all aspects of life. The third precept deals with debauchery. You get fifty demerits for having too many wives and concubines or for associating with people addicted to whoring. Ten demerits against you for lustful thoughts, using language to excite lust in women, or having pornographic pictures. A lewd dream is one demerit, unless it puts you into action; then it's five. The big-time demerits are saved for violating a chaste woman, selling a housemaid as a prostitute, or producing erotica. You get a thousand demerits for each. If you scheme to make a nun or a widow your concubine it's five hundred demerits. Encouraging a man to sell his wife is three hundred.

TRIVIA Throughout history, punishments for sexual offenses vary according to the culture and the offense. Adulteresses are cruelly punished: Their noses and ears are slit or cut off. Their genitals are mutilated. Some Zulu tribes thrust a cactus into the offender's vagina. The Vietnamese use a trained elephant to toss and trample the woman to death. Stoning is popular in some cultures, too. Adulterers don't get off the hook. Castration or murder by the husband is common. Facial mutilation and amputation of the hands can also be used. In ancient Rome, a fish with a spiny head is rammed into an adulterer's anus. Homosexuals are mostly put to death, but not before being ridiculed and castrated. Incest is dealt with severely in most societies. The Cayapa of Ecuador slowly roast the offenders over lighted candles.

1374 Believing their nighttime rituals are an excuse for sexual orgies, the church condemns witches as heretics, since many of their evening services are devoted to pagan gods. Under the rules of the Inquisition heretics are dealt with severely. A woman—most witches are women because they are believed to be unintelligent enough to be swayed—is considered guilty unless she can prove her innocence. If she confesses her guilt, the Inquisition is lenient: she'll be given absolution before being burned to death. By the mid-sixteenth century one officer of the Inquisition brags that over 30,000 witches have been burned during the last 150 years.

1450 The public baths at Bath, England, were refurbished three hundred years ago, and since then men and women have enjoyed nude bathing together, a practice that's believed to promote good health. But they're enjoying it too much. Since the spa is under control of the local bishop, he takes what action he can: anyone caught bathing nude in mixed company is excommunicated. A hundred years later there's still a problem. This time the rule is anyone over the age of puberty must wear a robe.

c. 1500 In addition to the four wives plus concubines, which men are allowed to have in the Ottoman Empire, the Turkish version of "Greek friendship" is rampant. Plus men are not limited to their own women. Women from conquered nations are absorbed into their lifestyle with ease. Why should there be any adultery? There shouldn't be. That's what the law says. Fallen women must buy an ass and ride through the city in shame. Men are flogged and required to kiss the executioner who delivers their one hundred lashes.

1533 England passes its first anti-sodomy law, the Buggery Act of 1533. The punishment is death but how it's meted out is politically or religiously motivated. Walter Lord Hungerford, accused of treason after asking his seers to prophesy the date of the king's death, is also accused of sodomizing his servants. He's beheaded. The headmaster of Eaton has his way with his students. He loses his job, not his head, and is later appointed headmaster at another school. The law is repealed until 1563, when it's reissued. It stays in place until 1967.

1559 No one, absolutely no one, can read any book on the *Index Librorum Prohibitorum*. This list of banned books includes any written work that contradicts Catholic church dogma, teaches

superstition or magic, or contains obscene matter. Punishment is meted out by the Inquisitors. Finding offenders isn't difficult: the church offers the accuser 25 percent of the convicted sinner's confiscated property.

1564 With moral reformation under way, Pope Paul IV orders the nude figures in Michelangelo's *Last Supper,* which adorns the Sistine Chapel, to be clothed. With Michelangelo's permission, Daniele da Volterra, his assistant, gets the job of clothing the nudes, earning him the nickname Il Braccatone, the breeches maker. By the 1580s pagan imagery and nudity in artwork are systematically done away with. In response to the *Index* and the censorship of art, an underground business in illicit materials booms.

1580 The fashions imported into London are giving the clergy a holy fit. When they see that the enhancement of feminine charms is more than a passing trend, they exert political pressure until an edict is issued. Any woman wearing a wig, cosmetics, high-heeled shoes, perfume, or other enticements that lead one of her majesty's subjects into marriage is dealt with as a witch.

1582 Prostitutes aren't having a good time in this age of Reformation. The growing bands of Protestant and Calvinist reformers call for their excommunication. Reformer Philip Stubbes has his own ideas: all prostitutes should be branded on their cheeks, forehead, and any other visible body parts. While you're at it, cut out the dancing. It leads to whoredom.

1583 Spanish lawmakers have had it with the saraband, an erotic dance that was imported from the Canary Islands by explorers, who taught it to their countrymen. Hips sway, breasts knock, lips kiss, and indecent positions and gestures are accompanied by castanets and tambourines. But no more. Anyone caught sarabanding is given two hundred lashes. Women are then exiled and men sent to the galleys for six years. The dance is later cleaned up and becomes a favorite at European courts.

1595 Francesco Carletti, in his book *My Voyage Around the World,* published this year, tells of the interesting way Korea deals with adulterers. Bound and put into a wagon, the man is castrated with enough of his pubic skin taken off to make a skullcap for the woman. A circular piece of flesh is taken from around the woman's vagina to make a garland for the man to wear. Then, naked, they're paraded through

Hardy pilgrims mete out heavy punishments for sexual misbehavior.

the streets until they slowly bleed to death. Needless to say, monogamy is very popular.

c. 1600 Chocolate's aphrodisiac qualities are well sung. Alone or as an accompaniment to other aphrodisiac foods, the French believe in its power. That's why monks are forbidden to drink it (chocolate is in liquid form only). They can have cocoa though. It's considered an anaphrodisiac.

1627 Dancing around the Maypole has long been a fertility rite practiced by numerous cultures. In Bohemia its power is taken so seriously that only virgins can do its circle dance. But when that "lord of misrule" Thomas Morton dares to erect an 80-foot Maypole in what is now Quincy, Massachusetts, then throws a beer bash and allows his workers and Indian women to boogie down for a few days, Puritan fathers say enough and cut it down. Morton and his men receive a stern lecture.

Puritan fathers frown on dancing around the Maypole.

1638 The hardy pilgrims who braved the sea to come to America don't have ice water flow-

Great Moments in Sex

ing in their veins and the women who make the trip are more gregarious than the norm. Connecticut's Puritan forefathers keep problems from starting by laying down the law. Adultery, homosexuality, and having sex with an animal merit the death penalty. Premarital sex gets the participants instantly engaged, whipped, fined, or all three.

1642 Theater ceases to exist in England under Oliver Cromwell after Parliament passes an ordinance closing the theaters so as to "avert the wrath of God." Players and spectators are marked as people of loose character and suffer penalties if caught at any play. For the next eighteen years the theaters remain officially closed until 1660, when Charles II takes the throne and reopens them.

1674 Keep away from my soldiers! That's the order Louis XIV sends to prostitutes, with an additional threat: any harlot found with a soldier boy within five miles of Versailles will have her nose and ears cut off.

1691 Virginia becomes the first colony in America to ban interracial marriage. Settlers, once too concerned for their own survival to differentiate color lines, now decide to protect their European roots. Any white woman who marries a Negro or mulatto, whether free or slave, is banished from the colony. A white woman bearing a black or mulatto child must pay a fine of fifteen pounds. If she's unable to pay, she becomes a slave for fifteen years. Massachusetts passes a similar law in 1705, with severe punishment for fraternization between the races. Maryland already has a law giving ownership of a child born of a liaison between a white woman and a Negro slave to the master of the slave.

TRIVIA The story of the wedding night of a young couple epitomizes the sexual repression of the Victorian era. Upon entering the bedroom, the groom finds his wife sprawled across the bed in a deep chloroformed sleep. The note pinned beside her reads, "Momma says you are to do what you like."

1698 English clergyman Jeremy Collier writes *Short View of the Immorality and Profaneness of the English Stage*. He blames the degeneration of public morals on the English theater, which portrays immoral characters as successful and admirable. Several playwrights defend themselves but Collier has the last say, sniffing out all forms of lewdness and attacking everyone. The theater becomes a more proper, if duller, place.

1722 Japan outlaws the presentation of popular love-suicide plays. Art imitates life. Lovers who are denied permission to marry are known to kill themselves together because they believe doing so unites them forever in the afterlife. The plays romanticize the suicides so much that couples emulate them even more. Anyone who survives a suicide attempt is severely punished. The corpses of non-survivors are displayed publicly like criminals.

1790> It's almost a contest from the very beginnings of the Victorian era to see who's more proper. The art world suffers as nude stat-

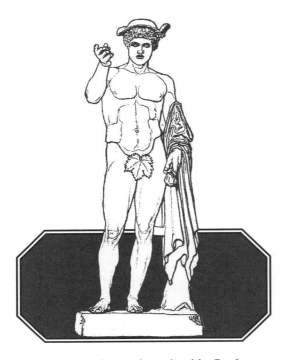

ues are draped or adorned with fig leaves. Nudes in artists' portfolios are secreted away and those shown lack sensuality. Books are burned and banned. And the English language takes a turn toward the ridiculous. Body parts are not said aloud. Legs are limbs, breasts are the neck, and chickens have bosoms. Underwear are unmentionables that are strictly unmentionable. Venereal diseases are social diseases, which you don't get if you practice the solitary vice (masturbation), which is forbidden. But then so is having a connection (sex) that could make a female (woman) enceinte (pregnant) until she is confined (gives birth). Animals aren't off the hook, either. A cockroach loses his cock and becomes a roach. A cock and bull story becomes a rooster and a male cow. An ass is an a———. A mid-nineteenth-century book on etiquette has the final say on priggishness. Books by male and female authors should never share the same shelf space. An exception is made if the authors are married to each other.

c. 1790 Dancing the waltz will either be the most wonderfully intoxicating thing you've ever done or it will condemn you to eternal damnation. Created in Germany, the waltz is a very fast spinning dance that requires partners to hold each other close. Some men wrap the women's skirts around them, pressing their material filled hand against their partners' breasts. Europe loves it. Or hates it. Whoever isn't dancing it is condemning it. It's called disgusting, immodest, degenerating, and polluting. Lord Byron, a trendsetter, scoffs at the dance because it won't "leave much mystery for the nuptial night." In the few years it takes to reach America, the waltz is toned down in speed, but it still meets with objections.

1818 Thomas Bowdler is a self-appointed censor who feels that "If any word or expression is of such a nature that the first impression it excites is an impression of obscenity, that word ought not to be spoken nor written or printed; and if printed, it ought to be erased." Bowdler rewrites Shakespeare, changing words and omitting characters. Then he moves on to Edward Gibbon's *History of the Decline and Fall of the Roman Empire* and deletes passages he considers immoral or irreligious. Bowdler dies in 1825 before he can damage more works. By 1835 the term "bowdlerize" is used to denote the modification or omission of anything considered vulgar.

1828 The French Revolution has left the English aristocracy sweating. Believing that France's loose morality was partly responsible England tightens hers, beginning with the upper classes, who are expected to set a proper example. Even nude swimmers are taken to task. Homosexuals get the brunt of the punishment.

The 1533 law against homosexuality is still in effect and this year the standards of evidence are relaxed. Proof of "actual Emission of Seed" is no longer needed, only proof of penetration. The first thirty years of the nineteenth century see the execution of more than fifty offenders. In 1861 the punishment is reduced to ten years to life imprisonment. The threat is enough to make some gay aristocrats leave the country and live abroad.

Sometimes You Can Try Too Hard

1833 Reverend John R. McDowall takes it upon himself to inform fellow clergymen and the public of the prevalence of prostitution in New York. In addition to trying to convert whores, he publishes *McDowall's Journal,* which details names and addresses so well that many refer to it as the Whorehouse Directory. He's brought before a grand jury whose members consider the journal "injurious to morals, and degrading to the character of our city." That doesn't stop him. He gathers up obscene books, prints, music boxes, playing cards, and snuffboxes and invites three hundred clergymen to view the display. At first they're astonished at the array, but they soon turn on him, charging that he's gone too far. McDowall is brought before the Third Presbytery of New York and suspended from the ministry. He dies a few months later.

1833 Noah Webster proves he's a wizard with words when he publishes his *American Dictionary of the English Language* in 1828. In 1833, he's not adding words, he's deleting them—from the Bible. Webster rationalizes that current society is refined and doesn't need the coarser passages. His purged edition of the King James Version loses words like "womb" and "teat" completely. "Lewdness" and its variant forms replace "fornicate," "harlot," and "whore." And men don't have "stones" (testicles) anymore. They have "peculiar members."

1837 Horseback riding for women is put on the no-no list in Donald Walker's book, *Exercise for Ladies.* Equine exercise is ill-advised, since it deforms the lower part of the body, which performs womanly duties.

1862 The United States passes legislation outlawing polygamy. There's little enforcement of the law, which is aimed primarily at the Mormons in Utah. Twenty years later, the Edmunds law is passed, defining polygamous marriages as bigamy.

1862 Abraham Lincoln sends General Benjamin Butler to occupied New Orleans, but the southern ladies don't take kindly to the Yankee troops. Their slamming windows shut

and spitting on northern troops are tolerated. But when belles flip up the backs of their dresses—sign language for "Kiss my ass"—and empty chamber pots from second-story windows onto soldiers below, Butler has enough. Hitting southern gentility below the belt, he issues General Order Number 28, stating that any woman showing contempt will be treated and punished as a prostitute. The ladies fall in line. No one is ever arrested.

1873 Anthony Comstock, founder of the Society for the Suppression of Vice, dedicates his life to ridding America of anything *he* considers obscene. He lobbies Congress to pass the Comstock Law, prohibiting the mailing of obscene, lewd, lascivious, or filthy matter, including books, contraceptives, abortifacients, and advertisements. Comstock is appointed special postal agent to help sniff out smut. His narrow-minded subjectivity, his inability to distinguish pornography from works of literary merit, and the fact that "lewd," "indecent," "obscene," and "lascivious," are not defined in the bill, has publishers editing words like "pregnant" and replacing it with "enceinte." Saying that "a single book or a single picture may taint forever the soul of the person who reads it," Comstock gloats, two years before his death in 1913, that "I have convicted persons enough to fill a passenger train of 61 coaches, 60 coaches containing 60 passengers each and the sixty-first almost full. I have destroyed 160 tons of obscene literature."

1878 Anthony Comstock doesn't like birth control in any form. That includes abortion. New York's Madame Restell, a self-proclaimed "woman's doctor," specializes and makes a fortune in abortifacients, contraceptives, and midwifery, sometimes performing abortions. Payoffs to the police and offering services women desperately need keep her in business—until Comstock shows up at her door and entraps her into selling him an abortifacient for his poor wife. He arrests her but the sixty-seven-year-old grandmother, who has already spent a year in jail and doesn't want to repeat the experience, slits her own throat. This is the fifteenth suicide that Comstock is connected to, including that of sex educator Ida Craddock, author of *Advice to a Bridegroom*, and the public is getting its fill of him. He is lambasted in the press for overzealousness, and even the clergy look upon Restell as a wronged woman. Comstock, unfazed, continues his crusade.

1879 Saint Louis's Social Evil Law is repealed, ending a decade-long experiment in legalized prostitution. The law, passed in 1870, requires brothel owners and prostitutes to register their businesses and pay a fee to the Department of Health to be used for medical checkups of prostitutes. It also limits the locations, thereby safeguarding the value of homes in "proper" neighborhoods. Problems begin when too many individual prostitutes register and then constantly move. Doctors get backlogged in their inspections and issue health certificates without examining the women. The clergy and some proper lay people complain. Feminists don't see why promiscuous men aren't forced to register, too. Missouri's state legislature decides to check things out and sends sixteen legislators to the district at night. Only three return on time. The next move is decriminalization. Police can only arrest streetwalkers for vagrancy. When prostitution begins to spread into better neighborhoods, the deal is called off. Prostitution is once again a criminal act.

Great Moments in Sex

"Hey, whiskers, going to ball me off?" a prostitute asked the Reverend Charles Parkhurst during an undercover investigation in New York City, 1892.

1892 The Reverend Charles Parkhurst admits to a grand jury that his allegations of police corruption and his statement that the city administration is a "lying, perjured, rum-soaked, and libidinous lot," are based on newspaper reports. Rebuked harshly, Parkhurst hires a detective and spends three weeks investigating brothels, opium dens, and dives. He gets his proof, even witnessing a police precinct captain enter a bawdy house. Parkhurst ushers in an era of antiprostitution that is aimed at ridding municipal government of underworld ties. Raids are numerous but mainly for show. Local politicians bail out the prostitutes as soon as

they're arraigned. Parkhurst's pressure leads to a few politicos and police admitting payoffs. But in a few years, the status quo returns. More importantly, the minister's tactics and goals serve as a model for other anti-vice groups for the next quarter century.

1906 Edward Bok, editor of the *Ladies' Home Journal,* agrees with a growing number of reformers who see a need for education and information in order to stop the spread of venereal disease. He publishes a series of articles on VD, putting emphasis on chastity and abstinence. For his efforts Bok loses 75,000 outraged subscribers.

1906 Rumors of Germany's imperial court being overloaded with homosexuals and threatening national security come to a head when journalist Maximilian Harden exposes the "conspiracy." It's true that upper-class gay men have been invited to join a defense league, which never materializes, and there are gay men at Wilhelm II's court. But Harden claims that an international brotherhood stronger than a monastic order threatens Deutschland and the king. Wilhelm is forced to demonstrate his heterosexuality to the point of switching political positions against England in order to seem more manly. Gay men are portrayed as effeminate and having the worst stereotypical female characteristics. It's not chic to be gay anymore. This sentiment will reach a peak during Nazi Germany.

1907 If you're a criminal, an idiot, an imbecile, or a rapist, the state of Indiana doesn't want you to procreate. A sterilization law passed this year gives the authorities the right to make sure you won't. About 120 operations are performed by 1921 when the state's Supreme Court rules that the law is unconstitutional, leaving criminals, idiots, imbeciles, and rapists free to reproduce once more.

1909 The National Board of Censorship is set up as a self-appointed review committee to monitor the moving pictures that are captivating Americans. From the time nickelodeons are introduced, newspaper editors, clergy, and watchdog groups fret over the movies' potential to exhibit the baser side of life, fearing that young minds will find the lifestyles of loose women, philandering husbands, and criminals too attractive. Risqué films can be made but they had better have a moral ending. Criminal characters must go to jail, and those who defy Victorian moral standards usually die a pathetic death.

1910 The U.S. Congress passes the Mann Act, prohibiting the transportation of women across state lines or international borders for "immoral purposes." The law is enacted to counter white slavery, which is sweeping the nation. The reported trafficking in women, particularly European immigrants, and forcing them into prostitution, angers the American public and results in the passage of the law.

1913 Irving Berlin may have penned *Everybody's Doin' It,* but conservative and religious groups are trying to stop it—the Turkey Trot, that is. A quick one-step, with arms flapping at the sides, the Trot is a newfangled dance that allows close body contact. The younger set loves it. But ramifications are on the way. The editor of the *Ladies' Home Journal* fires fifteen women in his office for trotting during lunchtime. A Methodist pastor in Clayton, New Jersey, calls it "hugging to music" and threatens to dismiss

church members who do the dance. Philadelphia bans it. And in New York the president of the International Art Society at the annual ball held at the Hotel Astor announces that anyone doin' it will be "escorted from the hall." The fuss isn't necessary. Like all fads, the Turkey Trot dances into the sunset after a couple of years.

1917 Josephus Daniels, the secretary of the navy, puts an end to Storyville, New Orleans's attempt at legalized prostitution. With America's entry into World War I, Daniels proclaims that no prostitution is allowed within five miles of a navy base. The mayor of New Orleans's protests are in vain. At the stroke of midnight on November 12 the madams lift their last glasses of champagne, and the girls pack their bags and leave the district. But not the profession.

1920s Bean Town's fondness for censorship makes the phrase "banned in Boston" a familiar one. Not limiting their clicking tongues to the burlesque houses, which usually have a second version of their shows—the Boston version— ready for those times when the police show up, Boston's censors regard the stage, dance, and literature as fair game, too. When dancer Isadora Duncan flaunts her sexuality and her Communist views, the mayor prohibits her from appearing on any Boston stage ever again. Eugene O'Neill's play *Strange Interlude* also gets the thumbs-down. At one time or another Boston banned all theatrical performances; the opera *Salomé;* Elinor Glyn's novel *Three Weeks;* Gabriele D'Annunzio's novel *The Triumph of Death;* and all of Leon Trotsky's works to name a few.

1920s As eager as flappers are to show off their legs, Philadelphia ministers are eager to cover them. A group of clergymen design a proper gown with a hemline exactly seven and one-half inches from the floor. Utah's restrictions are tougher: any woman brazen enough to show more than three inches of leg above the ankle is fined.

Will Hays: Hollywood's morality czar.

1922 In an effort to censor themselves before the federal government does, Hollywood moviemakers form the Motion Picture Producers and Distributors of America. They appoint Will Hays, a member of President Harding's cabinet and a church elder, to sit as the czar of morality. Moral-guidance groups like the General Federation of Women's Clubs are up in arms at the thought of their daughters turning into hedonistic, bobbed-hair vamps, and they blame Hollywood. Hays produces a list of dos and don'ts, mostly don'ts, for filmmakers: Marriage and family are to be glorified. Adultery is never justified. Passionate scenes cannot "stimulate the lower and baser element." Seduction and rape cannot be comedic subjects. Films should not be based on books or plays that offend the public's sensibilities. Creative directors find their way around the code. Innuendo and subtle, nonexplicit references let the knowing audience catch on while less sophisticated viewers can still enjoy the movie.

1933 The Roman Catholic church decides that movies are a "deadly menace to morals" and forms the Legion of Decency. Hollywood bows to the pressure of 10 million members vowing to boycott films. As of 1934 only movies with "correct standards" can be shown. There's no taking the name of the Lord, bedroom scenes are treated delicately, excessive kissing is out, and forget about perversions. Films are rated A (pure), B (problems exist, go see an A-rated picture), and C (it's condemned—see it and you sin). The Legion of Decency rules with an iron fist until 1956, when Elia Kazan's version of Tennessee Williams's *Baby Doll* breaks the mold. The Legion can't garner support to boycott the film. Theaters refuse the Legion's request not to show it. The board's bite loses its teeth, agreeing in the 1960s to give its seal to films like *Who's Afraid of Virginia Woolf?* and *The Pawnbroker*.

1938 Radio stations ban any song with the word "do" in its title because of the sexual activity it implies. So "You Do Something to Me" and you may want to "Do It Again," but you're not going to hear it on the radio.

1940 Birth control is a fact of life in most states, but not in Connecticut. An 1879 law prohibiting the use of contraceptives, even by married couples, makes it impossible to run a birth-control clinic in that state. The law allows for devices that prevent disease, such as a condom or a diaphragm, and no effort is ever made to stop doctors from supplying their patients. But the clinics are in blatant violation. The ban continues until 1965, when the law is ruled unconstitutional.

1950 The FBI is responsible for doing background checks on civil service employees, so

J. Edgar Hoover sets up an intricate nationwide system of informing on homosexuals. Hoover believes gays should be denied government employment because they are susceptible to blackmail. Ironically, Hoover's own sexual orientation comes into question when stories of his homosexuality and cross-dressing are revealed after his death. FBI agents are under even closer scrutiny. Any agent caught living with someone outside of marriage or having an affair is fired immediately.

1962 While the rest of the country is twisting away, the bishop of the Buffalo, New York, Catholic diocese bans the trendy dance in Catholic schools and at events sponsored by Catholic organizations. Nor can you sing it or listen to it. Other cities ban the dance at their community centers. Generations ago, moralists squawked when partners held each other too close. With the twist they complain that lusty frenzy can be had alone.

1965 Viewers in earlier years accepted the puzzling fact that TV's happiest married couples—Ozzie and Harriet, Lucy and Ricky, and Ward and June Cleaver, for example—never shared the same bed. This year viewers are faced with a mystifying sight when *I Dream of Jeannie*'s Barbara Eden appears in a bare-midriff harem costume but has no navel. It's simple: censors won't let it be shown.

1966 The era of free love and drugs has the National Association of Broadcasters on their toes. The NAB instructs all disc jockeys to filter out songs with hidden references to drugs or obscenity. No doubt underground FM stations play those records first.

c. 1968 Public schools expand their sex education classes, and not everyone is happy about it. Across the country PTA meetings become shouting matches. Conservatives form protest groups or join established right-wing organizations like the John Birch Society, which deems sex-ed a Communist plot and succeeds in getting some school systems to drop the course.

1968 The Motion Picture Association of America institutes a rating system for audiences to use as a guideline. Pictures rated G are guarantee a movie is safe for a general audience. M, for mature audiences, is later changed to GP (general patronage) and then to PG for parental guidance. Only those over eighteen are admitted to restricted films (R), while moviegoers have to be over twenty-one to see an X-rated film. The R rating is loosened to allow minors under seventeen in as long as they're accompanied by a parent or guardian. The X rating is replaced by NC-17 in 1990, in an effort to distinguish a film meant for adult viewing from pornography. Porno movies are happy to keep their self-proclaimed X, XX, and XXX ratings.

1973 The Supreme Court rules in the case of Miller v. California that censorship can be based on community standards. Chief Justice Warren Burger writes, "It is neither realistic or constitutionally sound to read the First Amendment as requiring that people of Maine or Missouri accept public depiction of conduct found tolerable in Las Vegas or New York City." Local censors applaud the freedom from national standards.

1975 Going to work every morning gets more difficult when federal courts expand their definition of sex discrimination to include sexual harassment. While no one questions the need for the law, the widely varying interpretations of people's actions force businesses to educate their employees about proper office behavior. Any employee who is a recipient of unwelcomed sexual advances or favors, or is forced to work in a hostile environment where there is offensive verbal or physical sexual conduct, may sue for damages. While blatant casting couch situations are easy to identify, those off-color jokes at the water cooler or the unclothed Miss February on your desk calendar may get you sued as well. Though women are the primary beneficiaries of the law, men also win suits against female supervisors. Same-sex cases are also heard.

1977 Former Miss America runner-up Anita Bryant forms the crusading group, Save Our Children, in an effort to pressure Florida lawmakers to repeal a gay rights ordinance passed earlier this year. The law prohibits discrimination against homosexuals in housing, employment, and public accommodations. Bryant, calling herself God's "vessel," sees the ordinance as a way to "legitimize homosexuals and their recruitment of our children." Attracting the national spotlight, she gains national support from other conservative groups. Although gay activists also rally on a national level, the ordinance is repealed by Dade County voters by late spring.

1978 Extracts from the writings of Iran's Ayatollah Khomeini reaffirm the traditional treatment for sodomized camels. Following a ruling found in the Bible, sodomized animals must be killed, but you can't use them for food.

You Can't Do That!

> SHIT
> PISS
> FUCK
> MOTHERFUCKER
> COCKSUCKER
> CUNT
> TITS

1978 You cannot say the above "seven dirty words" on radio, as WBAI in New York finds out after playing a George Carlin monologue one afternoon in 1973. The Federal Communications Commission files charges against the Pacifica radio station, but Pacifica challenges the action. The Supreme Court upholds the FCC decision, stating that different words can be used to express ideas, but the commission does not ban the words; it only regulates their use, saying they might be limited to late night hours.

1979 The reverend Jerry Falwell's coalition of fundamentalists and other religious right-wingers form the Moral Majority in an effort to straighten out American values. Waging a war on immorality, they claim success with the election of President Ronald Reagan, and they campaign for conservative issues, such as returning prayer to the classroom, outlawing abortion, and ridding store shelves of skin magazines. They are antifeminist and antihomosexual (Falwell preaches that homosexuals will spend eternity in hell), and they demand the quarantine or imprisonment of AIDS-infected gays who continue to be sexually active. They use or threaten to use boycotts to achieve their goals. Detroit Girl Scouts drop birth control and abor-

tion from an adult training program after a threatened boycott of their cookie sale. Cover Girl and Maybelline cosmetics drop their ads from the teen magazine *Sassy* when the religious right finds its articles too suggestive and demands that advertisers back out. Falwell opens Liberty College, where freshmen and sophomores are restricted from dating and the entire campus is free from the influence of rock 'n' roll and country and western music. In 1989, saying that "our mission is accomplished," Falwell disbands the Moral Majority.

1984 Miss America pageant officials decide that it's inappropriate for any Miss America to have appeared in nude photographs. The decision is made after nude lesbian photos of Vanessa Williams, the first black Miss America, are printed in *Penthouse* magazine. A nationwide controversy erupts over whether the pageant, which parades women in swimsuits to have their bodies judged, is in any position to be judgmental. Williams is forced to relinquish her crown but has the last laugh. She moves on to a successful singing and acting career.

1984 The Indianapolis, Indiana, City Council passes an ordinance that prohibits pornography because it discriminates against women. The law would allow damages on a civil rather than a criminal basis. The ordinance is drafted by law professor Catharine MacKinnon with the support of feminist writer Andrea Dworkin. Both women believe pornography subordinates women, negates their chance for equality, and promotes violence against women. (Both women also believe that consensual heterosexual sex is subordination and desecrates women.) A federal judge enjoins the city from applying the law, and the case makes its way to the Supreme

Court. In a 6–3 decision the court rules the ordinance unconstitutional based on the First Amendment right to free speech. Says one Justice, "This is thought control."

Obscenity is whatever gives a judge an erection.

Anonymous, from The Cynics Lexicon, *1984*

1985 One of the most popular magazines offered in Braille by the Library of Congress is *Playboy.* But Representative Chalmers Wylie of Ohio doesn't see it as a service. After his requests to discontinue the magazine are turned down by the library, Wylie promotes a house bill that deducts $103,000—the cost of producing the magazine in Braille—from the program's budget. It passes. Wylie gets his wish. And the Library of Congress gets sued. Playboy Enterprises, the American Council of the Blind, the Blinded Veterans Association, three blind individuals, and the American Library Association sue to reinstate the skin magazine. The court agrees with the plaintiff and orders the library to reinstate the magazine and supply any back issues it missed during the litigation.

1986 Over 4,500 7-Eleven stores announce that they will no longer carry *Playboy, Forum,* and *Penthouse* magazines, citing a possible connection between adult magazines and violence and child abuse. For a couple of years reli-gious right-wing groups have picketed and threatened to boycott the stores nationwide. A commentary in the December 1986 issue of *Playboy* is quick to point out that magazines showing a nude murdered man, a young stabbing victim tied to a tree, decomposed corpses, and bare breasts and buttocks in women's magazines are still available at the stores.

1986 The Supreme Court rules in Bowers v. Hardwick that a constitutional right to privacy does not extend to homosexual sodomy, even between consenting adults. The Court upholds a Georgia statute prohibiting sexual acts involving "the sex organs of one person and the mouth or anus of another," which is punishable by up to twenty years in prison. Twenty-four other states have anti-sodomy laws, but they are seldom enforced.

1992 New York City's Court of Appeals rules that it's sex discrimination for men but not women to be able to go bare-chested in public. As long as they don't behave in a lewd manner, women are free to be topless. While guys salivate, commentators are quick to remind the public that not all women are built like Cindy Crawford and that breasts, which are enticing when covered, may lose their sexual significance with constant exposure.

Nothing is so much to be shunned as sexual relations.

St. Augustine

1993 Pope John Paul II issues the 179-page encyclical *Veritatis Splendor,* restating the church's position on contraception, homosexuality, masturbation, premarital sex, and abortion. The church's position, in the same order: no, no, no, no, and no.

I was never yet once, and commend their resolutions who never marry twice. . . . I could be content that we might procreate like trees, without conjunction, or that there were any way to perpetuate the world without this trivial and vulgar way of union; it is the foolishest act a wise man commits in all his life; nor is there anything that will more deject his cool'd imagination, when he shall consider what an odd and unworthy piece of folly he hath committed.

Sir Thomas Browne

1995 The Mexican economy lends a helping hand to wives who want their husbands to be faithful. It's common for husbands, both blue-collar and white-collar, to keep a mistress and to pay for her apartment, credit cards, and romantic getaways. In many cases men support a second family. But the peso has tanked, and gone are the expense accounts and the jobs that financed *la casa chica.* With inflation looming at 50 percent and with a 70 percent interest charge on credit cards, wives begin to look better. Mistresses start swelling unemployment lines.

1995 Germany tells CompuServe it's violating their pornography laws. Without so much as a whimper of protest the on-line service shuts down subscriber access to alt.sex discussion groups—worldwide. While trying to censor all sites with the word "sex" in it, which closes down religious, health, and wire service groups along with pedophiliac, fetish, and bestiality groups, it censors nothing. The groups are part of Usenet, a computer conferencing system that is easily accessed through other on-line services. CompuServe is jeered for being spineless and scampers to find a way to block out only the offended country.

1996 Congress passes the Telecommunications Deregulation and Reform Bill, which includes an amendment regulating pornography on the Internet. Initiated by Senator James Exon who is disgusted that images from alt.sex groups such as bestiality.hamster.duct tape and erotica.female.anal can be downloaded by minors, the law institutes criminal penalties for knowingly transmitting obscene material to underage Internet users.

Great Moments in Sex

Chapter Ten
UNDERLINE THESE PARTS

B.C.

c. 974 Solomon, king of Israel, writes the Song of Songs, the most sensuous love poem in the Bible. Solomon's known for his randy lifestyle: note his 700 wives and some 300 mistresses. But the passage written as an invitation to make love leaves no doubt that he's a romantic. She has "lips like a thread of scarlet," a navel like "a round goblet," and breasts that are "like two young roes that are twins." His hair is "bushy, and black as a raven," his legs "are as pillars of marble," and "his mouth is most sweet: yea, he is altogether lovely." Love is promised to be made outdoors: "our bed is green. The beams of our house are cedar, and our rafters of fir." Early uptight scholars say the poem is not between a man and a woman but between the church and Christ, or God, and Israel. One scholar makes boobs out of Moses and Aaron when he insists that they are the two breasts.

I have compared thee, O my love, to a company of horses in Pharaoh's chariots. Thy cheeks are comely with rows of jewels, thy neck with chains of gold. We will make thee borders of gold with studs of silver.

While the king sitteth at his table, my spikenard sendeth forth the smell thereof. A bundle of myrrh is my well-beloved unto me; he shall lie all night betwixt my breasts. My beloved is unto me as a cluster of camphire in the vineyards of En-gedi. Behold, thou art fair, my love; behold, thou art fair; thou hast doves' eyes. Behold, thou art fair, my beloved, yea, pleasant: also our bed is green. The beams of our house are cedar, and our rafters of fir.

SONG OF SOLOMON

c. 580 The Greek poet Sappho writes poetry on the isle of Lesbos. The founder of a girls' finishing school, she pens love poems to her students, which Ovid describes as a complete guide to female homosexuality. Her poetry is so prized by Greeks that her contemporaries refer to her as the Tenth Muse. Too bad Pope Gregory VII doesn't share their opinion. In 1073 he has the vast majority of her works burned because he regards them as a menace to morality. Out of 12,000 lines that filled nine books, only some 600 lines survive.

c. 450 The Greeks depict their sexuality on their pottery. Artwork runs the gamut from pederasty to young lovers to fun with the hetairai with various positions and levels of passion and emotion. Fondling, kissing, and full erections leave no doubt that the Greeks see themselves as sexual beings and enjoy experimentation.

Oedipus Rex: the original mother complex.

c. 430 Sophocles gives Sigmund Freud a name for his mother-complex when he writes *Oedipus Rex,* based on the legend of a king of Thebes. When oracles warn his father, the king, that one day the boy will kill him and marry his own mother, the father abandons Oedipus as an infant. The tragic hero later unknowingly kills his father in an argument, then saves the king's city and is permitted to marry the widowed queen, his mother. When their relationship is revealed, his mother hangs herself and Oedipus puts out his eyes and lives in the darkness with the evil he has done. Incest never amounts to anything good.

c. 350 Praxiteles creates one of the first nude female statues—the first nude goddess—when he sculpts the Aphrodite of Knidos. The statue is made for the citizens of the island of Kos but they are too shocked by its complete nudity. The people of Knidos, on the other hand, think she's dandy and place the beauty in a circular temple where she can be seen from all sides. So alluring is the original that legend tells of a young man who spends the night alone with her, resulting in a spot on her left thigh. Unfortunately, only copies of the statue remain.

161 When the notion of love enters Roman relationships, the plays of Terence reflect it. In *The Eunuch* he gives his courtesan heroine a heart, even though she sleeps with men other than her lover, who isn't rich enough to have her to himself. The play reflects the contemporary Roman view of marriage. The lover finally does get the heroine to himself, but they never marry.

30 A series of humorous obscene poems comprise *Priapeia,* which is ascribed to the Roman poet Vergil, though some sources believe Ovid and a few others have their hand in the poetry to and about Priapus, the god of fertility. The work disappears but resurfaces during the fifteenth century. By that time no one wants to believe that such an esteemed poet could have penned these obscenities. The poems are included in the complete works of Vergil, but many readers remove them from their copies.

Though I be wooden Priapus (as thou see'st),
With wooden sickle and a prickle of wood,
Yet will I seize thee, girl! And hold thee
*   seized*
And This, however gross, 0 withouten fraud
Stiffer than lyre-string or than twisted rope
I'll thrust and bury to thy seventh rib.

PRIAPEIA, NO. 5 *(TRANSLATED BY L. C. SMITHERS*
AND SIR RICHARD BURTON)

A.D.

50 *The Satyricon,* a best-seller by Petronius, is a collection of probably sixteen satirical books, of which only two remain. It is ribald in plot, language, and characters and gives a detailed picture of life in Rome. The central character is the slave Trimalchio, well loved by both the master and mistress of the house, who becomes wealthy from their presents and builds an estate where his enormous appetites are filled. Petronius also writes another piece of erotica, this one non-fiction: in his will he leaves a detailed account of the sexual peculiarities of his friend Nero.

c. 150 Lucius Apuleius writes *Metamorphoses,* or *The Golden Ass.* His licentious hero wants briefly to be turned into an owl, but he drinks the wrong magic potion and is turned into an ass. While second-century readers enjoy these tales of intrigue and love, early twentieth-century readers are prohibited from reading them: *The Golden Ass* is banned by the U.S. Customs Department until about 1930.

c. 200 Heliodorus of Emesa puts a Christian emphasis on preserving chastity in his *Aethiopica,* or *Egyptian Tales.* In the story of two love-struck youths captured by pirates, Heliodorus puts his heroine through some narrow escapes but keeps her intact while espousing the virtues of feminine modesty.

<800 The Moche of Peru not only like sex, they have fun with it. Little is known about the customs of the Moche, but their pottery is of unusual interest. Unlike symbolic erotic art, the Moche pottery depicts various acts of sex humorously. Artistically advanced and explicit, some of the vessels force the user into participating in mock sex. One vessel with a spout in the shape of a penis has holes around the brim so that it's impossible to drink without putting the penis in your mouth. A pan for roasting maize has a penis-shaped handle. Others have openings in the shape of a vulva. Anal and oral sex, masturbation, lesbian and homosexual acts, and zoophilia are also depicted in Moche artwork.

c. 1160 If Eleanor of Aquitaine defines courtly love and Andrew the Chaplain sets forth its rules, then it is Chrétien de Troyes who writes its story. *Le Chevalier à la Charette* is the story of Lancelot and his love, King Arthur's wife, Guinevere. Chrétien de Troyes writes the story for Countess Marie of Champagne, Eleanor's daughter, who supplies the story line based on early legends.

c. 1237 The most widely read book of the Middle Ages is *Roman de la Rose,* a 4,266-line allegorical poem by Guillaume de Lorris. The hero, in a dream, encounters in the Garden of Love the most beautiful rose (his lady love) he has ever seen. But it is surrounded by thorns and thus unattainable. Virtuous life tangles with life's baser moments. Does our hero pluck his rose? Guillaume dies without finishing the poem. Readers wait forty years for Jean de Meung to pick up where Guillaume de Lorris left off. But Jean isn't romantic and turns the last 22,000 lines into a satire. After Jean goes on about the evils of marriage and reminisces about a time when life was communal, the Lover is admitted to the inner shrine where the Rose is and plucks his heart out.

c. 1353 One of the most famous books in all of literature is written by Giovanni Boccaccio.

The Decameron, one hundred tales told by ten men and women on a journey to escape the plague, does have its naughty moments. The book is burned in 1497, put on the papal index of banned books in 1559, and condemned in France in the early nineteenth century. The United States and England are wary of the book also. As late as the 1950s copies of the masterpiece are destroyed.

1425 Women are advised not to read Antonio Beccadelli's *Hermaphroditus* in its introduction. The words are too game for gentle ears. Beccadelli's hermaphrodite, of course, has both a penis and a vagina and takes them on excursions through schoolrooms, libraries, and brothels. The work is popular, but it's condemned by clergy and scholars alike, causing the author to withdraw the dedication to his patron, apologize profusely for the affront, and leave the city in disgrace.

1501 Michelangelo treats the ladies to the ideal male form with his statue of *David.* The Renaissance brings beauty to and places emphasis on the male body, but Michelangelo takes it a step further. The statue depicts David from the biblical story of David and Goliath. Instead of making him the youth in the story, the artist ages him slightly and gives him the power, sensuality, and intensity of a mature man. Male genitalia on statues have always been small with the exception of males cast in a negative connotation. But *David* is well equipped to satisfy any woman. Originally created to adorn a buttress on a Florentine cathedral, the work is deemed too good to be ensconced where no one can admire it. *David* is later moved indoors to protect it from the elements.

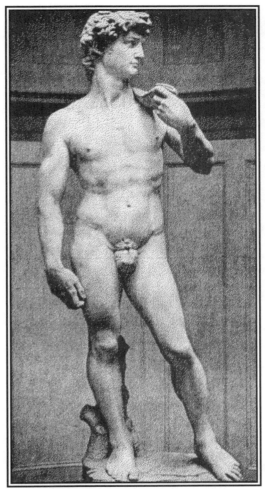

David, the statue, is more manly than his biblical character.

1514 The great humanist Erasmus publishes *Forms of Familiar Conversations,* a Latin textbook that is packed with a lot more information than how to conjugate verbs. Erasmus includes stories and lessons warning young ladies of the darker side of the clergy, advising them to stay away from "those brawny, swill-bellied monks. . . . Chastity is more endangered in the cloister than out of it." In its time the book is so popular that only the Bible outsells it.

1525 Antonio Vignali's *La Cazzaria* is pornography for and about the erudite. The story revolves around a homosexual relationship that develops between Arsiccio and Sodo, a student of philosophy. Arsiccio maintains a library of porn and introduces Sodo to things sexual, blending the pornographic with the philosophical, all the while emphasizing the need to keep such matters away from the common folk, who ultimately debase all things. Vignali satirizes the turmoil of the political families of Siena in the story of a struggle for power between the Big Prick, Pricks, Cunts, Balls, and Asses, and sets the tone for satirical pornography that lasts into the eighteenth century.

1527 When Marcantonio Raimondi publishes sixteen engravings by Giulio Romano depicting sixteen sexual positions in 1524, he is promptly thrown in prison by Pope Clement VII. For a year, Raimondi stays behind bars while artists and writers beg for his release. They secure his freedom, promising to destroy the plates, but one of the writers, Pietro Aretino, wants to see them first. When he does, he picks up his pen and writes bold, lusty sonnets to accompany each engraving and, in 1527, becomes the first pornographer of the modern age. The book is known as *Aretino's Postures* and inspires a whirlwind of copycats, each vying to present more positions than the original. Known to his admirers as "the Divine Aretino" and to his detracters as "the scourge of pricks," the author also pens the pornographic *Ragionamenti,* a book of dialogues.

1532 François Rabelais writes *The Horrible and Dreadful Deeds and Prowesses of the Most Renowned Pantagruel,* which is later joined by four other volumes to become *Gargantua and*

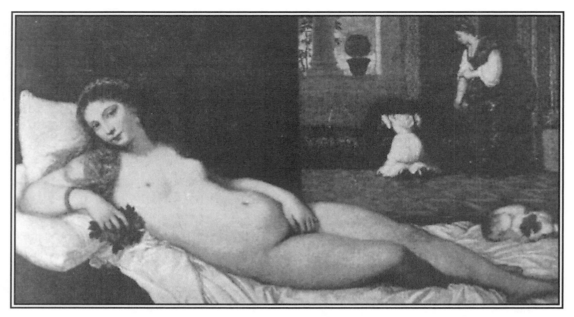

Titian's "Venus of Urbino" is a wide-awake temptress.

Pantagruel. The work is based on French tales of Gargantua, a kindly giant, and Pantagruel, his son, but Rabelais expands the lore and adds debauched characters. As each volume is published, it's condemned by the monks but forgiven by King Francis I, who laughs heartily. The most colorful characters in the tale are Pantagruel's sidekicks, Panurge—a lecher, rogue, and drinker, who is "otherwise the best and most virtuous man in the world"—and Friar John, who advises Panurge that if he wants sex, have it often, else his seed will dry up and his penis "will serve thee only as a pipe to piss out at." The volumes become the most-read books in France, bested only by the Bible and *Imitation of Christ*.

1538 Titian bases his painting *The Venus of Urbino* on Il Giorgione's earlier work, *The Sleeping Venus*. While Il Giorgione's nude *Venus* exposes herself innocently in slumber

with her hand falling gently over her genitals, Titian's nude *Venus* is wide awake with her hand not so restfully touching her pubic area. Titian's painting, considered his most beautiful nude, delights his patrons.

1558 Queen Marguerite of Navarre's *Heptaméron* is published ten years after her death. She wanted to write her own *Decameron* but died with only seven days completed. Stranded by a flood, Marguerite's characters spend their time telling stories, many of which are believed to be true accounts of members of the court, including Marguerite herself. The *Heptaméron* shares another commonality with *The Decameron:* in the twentieth century it, too, is banned in the United States.

1630 The best Spanish play ever written introduces the famous character of Don Juan to the ages. *El Burlador de Sevilla y convidado de* piedra (*The Jokester of Seville and the Guest of Stone*) is written by a friar, Tirso de Molina, who has been rebuked for the obscenities and vices found in his plays. The good friar creates a fast-living libertine in Don Juan but remains faithful to God and punishes his hero with eternal damnation.

c. 1650 Diego Velázquez's visit to Italy, where he is influenced by Venetian artists, results in his erotic nude, *The Toilet of Venus*. Nude paintings are frowned upon in Spain, so Velázquez skirts the problem of exposing genitals by showing his *Venus* from the back, giving the art world one great butt shot. Her curves are accentuated by her lying on her side with her arm thrown forward. Men find the painting arousing, but an early twentieth-century suffragette takes offense and slashes the masterpiece. The *Venus* is later restored to its former beauty.

c. 1650 Li Yü writes the popular pornographic novel *Prayer Cushions of the Flesh*. The hero of the story, Wei-yang-shêng, has a thief for a mentor whose work obliges him to hide in houses where he learns various sexual techniques by observation and passes them on to Wei. The book covers in detail nearly every sexual practice. Wei finds redemption as a Buddhist monk and is told that his past life was necessary for his enlightenment. The novel maintains its popularity for two hundred years in both China and Japan.

1655 Though the author of *L'École des filles* is unknown, the two publishers of the book are tried and imprisoned, and one is burned in effigy along with almost all the copies of the book. The slim volume is based on the conversations between two cousins, Franchon, the innocent, and Susanne, the all-knowing. Susanne lists the ways a lover can please her, when she allows it, while Franchon relates the experiences she's amassing under Susanne's tutelage.

1722 Daniel Defoe's classic *Moll Flanders* is added to the list of immoral immortals. Moll is an abandoned infant who grows up to become a whore. But Defoe tells the tale more completely in the original caption: *The Fortunes and Misfortunes of the famous Moll Flanders, who was born in Newgate, and during a life of continued variety, for threescore years, besides her childhood, was twelve years a Whore, five times a Wife (thereof once to her own brother), twelve years a Thief, eight years a transported Felon in Virginia, at last grew rich, lived honest, and died a penitent, Written from her own Memorandums.* The U.S. Customs Department allows Defoe's Moll into the country in the 1930s.

1734 English painter William Hogarth creates series of paintings based on "modern moral subjects." Rich in detail and wit, Hogarth considers them dramatic plays even though his "actors" cannot speak. Art lovers view the fall of the English country girl succumbing to the temptations of city life or, in *The Rake's Progress*, the downfall of a young hedonistic aristocrat who indulges too much in wine and women. Affordable engravings of the paintings make them even more popular.

1747 "The Speech of Miss Polly Baker," given by a young woman on trial in New England for bearing her fifth illegitimate child, is published in London's *Gentleman's Magazine*. Miss Baker is guilty of violating again and again the moral laws of the colony, but she asserts the law is unreasonable. She supports her children. The colonies need more people. She's following God's injunction to increase and multiply. And it isn't her fault that she's not married; the men who love her and leave her are to blame. The law would be better served if men were obliged to marry and fined for fornicating if they didn't. Who wrote this? Ben Franklin in what is considered his greatest hoax.

1748 *Thérèse philosophe* is published anonymously in France. Caught masturbating, Thérèse is shipped off to a convent. Later on, she becomes a philosopher as well as an adventuress. Through her journeys, the heroine expounds on her sexual escapades and waxes philosophic, pointing out that nature gave us a need and the tools to fill that need. To act otherwise is to go against nature. The book violates French law. Everyone affiliated with it—the financial backer, the printer, the distributor, even the woman who bound the pages together—is tossed into jail.

1748 English novelist Samuel Richardson writes *Clarissa,* and everyone in England, France, and America is reading it. The innocent rich girl is a victim of the libertine Lovelace, who, in order to break her hymen, imprisons her in a brothel, drugs, and rapes her. Richardson's novel sets a precedent: other writers adopt Richardson's trick of ravaging his heroine while maintaining her innocence—she was *drugged* and raped—even if the lady's innocence doesn't occur until the end of the book.

1749 John Cleland writes *Memoirs of a Woman of Pleasure*—a.k.a. *Fanny Hill*—and is called before England's Privy Council along with his publisher on obscenity charges. The story, written in diary form, tells of the

Richardson's Clarissa is an innocent victim.

escapades of a fifteen-year-old orphan girl who commits thirty acts of copulation and perversion. Cleland strikes a deal with an influential relative not to write any more memoirs, and he and his publisher are set free without a fine. Not so for an English publisher who is pilloried in 1761 for peddling the novel. In 1821 a Massachusetts court finds Peter Holmes guilty of publishing an illustrated edition. Anthony Comstock calls it "the most obscene book ever written." Frolicking *Fanny* stays underground until 1964 when, falling under the protection of the First Amendment, she is set free and published by G. P. Putnam's Sons.

1749 Henry Fielding perfects the comic romance genre with *Tom Jones, or the History of a Foundling.* Tom is an irascible rascal who is in love with Sophia. Alas, every female he meets is enamored with our hero, impeding the road to his true love. Fielding writes a contemporary novel that is so lusty and risqué that, while many hail the work, a 1750 London earthquake is thought by some to be the outpouring of God's ire at the overwhelming success of the book.

1791 The Marquis de Sade publishes his first novel, *Justine, or the Misfortunes of Virtue,* and France gets its first taste of sadistic literature. De Sade's victim, or heroine, is a young woman deserted by her bankrupt, widowed father and left to fend for herself. Throughout the book she is tied, flogged, her flesh pierced, her life lustily endangered, raped, and humiliated—as is her sister in pain, the protagonist of de Sade's next novel, *Juliette* (1796). De Sade rationalizes his deviance. He believes that nature is basically evil; therefore the actions of his tormentors are in accordance with the universe. The books are successful, but France eases the ladies' pain by banning both books in 1815.

1796 Matthew Lewis spins a sadistic tale in *The Monk.* Pious Ambrosio is seduced by Matilda, an agent of Satan (we find out at the end). Under her direction, he murders two women—one of whom turns out to be his sister—but not before seducing them and subjecting them to horrors. Lewis, who earns the moniker "Monk," completes the work in ten weeks.

1808 Francisco Goya paints two of his most famous paintings, *The Naked Maja* and *The Clothed Maja.* For both paintings he uses the same model, a woman whose identity is still a mystery. Goya crosses the line on two counts. First, nudes are not permissible in Spanish art. More important, Goya's maja is no goddess. She's a real woman and makes no pretense of being anything but. In full contact with her sensuality, the naked maja reclines confidently, her alluring body in full unspoiled view. Even clothed the maja retains her sensuousness. Goya

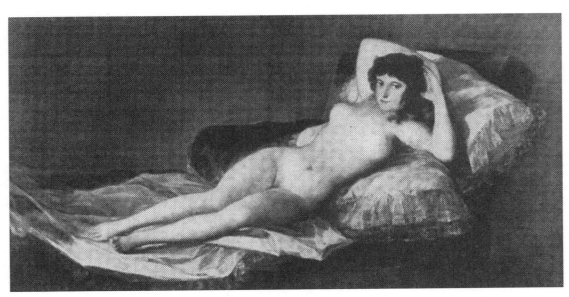

Goya's model for his Majas remains unidentified, but her sensuality is well known.

is brought before the Inquisition, but a well-placed friend, presumably the king, intercedes, and the artist goes unpunished.

And this coarsest of men, having placed me on a sofa in the attitude most propitious to his execrable pleasures, had me held down by Antonin and Clement. . . . Raphael, the depraved Italian monk, satisfied himself outrageously—without my ceasing to be a virgin. Oh, most awful of aberrations! It seemed that each of these crapulous men felt his glory to lie in leaving nature outside his choice when indulging his infamous pleasures. . . .

Clement was the next to approach me. Already inflamed by his superior's behavior, he was even more excited by the things he had done while observing this. He declared that he would represent no more danger for me than his confrère had done, and that the place where his homage was to be uttered would leave me without peril to my virtue. He made me get down on my knees, and fastening himself to me while in this position exercised his perfidious passions on me in a place which prevented me, during the sacrifice, from expressing any complaint as to its irregularity.

MARQUIS DE SADE, JUSTINE OR
THE MISFORTUNES OF VIRTUE

1810 While he is Prince Regent, George IV of England commissions a series of naughty drawings from artist Thomas Rowlandson. Rowlandson responds with ten lewd scenes that occur in common social settings such as a music teacher and his student. To each drawing he adds a verse that matches the picture's lewdness. Women's skirts are flung back to reveal the object of the man's passion, while the male subjects are drawn ready for action.

1828 *The Lustful Turk* is not a milestone in literature. But the tale of young English girls kidnapped and sold into the harem of a Turkish master, the dey, who deflowers them vaginally and anally, then somehow manages to capture their lustful young hearts, is an absolute for the underground reader. Toward the end of the century Anthony Comstock bans the book. What happens to the dey? One of the ladies isn't fond of the idea of anal sex. Before he has a chance to violate her, she pulls out a knife and castrates him.

1835 In Théophile Gautier's *Mademoiselle de Maupin*, Chevalier d'Albert searches for the ultimate woman: "It is not woman whom I desire; it is a woman, a mistress." De Maupin and d'Albert meet and spend one night together, each achieving the bliss they have yearned for. In the twentieth century the New York Society for the Suppression of Vice tries to ban the book but fails, setting a precedent for the acceptance of classic literature.

1844 It's a morality tale. It's pornography. No, it's *The Quaker City* by George Lippard. Set in Philadelphia, the stories of misbehavior at Monk Hall, an old mansion used as a secret clubhouse, include the deflowering of virgins, orgies, adultery, and sadistic acts described in erotic detail. The book is a huge success and it's not banned. Lippard's wild erotica is balanced by his frequent sermons and condemnations of immorality and social injustice interspersed

Great Moments in Sex

between the good parts. This first novel sells 300,000 copies in ten years.

1856 Walt Whitman's *Leaves of Grass* violates every theme Victorian society bans. The poet speaks of the human body, the physical love between a man and a woman, and between a man and a man. Whitman self-publishes the first edition, but booksellers return the copies after they read it. The second publication is returned by his publisher who fears charges of immorality. Europe praises the poet, but here at home Whitman temporarily loses his civil service job when the bluenoses raise a fuss. Thirty-seven years pass before the book stays in print and becomes a masterpiece of American literature.

1870 When Leopold von Sacher-Masoch turns his fetish for fur and his penchant to get off while being punished into novels, he taps into a ready-made audience. Sacher-Masoch's *Venus in Furs* is a bible for the well-beaten deviant. His hero, Severin, is trapped by Wanda, the beautiful, domineering aristocrat who parades around in a fur-lined red robe, demanding complete obedience and submission, usually with a whip. Sacher-Masoch's first marriage doesn't last (want to guess why?), but he has at least one lover upon whom he models Wanda.

1876 Mark Twain writes the hilarious *1601* but doesn't agree to its publication until 1882, and then only fifty copies are printed. Twain reports an imaginary conversation in Queen Elizabeth's court, supposedly recorded by Her Majesty's cupbearer. The participants include such luminaries as Walter Raleigh, Ben Johnson, the queen, and Shakespeare. Written to practice British dialogue for his upcoming novel, *The Prince and the Pauper,* the dialogue covers farting, masturbation, and intercourse in the forthright manner Twain believes was used in Elizabethan times.

1884 John Singer Sargent's reputation as a portrait painter is unquestionable. What is questionable is his *Portrait of a Great Beauty*. The affairs of Madame Gatreau, the wife of a Paris banker, are well whispered. When the portrait is unveiled in Paris it causes a scandal. The shameless woman stands in a stiff black sleeveless gown, with a low-cut bodice. Sargent has caught her lavish use of cosmetics and lavender body powder. The painting today is far less shocking than the original. When it's first shown, one of her diamond-studded shoulder straps falls off her shoulder, a visual symbol of her daringness. Sargent repaints the strap but refuses to comply with her mother's wishes to remove the painting from view.

1885 – 1888 Sir Richard Burton publishes his sixteen-volume translation of *The Arabian Nights*. Burton founded the Kamashastra Society to publish his translations of erotica including the *Kama-sutra, The Perfumed Garden,* and *The Priapei*. The tales of the Arabian nights are ages old and have been rewritten by various cultures. While many of the tales aren't sexual, those that are give westerners an extra punch, since the Muslim culture of the day permitted polygamy and concubinage. Before the erotica begins Westerners are shocked at the lifestyle. Pederasty, anal intercourse, bestiality, and adultery are all themes—at least in Burton's translation. While some editions are fit for children because they omit the erotica, Burton's work is considered the hottest.

1887 A classic work of Victorian pornography, *The Autobiography of a Flea* is written anonymously in London. The story is told from the viewpoint of a flea who happens to live in the genitalia of Bella, a beautiful young virgin who doesn't stay in that condition for very long. The flea gives detailed accounts of his mistress-host's love life, including her encounter with her confessor when she repents her sins.

He was already upon her body. His great bulk covered her figure most powerfully and completely. His distended member bore hardly [sic] against Bella's stomach, and her clothes were already raised to her waist.

With a trembling hand Ambrose seized the center chink of his wishes—eagerly he brought the hot and crimson tip toward its moist and opening lips. He pushed, he strove to penetrate—he succeeded: the immense machine slowly but surely entered—already the head and shoulders had disappeared. A few steady, deliberate thrusts completed the conjunction, and Bella had received the whole length of Ambrose's huge, excited member in her body.

The ravisher lay panting upon her bosom in complete possession of her inmost charms.

ANONYMOUS, THE AUTOBIOGRAPHY OF A FLEA

---

c. 1888 An aristocratic Englishman contracts with a printer to print six, and only six, copies of a manuscript he has written detailing his entire sexual history. No one knows how many copies are actually printed, but by the turn of the century *My Secret Life,* by "Walter," is a classic. The eleven volumes are more important to social historians than to porno collectors. It is a graphic nonfiction account of the social and psychological interaction between the classes. Walter has his share of prostitutes but views every lower-class woman as someone who can be bought. Shopgirls, factory workers, and chambermaids can all be had, or at least groped, for a shilling or so. Servant girls are as good, since they're conveniently located in his house. If they don't acquiesce they can be put out without a reference. If they comply and are caught, they can suffer the same fate. Both situations doom most of them to prostitution. He goes through woman after woman after woman, including some virgins, as young as ten and twelve. Walter is more comfortable when he pays the woman, but he never feels a shred of guilt or remorse, even when raping a few of them.

Aubrey Beardsley's illustrations are privately printed.

Great Moments in Sex

There the first thing she said was, "Oh I'm so full and so sleepy, let me lie down."—"My love, you shall but take off your things."—A little soft persuasion and she was soon in her chemise.—"Did you ever see a man naked." —"No,—he,—he,—and don't want."—"Yes, you do."—Stripping to my shirt, I pulled it up to my arm pits, and with prick in randiest glory, went up to her as she sat on the sofa, and made her handle and kiss it.—She was not loath.—"Come to the bed dear."—"What are you going to do?" "To give you such pleasure.— I must see and kiss that dear little cunt, it will give you such pleasure, now I will, it's no use your struggling."—After a few minutes of voluptuous persuasion, she was lying at the side of the bed with legs wide open and I on my knees gloating on her virgin treasure.

"WALTER," MY SECRET LIFE

c. 1896 Artist Aubrey Beardsley goes against current art standards and illustrates an English translation of *Lysistrata* and *The Story of Venus and Tannhäuser* as only Beardsley can. In minute detail, oversized penises and testicles burst out hungrily from otherwise clad male characters toward the anatomically correctly drawn genitalia of the female characters. Women are amply gifted by the artist's nature. Beardsley gets away with his drawings simply because the book is privately printed. A public publication would have brought prosecution.

1896 Pierre Louÿs's *Aphrodite* is set in Egypt in the first century B.C., which gives his characters ample room for sexual license, and they take it. A courtesan sends an enamored sculptor on an errand to prove his love. While she waits for his return, she engages in lesbian and heterosexual pursuits and orgies. Though the sex scenes aren't detailed, the mere multitude of deviations, including the offering of a slave girl to all the male guests at a banquet, is enough to get the book banned in the United States in 1930 by a New York judge who calls the book filthy.

1900 *Sister Carrie* is a landmark in American literature, but it doesn't start out that way. Theodore Dreiser's Carrie uses her good looks to make her way out of poverty by living with two successive lovers and parlays her beauty into success on the stage. That she does this without punishment or some moral awakening worries the publisher, Frank Doubleday, who does everything he can to ensure that the novel won't be a success. Critics agree. They're revolted and call it a disgrace. With only 456 copies of the book sold, it's withdrawn from circulation because it's too sordid and pornographic.

1913 Paul Chabas's *September Morn* is displayed in the window of Braun and Company, art dealers in New York. Moralist Anthony Comstock walks by and gets his knickers in a knot. Comstock orders the clerk to remove the picture, which is done. The manager comes back from lunch and promptly returns the painting to the window, and the battle is on. Newspapers print the painting along with the story, and suddenly *September Morn* is gracing calendars, cigar boxes, watch fobs, and living room walls. Chabas gains international recognition but doesn't make a dime from the use of his

The flurry over displaying "September Morn" in an art dealer's window makes the painting famous.

painting. Says he, "Nobody has been thoughtful enough to send me even a box of cigars."

1919 *Jurgen* isn't the first American novel to be deemed obscene. It is the first book by a major American author to be tested in the courts. Written by James Cabell, who uses double entendres and makes thirty changes in the manuscript to prevent it from being suppressed, Jurgen, the main character, travels outside ordinary dimensions in search for his wife who has been kidnapped by a god-devil. In his journeys he encounters and makes love to legendary and mythical figures and presents sex as a major preoccupation of people. One of the reasons the book isn't banned is that the judge believes the novel can be read and understood by only a handful of intellectuals.

1922 The cause célèbre of the 1920s is James Joyce's *Ulysses,* a stream-of-consciousness novel that is as difficult to read as it is to get past Customs. Immediately considered a classic, the only way to get a copy is to smuggle it out of Paris. Vacationing in France and returning without a copy is considered a waste. Publisher Bennett Cerf at Random House in New York decides to bring the censorship battle to a head. He imports the book, and the Customs Department seizes it. In the court case that follows, Judge John M. Woolsey finds that "in spite of its unusual frankness, I do not detect . . . the leer of the sensualist. I hold therefore that it is not pornographic." The book is published in America in 1934.

1927 Mae West is jailed for ten days and fined $500 for her appearance in her play, *Sex.*

The Broadway production was okayed initially by police but a year's worth of rewriting causes them to reverse their decision. West plays a prostitute as only West can. One police official claims that the actress "moved her navel up and down and from right to left" in a belly dance that the Society for the Suppression of Vice believes can corrupt the "morals of youth."

1928 D. H. Lawrence writes *Lady Chatterley's Lover,* the story of a woman who is married to a crippled and emotionally cold man who finds her sexual awakening with the earthy and potent groundskeeper of her estate. The groundskeeper's approach to sex, including anal sex, worries some, but it's Lawrence's use of four-letter words that gets the book banned in England and the United States. It isn't until 1960 that the ban on the Lady is overturned and her exploits can be read by the public.

1928 Marguerite Radclyffe Hall's lesbian novel, *The Well of Loneliness,* is published in England but is soon judged obscene. All copies of it are seized and burned. It's published in Paris but the British obscenity ruling kills its chances in the United States. Though only one scene in the book is remotely specific, Radclyffe Hall makes an impassioned plea for acceptance of homosexuality. The book is reissued in Britain in 1949 and sales are brisk. The author never sees her book sell over 100,000 copies a year. She dies in 1943.

1932 Erskine Caldwell writes *Tobacco Road* and follows it up three years later with *God's Little Acre.* Both novels are based on poor southern whites and filled with bawdy humor and earthy sexiness that make them best-sellers. Moves to ban *God's Little Acre* and the play

based on *Tobacco Road* fail, although a few public libraries refuse to carry either of the Caldwell works.

In this class we include those who by fraud or intimidation have been thrust into that life of celibacy where they were allowed to fornicate but not to marry; so that if they openly keep a concubine they are Christian priests, but if they take a wife they are burned. In my opinion parents who intend their children for celibate priesthood would be much kinder to castrate them in infancy, rather than to expose them whole against their will to this temptation to lust.

Erasmus, on the celibacy of priesthood

1932 The sexual growing pains of a Catholic boy from the South Side of Chicago are the subject of *Young Lonigan,* which James Farrell expands into a trilogy. Jockeying for position among his friends and securing a sexual identity are the goals of Studs Lonigan who gets his first piece in a "gang-shag," thinks about parents "doing it," peeks into a window of a whorehouse, and suffers normal teenage angst. The book is issued in a special edition sold only to physicians and professionals interested in adolescent psychology.

1934 Henry Miller's *Tropic of Cancer* is published and for the next thirty years is the subject of censorship and litigation. The book is published in Paris in English, which exempts it from French pornography laws. *Cancer*'s first court case comes in 1950 when the American Civil Liberties Union of California imports it and *Tropic of Capricorn,* forcing a confrontation. They lose when the judge finds that a "well-written" dirty book is more dangerous than a badly written one. Grove Press publishes it in 1961, becoming the target of over 60 lawsuits. While the book is selling briskly (68,000 copies in one week, one million in paperback sales), Grove Press gets its chance in front of the Supreme Court. The nine jurists find for *Tropic of Cancer* and, by implication, *Tropic of Capricorn,* but their opinion contains no explanation of why they find it acceptable.

So we can dismiss the idea that sex appeal in art is pornography. It may be so to the grey Puritan, but the grey Puritan is a sick man, soul and body sick, so why should we bother about his hallucinations?

D. H. Lawrence

1939 Georgia O'Keeffe denies that her flower paintings are erotic or that they represent sexual organs, insisting that it's the viewer who applies those associations to her art. That may be, but O'Keeffe's flowing depiction of irises and cannas, along with her vibrant and gentle colors, magnifies the resemblance to the vagina, and her calla lilies are blatantly male.

1944 An interracial sexual relationship is at the heart of Lillian Smith's *Strange Fruit.* The woman author not only broaches a taboo subject, she uses the word "fuck" twice and talks about the frigidity of white women. The book is held obscene in 1945, but it wins two literary awards and sells three million copies.

1948 Harold Robbins begins his career as a writer of "smutty potboilers" and "pulp classics" with *Never Love a Stranger,* which is put on trial with classics like *God's Little Acre* and Faulkner's *Wild Palms. Stranger,* the story of an orphan whose penchant for survival propels him to the top of New York's criminal circles, is considered tame next to the rest of Robbins's work. Known for his erotic scenes, the author excels at getting his characters off in subways, cars, boats, and elevators. His formula works. All of his books, including *The Carpetbaggers,* sell at least 600,000 copies.

1954 Dominique Aury writes *The Story of O* under the pseudonym Pauline Réage as a show of love for her married lover, French writer Jean Paulhan. The novel depicts the love life of a woman whose total submission to two lovers results in bondage, domination, anal sex, lesbianism, group sex, labia piercing, branding, and humiliation and ends with permission from her lover to commit suicide. Rivaling, if not surpassing, de Sade, the book is never officially banned. It makes its U.S. debut in 1965 and has never gone out of print.

1955 Unable to find an American publisher, Vladimir Nabokov's *Lolita* is published in France by Olympia Press, a house known for its pornographic titles. But *Lolita* is literature and disappoints their hard-core readers. Brought to light by Graham Greene, it is the story of Humbert Humbert who is so entranced by a twelve-year-old nymphet that he marries her irritating mother to be near her. When Mom catches on to hubby's fixation, she runs out of the house and is killed by an oncoming car and Humbert is forced to be with Lolita, now his stepdaughter, ward, and mistress. When it's published in the United States in 1958, the book sells 100,000 copies in three weeks, the first book to sell that briskly since *Gone With the Wind*.

1956 *Peyton Place* takes America by storm. Grace Metalious patterns the book after her hometown, Gilmanton, New Hampshire. Her characters are run-of-the-mill townspeople who have torrid affairs, sexual awakenings, heaving bosoms, hard body parts, incestuous relationships, and abortions. The few libraries that do carry the book sneak it out of the back room to favored patrons. Most readers prefer to buy *Peyton Place*. It sells 20 million copies and spawns a TV series.

1957 A historic ruling regarding the use of obscene words is handed down regarding Allen Ginsberg's *Howl and Other Poems*. Ginsberg receives literary acclaim for his poetry but his use of words to describe men in homosexual and heterosexual orgies is deemed obscene—that is, until Judge Clayton Horn rules that "an author should be . . . allowed to express his thoughts and ideas in his own words."

If there's a decent word in it, it is because I overlooked it.

Mark Twain, to a Cleveland librarian on his underground pornographic classic *1601*

1958 *Candy,* a lewdly hilarious satire, written by Mason Hoffenberg and Terry Southern under the pen name Maxwell Kenton, is about "a fabulous, blue-eyed, pink-nippled, pert-derrièred" American girl whose humanist philosophy leads her into encounters with minorities, professionals, priests, and a hunchback, who have their way with her in every way possible. Searching for solace, she travels to the Far East and attains the peace she desires, her last earthly act to be screwed by the nose on the statue of Buddha when the temple she is in is bombed. The book is smuggled into America from France until 1964 when it's published in hardcover and sells over a million copies.

1962 Prominent authors come to the defense of *Naked Lunch* by William Burroughs when it's banned in Los Angeles and Boston. This surreal and hallucinogenic novel exposes the destructiveness of a drug society. Burroughs doesn't cut corners when describing orgies, manipulation through drugs, and porn movies. The drug society has its effect on Burroughs. He's under the influence while writing the book and, in his introduction, admits that he does not remember writing it.

1964 Richard Berry's "Louie Louie" starts off as a slow-moving song about a Jamaican sailor who tells a bartender (Louie) how much he misses his girl back home. When the Kingsmen get hold of it, they speed it up, record it in a primitive recording studio which muffles the voices, and the first "pornographic" rock 'n' roll song is born—even though there's nothing pornographic about it. Listeners swear they hear the sexually explicit line, "I got my boner high in her hair," which, according to Berry's lyrics is "I smell the rose in her hair." FCC officials investigate but they find "the record to be unintelligible at any speed." Indiana governor Matthew Welsh doesn't care what the words are. He deems it pornographic and wants the state's radio stations to ban it. The song, which Berry sold the rights to for $125, sells 12 million copies.

1966 When *Valley of the Dolls* is published, intellectuals see it as proof positive that great literature is dying out. Its author, Jacqueline Susann, doesn't care. The novel about three starlets who sleep their way to the top and use drugs to cope with failure and aging heads the best-seller list for twenty-eight weeks.

I've put off reading Lolita *for six years, till she's 18.*

Groucho Marx

1968 John Lennon and Yoko Ono release their first album, *Unfinished Music No. 1—Two Virgins.* The cover of the album, which is wrapped in brown paper for retail sale, features a photo of the lovers buck naked in a full-frontal pose. The next year the couple makes headlines again with their "bed-in" protest where they record "Give Peace a Chance."

1969 Masturbating with a piece of liver, "chasing cunt," "shtupping it," "thinking about it," and impotence are the result of man's natural sexual instincts being repressed. That's the story of Philip Roth's *Portnoy's Complaint,* a tale of a sexually frustrated Jewish adolescent. The street language and the book's directness make it a best-seller with over 300,000 books sold in less than a month.

1969 Miami, Florida, charges Jim Morrison of the Doors with lewd and lascivious behavior after the lead singer exposes himself on stage during a concert and simulates masturbation and oral sex. Morrison is acquitted of that charge but found guilty of indecent exposure and profanity. He's fined and sentenced to eight months of hard labor but dies of an overdose while the case is pending appeal.

1971 The Rolling Stones' new album, *Sticky Fingers,* contains the classics "Brown Sugar" and "Wild Horses," but it's the album cover that catches the eye. Designed by Andy Warhol, a lower male torso and thighs in jeans comes with a workable zipper fly that, when opened, reveals Mick Jagger's lips and tongue. Five years later, their *Black and Blue* album causes a controversy when billboards promoting it feature a bruised woman, gagged and tied, with the message, "I'm black and blue with the Rolling Stones and I love it."

1972 *The Oxford English Dictionary* legitimizes the use of four-letter words. Included in this year's supplement is the word "fuck."

1973 Erica Jong introduces the "zipless fuck," the ultimate woman's fantasy in which a woman yearns for, acquires, and uses a man's body without emotional attachment or knowing his name—the quintessential one-night stand. In *Fear of Flying,* Jong has no fear of expressing female sexual needs, including masturbation, fantasizing, and controlled rape. The novel that sets forth women's sexual needs causes some men to see it as a man-hating book. *Fear of Flying* achieves success in the feminist and free-love movements.

1975 The backlash against the zipless fuck is delivered in Judith Rossner's novel, *Looking for Mr. Goodbar*. After a series of failed relationships, Theresa picks up men in a bar for one-night stands, finding pleasure without pain. Her last one-night stand culminates in her murder during which she comes face-to-face with the futility of her existence. The novel, which is based on the 1973 murder of a teacher in New York, changes the dating habits of thousands of women.

1987 George Michael's single "I Want Your Sex" is banned by 30 percent of American radio stations and inspires protests in England where some feel the song is too suggestive in the age of AIDS. Michael counters that the song promotes monogamy, citing the use of his girlfriend in the video's starring role (MTV edits the video three times before airing it). The song soars to number one on the *Billboard* charts. Michael apparently changes his position on monogamy and gender preference in 1998. He's arrested for committing a "lewd act" in a public rest room in a park in Beverly Hills that has a reputation as a gay pickup spot. Three days

after his arrest, George Michael announces that he is a homosexual.

1990 Photographer Robert Mapplethorpe's photographs stir up controversy in Cincinnati, Ohio, where the director of the Contemporary Arts Center is put on trial for obscenity for exhibiting the late artist's work. The black and white photos, including one man urinating into the mouth of another, a forearm inserted into a rectum, a finger inserted into the head of a penis, and two photos of nude children, are found not obscene. That Dennis Barrie, the CAC's director, is the first museum director to face criminal charges is where the real damage lies. The fear of prosecution could influence other directors' choices of exhibits.

1990 2 Live Crew earns the distinction of having the first record to be deemed legally obscene. Their album, *As Nasty as They Wanna Be,* is so judged by a Fort Lauderdale, Florida, court because it contains over two hundred uses of the word "fuck," descriptions of oral sex, incest, sadism, masochism, hard-ons, and moaning. Group members Luther Campbell, Mark Ross, and Chris Wong Won are arrested in Florida for performing songs from the album. The attention causes the record's sales to skyrocket. A jury rejects the charges against the group and the court of appeals overturns the obscenity ruling.

Chapter Eleven
TURN-ONS AND TURN-OFFS

B.C.

✎**c. 3000** Ancient Egyptians work hard at being sexy. Being clean isn't just a turn-on; it's a must and requires three baths a day. *All* body hair is removed with a pumice stone, and the entire body is perfumed. (The ultimate act of cleanliness is circumcision, writes historian Herodotus. Egyptians consider "it better to be cleanly than comely.") After bathing, the women don finely woven transparent sheaths. Covered breasts are optional. Men wear loincloths and belts, revealing slim waists, muscled chests, and great legs. Women fortunate enough to have the veins that show through the skin on their breasts and legs highlight them further with blue dye. Gold jewelry and cosmetics complete their come-hither look. Egyptian women entice their men on an intimate level, inserting small perfumed pads in their vaginas before sex. It's the total sensual experience.

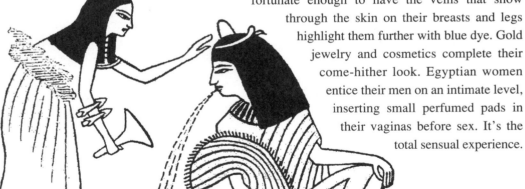

☞ **c. 3000** Egyptians take care to protect the corpses of beautiful and noble women from embalmers who sometimes practice necrophilia. To restore a dead man's virility—the Egyptians are firm believers in the afterlife—a pseudo sex act is performed. Dead women, however, need no such restoration.

☞ **c. 1100** The practice of removing all or part of the male reproductive system begins in China as punishment. These manless males are then employed by the imperial family mainly to run the harem. Castration co-evolves in or spreads to Assyria and then to Egypt, Persia, India, and Africa. Not all castrates are clean shaven (penis and testicles removed). The penis or the testicles can be removed or the balls can be crushed. The demand for eunuchs always exceeds the supply, whether for use in harems or to fill political offices where they are deemed trustworthy, or, later, to sing in church choirs. Some poor men give up the family jewels as a means of securing a good position. Castration remains a punishment for misdeeds such as adultery, and it is also performed by victorious armies on enemies.

👍 **c. 1000** Mandrake, a plant indigenous to the Mediterranean area, is used to cure barrenness and sterility. Its root makes it a prized commodity. Nearly twelve inches long, it bears a striking resemblance to a man, penis and all. Carried as an amulet, it's a love charm. Digested, it's relaxing and induces sleep. It's so powerful and humanlike that mere men don't dare harvest it. A dog's tail is tied to the plant and then the dog is tempted with meat held just out of reach.

👍 **c. 1000** Egyptian women find many uses for the country's abundant gold. Rings, bracelets, and elaborate ornamental collars attract attention but not as much as gilding their nipples with gold paint.

👍 **c. 600** The dress of the day for Spartan women is a plain knee-length chiton. Most Grecian women secure the sides of the garment. But Spartanettes leave the slits open, earning them the enmity of sister Greeks and the nickname "thigh showers." It adds to their reputation for sexual aggressiveness.

👍 **c. 500** Perfuming one's body is important, and a complete body dousing is called for if you want to be up to snuff. Roman women employ an unctor, a slave whose duty is to anoint his mistress after her bath. Egyptian women use frankincense, myrrh, and sesame oil. The Bible

Mandrake.

Opium smoking produces an erotic dream state.

tells how concubines are soaked for a year before being presented to the king. Men cause nostril twitching, too. Mesopotamian soldiers are sometimes paid in perfume. Assyrian males glob their locks. All of this is not to cover up body odor; it's meant to enhance it.

c. 500 Spanish fly is made from powdered dried meloid beetles and slipped into food or drink. It's said to produce passionate erections. The powder is so lethal to humans that one ten-thousandth of an ounce can cause kidney failure. A little more brings on convulsions or death. Why the love-maker reputation? Meloid beetles contain cantharidin, a urinary tract irritant that causes priapism, an immediate, persistent, and agonizing penile erection. It's used well into the nineteenth century. Men wise up and stop taking it themselves, but start slipping it to women, hoping it will turn them into nymphomaniacs. Alas, its disastrous and deadly effect extends to women as well.

c. 350 The quickest way to get it down and keep it down? Says Aristotle in one word: cold. Toss the sandals, walk barefoot, and take plenty of cold baths. Drinking cold water keeps the hormones in check, too.

A.D.

c. 20 Ovid gives helpful hints on how to be attractive to the opposite sex: Be clean, neatly attired, and brush your teeth and hair. To really welcome love, nothing beats idleness, partying, and hanging out with people. Except cabbage and onions which are aphrodisiacs.

40 Roman legislators decide that all prostitutes must dye their hair blond or wear a blond wig. But dark-haired women soon notice that men are taken with golden locks, and soon non-pros are using yellow pomades and gold or silver dust to prove that blondes have more fun.

c. 50 Social historian Pliny doesn't think much of birth control so he emphasizes anaphrodisiacs. He's a big believer in excrement. To cool the libido, mouse dung applied in the form of a liniment or snail or pigeon droppings is taken with oil or wine—lots and lots of wine. If a man urinates into a puddle of dog urine or drowns a lizard in his urine, that also douses the fires of passion—for him and the lizard.

c. 50 Pliny's not always a wet blanket. To get your vim and vigor back he suggests ingesting the herb wormwood. If that doesn't work, wear a couple of crocodile teeth tied to your right arm.

c. 160 Too much desire? Too many wet dreams? Roman physician Galen has the sure cure for both. Cold lead plates. For the former

problem put them on your calves or kidneys. For the latter, place them over the loins. Pleasant dreams.

c. 600 Opium finds its way into the Far East as a medicine. As its relaxing qualities are realized, it's used as an aphrodisiac. When pipe smoking is introduced in the seventeenth century, the effects of the drug are much more dramatic. Inhibitions are reduced, an erotic dream state is induced, and impotency is occasionally cured. But prolonged use decreases desire. The addiction to the dream state becomes more desirable than having sex, and the user is left alone in a fog. The Chinese government watches helpless as the number of users grows, eventually leading to wars to stop importation of the drug. To this day all drugs that are derivatives of opium, synthetic or natural, including morphine, methadone, and Demerol, affect sexual desire and performance.

c. 1000 The practice of footbinding begins in China. The Golden Lotus, as the deformed

IN OTHER PARTS OF THE WORLD

• Trukese men are turned on when their partners urinate as they reach a climax. In turn, the women expect their partners to urinate inside them after an orgasm.
• On the morning after their first night of sex, the Bantu-lla bride plucks out all of her new husband's pubic and chin hair. An old woman comes in later and manually inspects the job.
• The Marquesans of Oceania practice ménage à many. A group of men have sex with one woman in public. But etiquette must be followed. Last man out must suck the semen from her vagina.
• In Java it was once custom for peasant couples to copulate in the rice fields to ensure the crops' fertility.

foot is called, is painfully achieved, starting when a girl is age five, by bending back the big toe and folding the remaining four under against the sole with tight bandages. The heel is brought forward to the ball of the foot, resulting in a macabre built-in high heel and feet compacted so small that walking is difficult if not impossible. Why this gruesome torture that can cause gangrene to rot the feet and kill one woman in ten? Chinese men consider the small misshapen foot so erotic that women who aren't deformed are unmarriageable. The foot plays an important part during the mating process. If a man feels he's on the right track, he drops his chopsticks or some other prop and when he stoops to pick it up, he touches the lady's foot. An accidental brush against any other body part can be explained away. The foot touch can't. If the woman doesn't vigorously complain, he can continue with physical contact. The ideal Golden Lotus is a mere three inches long. A wife with small feet is a status symbol, for everyone knows her husband must be rich enough to support an idle woman. The practice continues for nearly a thousand years.

c. 1100 Gone are plain unisex nightshirts. In this era, everyone sleeps in the nude. By the fifteenth century the naked body is so accepted that people barely clothe themselves for the walk to the public bath.

c. 1100 The twelfth-century female physician, Trotula—whose beauty advice is followed unhesitatingly (even when she prescribes cow dung)—suggests herbal cures to tame the gung-ho libido. "Cooling" herbs such as willow, camphor, lettuce seed, Saint-John's wort, henbane, rue, vervain, and columbine ice sexual tendencies.

Why the Wolf Howls

c. 1200 To curb the sex drive of a wife or daughter, take the penis of a wolf, his eyelid hair, those under his beard, burn them and secretly put the ashes in her drink. Of course, she can retaliate using another wolf's penis. With it in hand, she stands near your door and calls to you. When you reply, she ties up the penis with white thread and you're impotent as if you "were indeed a eunuch." The one who gets the worst of the deal is, of course, the wolf.

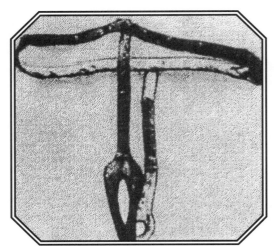

Chastity belts lock up the goods while hubby's away.

👎**c. 1300** The chastity belt is invented, most likely in Italy since it's referred to as the Florentine girdle. Developed to prevent rape—a needed protection against marauding armies—husbands off on business or war lock up their wives' treasures to ensure faithfulness. The belt is usually made up of a metal piece around the waist, with pierced-metal straps that restrict access to the vagina and anus while allowing for waste elimination. Hopefully there's only one key, which stays in the husband's possession. Chastity belts are worn as late as the nineteenth and twentieth centuries. In modern times their primary function is to prevent masturbation.

Codpieces protect and exaggerate one's manhood.

👍**1348** After the Black Death sweeps across Europe, reducing the population by more than a third, repopulation becomes a priority. Fashionable clothes show off men's legs, décolletages bare women's cleavage. Faces are painted and powdered. Men wear heavy chains of gold.

People watch their weight. It must work. Human beings escape the endangered species list.

👍**c. 1400** The male of the species struts his stuff with the aid of a codpiece. Initially used as a separate covering to protect one's manhood in war, the covering becomes a fashion statement of virility. Knights use metal protectors. Peasants use leather. Commonplace is a padded, decorated elongated phallus that jauntily protrudes between the man's legs, which are covered in skintight pants, and out from under a coat that strategically ends where the codpiece begins. Always in a state of erection, the codpiece—"cod" is an Old English word for "scrotum"—is bejeweled with gemstones, gold, and ribbons. Some have a face of their very own. Later a pocket is added in which the gentleman can carry his coins, handkerchief, bonbons, and fruit, which he offers to the ladies. Laws are passed later allowing only noblemen to stick their heads out. By the end of the sixteenth century all of the little fellows will have gone back into hiding.

👍**c. 1400** Venetian women wear chopines—platform shoes that make the faddish platform shoe of the 1970s look like baby booties. Chopines can reach a yard high giving even the most diminutive woman a penthouse view.

Chopines put a woman heads above the rest.

There's only one problem: the woman can't walk. A rich woman is braced by servants who hold their mistress upright, which doesn't work all the time. Mistress winds up looking more like Humpty Dumpty than Saucy Flossy. The government tries to legislate against the shoe, but the protruding butt caused by the change in posture, the uncertain walk, and the overtones of bondage are considered erotic, and the fashion endures.

👍 **c. 1400** Breasts defy gravity in the fifteenth century. A tight-fitting bodice shoves the mammaries high, creating a platform so stable that "a candle could be stood upon them." Necklines are wide and deep, revealing the upper portion of the orbs. Some women are confident enough to expose the entire breast. Showing a hint of nipple is acceptable only for virgins.

I Can't Believe My Thighs!

👍 **c. 1500** Botticelli paints the ideal beauty. Along with small, round perky breasts, dreamy eyes, flowing hair, and plenty of romantic sex appeal, there's one more thing she has plenty of: thighs. Ample and round, they're attached to fleshy hips. They can't be seen when she's dressed, but at night that's what turns the guys on.

👎 **1533** Poor Catherine de Médicis. She's wed to the king of France, but he has a mistress who's everything she's not. Catherine's short and scrawny with bulging eyes. But she does have great legs. Underneath her gown, she wears form-fitting trousers and invents a new way to sit on a horse—sidesaddle. The traditional womanly way is mounted sideways, resting the feet on an attached stool. Catherine keeps her left foot in the stirrups and wraps her right leg around the saddle horn, which pulls up her skirts, revealing her prized possessions. It's not enough. The king refuses to give up his mistress.

👎 **1542** A healthy salad for lunch may be good for your waistline, but according to Andrew Boorde in *A Dyetary of Helth,* lettuce won't do much for your sex life. "Lettyse doth extynct veneryous actes," he writes. If you chow down at the salad bar, add a few figs to your meal. They "stere a man to veneryous actes, for they doth urge and increase the sede of generacyon."

👍 **c. 1550** Sixteenth-century men are virile. Their broad chests, muscular arms, and well-formed calves turn women on. But hold on a second. Long before padded bras, men pioneer the art of padding. Those doublets are doubled by what's stuffed into them: animal hair, rags, and bran. The sleeves, hose, and pumpkin breeches get the stuffed-turkey treatment too.

The padding does provide warmth and offer a safety cushion from daggers. On the downside, bran encourages lice and leaves a Hansel and Gretel trail when it leaks out. And then there's reality: you do have to get naked sometimes.

1561 Elizabeth I receives a pair of black silk stockings made by her silk woman and wants nothing else next to the royal gams. Neither do men who put in a command performance for any lady wearing them.

1572 They say the apple doesn't fall far from the tree, but in the case of Catherine de Médicis and her daughter, Margaret of Valois, the apple fell in a different orchard. Margaret's a brunette, but she wears blond wigs which complement her fair skin. She discovers another way to highlight the whiteness of her flesh: black satin sheets on which she entertains any number of lovers.

c. 1580 The Elizabethan woman offers her sweetheart a "love apple" and says, "Take this as a token of my love and remember me." It's a peeled apple she keeps under her arm until it's soaked with sweat, which doesn't take long considering the infrequent bathing habits. Sweetheart inhales the apple to excite him.

c. 1600 Spanish women are covered from head to ground. A *tapado,* or cloak, covers everything but the left eye, while their gowns hit the floor. Spanish men don't want anyone to see their women's feet. Carriages are fitted with special doors that hide the shoes of dismounting ladies. The Queen, a tripping victim of fashion, suggests that hemlines be raised but only raises the ire of men who would rather see their wives dead than share the sight of their feet.

c. 1600 Kissing comfits are sold in England. Made by apothecary Robert Burton, the confection is made from sea holly, which grows wild along England's shores. The roots of the plant are candied and snacked on for their restorative, stimulating, and aphrodisiac properties.

c. 1690 Patches are tiny black silk or velvet cutouts that are glued to the face, neck, and bosom if you're daring enough. They cover unsightly blemishes and pockmarks and have a language of their own. Worn on the outer corner of the eye, a patch speaks of passion; beside the mouth, a kiss. The middle of the cheek connotes a fine lady; just below the lower lip, you're a flirt. If it's worn on the nostril, it suggests impudence or maybe a remnant of a bad cold. Some wear up to fifteen patches, making them look like walking connect-the-dot games.

c. 1700 The breast makes a comeback, getting more pushed, powdered and pampered with each passing decade. Gown bodices are tight, and corsets push chests out and shoulders back. Those heaving white necks are made whiter by powdering them with ceruse and chalk, which takes a toll on the skin. The resulting inflammation and scabs require more ceruse and chalk. Bosom bottles are stuck in the cleavage to hold flowers. In the late 1700s false bosoms are introduced. Unlike falsies, which only cover or pad out the breast, the false bosom augments the entire breast to the shoulders.

👍 **1709** Italian chemist John Farina mixes orange, alcohol, bergamot, lemon oil, and rosemary and sells it under the German name Kölnisch Wasser. It's so popular in Europe that aside from making the wearer sweet-smelling, it's attributed with the power to cure headaches, stomachaches, and the vapors. It's manufactured in Cologne and renamed in the international language of French. And that's how eau de cologne is born.

French women dampen their dresses to make them even sexier.

👍**c. 1750** The young lady takes refuge behind her fan. But wait. She presses it to her lips, a signal to her lover to kiss her at the earliest opportunity. A partially opened fan tells what hour to meet her by the number of struts displayed. A wide-open fan tells him to be passionate. More than fifty gestures signal amorous aims which helps fan their popularity worldwide. Ladies take them to church but clergy protest their highly decorated, erotic, mythological scenes. That's taken care of with Sunday-go-to-meeting fans. Now, how do you signal "Pass the collection plate"?

👍**c. 1790** Men's trousers have never been tighter. Those toned-up legs and thighs are all but sewn into pants and are further displayed by a top coat that's cut away from the waist to narrow tails. The fashion is accepted in Europe and America but not in the Papal States. Penalties await any dandy who dares to strut his stuff.

👍**c. 1795** The French Revolution revolutionizes ladies' dress. The chemise is made from nearly transparent muslin, linen, or cotton. The Greek goddess–style dress falls from an Empire waist and flows along the natural lines of the body. Worn over a silk body stocking, the dress is sometimes slit up the right side to reveal the legs. Not sexy enough? Before going out, French ladies dampen their dresses to make them cling more.

c. 1800 Italian courtesans don underpants but they're considered masculine attire and respectable women go without. By the end of the eighteenth century, most women begin wearing them for warmth and to cover up. Men are infuriated. Not only are women encroaching on a male domain, but the chances of catching an accidental glimpse of a bare derriere or, even better, genitalia, are severely curtailed. The complaining ceases when panties take on a more feminine look. The voyeur is as aroused, if not more, at the sight of lace and silk. By the late 1800s women's underwear is an accepted and expected part of daily attire.

1800s As the Victorian era is ushered in there is a pronounced rise in flagellation, masochism, sadism, and fetishes, especially in England, though other countries share the interest. There is a correlation between the English schoolboy who is spanked by a sexually attractive governess or schoolmarm and the eventual adult who pays a prostitute to don furs or a nun's habit and beat him into excitement. Some brothels specialize in whipping and humiliating their clients. Even England's George IV, when he is Prince of Wales, pays an occasional visit to a flagellation bordello. Fur, silk, velvet, and leather become part of the harlot's wardrobe. The only client brothels don't cater to is the sadist. When they do oblige him, the fees are outrageous. Mostly the sadist is left to his own devices to find his victims.

c. 1830 Men's trousers come equipped with a button fly. Traditionally trousers are buttoned on the side. Buttons have long been thought of as immoral. You could get out of clothes too quickly. Some people still carry that sentiment. Mormon leader Brigham Young refers to the button-down trousers as "fornication pants."

c. 1840 Dr. C. A. Weinhold, a staunch believer in population control, sees a solution to the problem: he suggests that infibulation be performed on all males at the age of fourteen and not be reversed until a man can afford a family. Infibulation includes pulling the foreskin over the head of the penis and putting a wire ring through it, which is soldered and stamped prohibiting its removal. Thus ends a man's sex life until he can afford to have children. If he never saves enough, thus ends his sex life. Fortunately, no one takes Weinhold seriously.

1850> Repression in the Victorian era brings out some strange tastes, one of which English brothel owners willingly meet: a fresh supply of virgins is on hand for deflowering by clients who are willing to pay the price. One reason for its popularity is the myth that sex with a virgin will cure VD, which is running rampant through England. For 100 pounds you get the girl and a gander at a medical certificate verifying that she's intact. Of course, the doctor is employed by the house, and girls lose their virginity more than once. A blood-soaked sponge inserted in the vagina releases fluid with pressure. A few stitches or fumigation with vinegar steam and everything's sealed up tighter than a drum. Acting the part with well-placed tears and screams helps out, too. Are men easily duped? Of course. But some must catch on. By the end of the century, the price has fallen to 5 pounds.

allowed in lecture halls. Wearers have their morals questioned on the street by children who pelt them with snowballs. It's no wonder the fashion fades away quickly.

1856 Wet dreams got you down? The answer may be L. B. Sibley's sleeping ring. Worn to bed, the penis ring is studded with metal spurs that dig in as the penis becomes erect. The man awakens and voilà! The wet dream is averted.

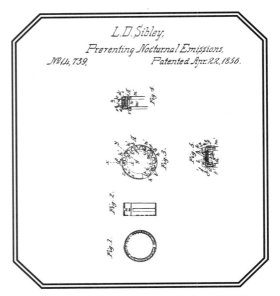

L. D. Sibley,
Preventing Nocturnal Emissions,
№ 14,739,   Patented Apr. 22, 1856.

The metal-spurred sleeping ring that fits over the penis puts an end to wet dreams.

1860s The hourglass figure takes center stage. A waspish 16-inch waist is considered ideal, though some women tight-lace themselves down to a mere 13 inches. The bisection of the body is achieved with corsets that require a second person to pull the corset strings tighter and tighter month after month, year after year, until the ribs and internal organs become compressed. The lowest ribs are sometimes surgically removed to achieve perfection. Breasts are pushed up, and, because

Bloomers are a short-lived attempt to give women more freedom of movement.

1851 Bloomers are introduced by feminists as a reasonable alternative to unmanageable hoopskirts. Named after Amelia Bloomer, one of the first women to wear them, bloomers are Turkish trousers worn under a knee-length dress. The outfit allows women freedom of movement. Male voices rise in protest. Clergymen throw bloomer wearers out of church. They're not

the diaphragm is solidly encased in whalebone or metal stays, breathing is limited to shallow breaths from the top of the lungs, making breasts heave. Hips remain full with a bustle picking up the rear. As anti-sex as society is, the fashion—with the rising and falling breasts, the sashaying behind, and restrictions that promote vulnerability—makes females more alluring.

1870s Regarding those heaving bosoms mentioned above, well, some women can push things up and still never acquire a substantial enough heave. So they wear a palpitator, or false bosom. Available models include inflatable bodices, pads, rubber shapes, and camisoles with a built-in spring mechanism that allows for a selection of sizes. They're one-piece, provide no cleavage, and worst of all, there's no heaving. Without that gentle up-and-down movement, everyone knows you're augmented.

1876 Englishmen who attend the Grand Opéra Bouffe at the Alhambra Theater are panting over French dancers who introduce garter belts to the isle. The flesh of the women's naked

thighs is titillatingly broken by the ribbon of the garter that reaches across soft skin to meet stocking tops. Men swoon. It isn't long before garters come off the stage and star in real life.

c. 1880 Victorian women are believed to be sexless creatures, but occasionally one gets born with feelings. If she explores those feelings by playing with herself, the medical profession deals with it. First, a diet of cold liquids, bread, ripe fruits, and buttermilk with a little saltpeter. Then tepid baths and quiet activity, like reading, is prescribed. Exercise isn't recommended because it might rub the labia and start everything up again. If all else fails, there's the clitoridectomy—the surgical removal of the clitoris. The clitoridectomy isn't a new proce-

TRIVIA At the turn of the twentieth century, a growing propaganda campaign is under way to make men clean-shaven. In France two men—one bearded, one not—are walked through the streets of Paris to a laboratory where each kisses a girl! The girls' lips are then swabbed and the swab deposited in a sterilized solution and sealed for four days. Aha! Only harmless germs are passed by the clean-shaven gent. The bearded fellow's kiss swarms with "malignant microbes." Women, one magazine reports, are the final arbitors, and in their view facial hair is "obnoxious." Anyone got a razor?

If warm baths don't cure a woman of masturbating in the late 1800s, doctors may resort to performing a clitoridectomy.

dure. Certain Muslims and other African societies routinely perform the operation on girls as a rite of passage into womanhood by removing her womanhood. This sadistic operation is performed as a cure into the twentieth century.

1880s Cases of husbands infecting their wives with venereal disease after visiting prostitutes are on the rise. When condoms become available, wary wives do not protest their use, especially since they cut down on pregnancy. It finally becomes possible for a woman to claim some of her sexuality and be alluring to her husband. It's no wonder that ultra-feminine nightgowns and negligees become popular.

c. 1890 Some Victorian ladies choose to wear jewelry where no one—well, almost no one—can see it. Breast piercing becomes a quiet rage. During the day small gold rings are worn. At night, husbands spring for more costly gems. Whatever hangs on the earlobes also hangs on the nipples. Some women drape a string of pearls from one breast to another. Wearers admit

being titillated by the jewelry's rubbing against clothes. Others believe it's a way to make their breasts larger, rounder, and firmer.

1890s There's nothing more exciting to the man on the street than the sight of a well-turned ankle. Breasts, waists, and hips have been

The sight of a bare ankle in the late 1800s is elusive and eye-opening.

emphasized. Shoulders have been bared. But legs are covered up and not to be mentioned. When a skirt is blown up or slightly lifted, exposing part of the forbidden limb, men's hearts and other body parts start throbbing.

Doctor, Doctor, Write Me a Prescription!

👎 **1890s** Hysteria is a problem for some Victorian women. Fortunately there are doctors who provide a cure for this condition, which causes women to be interested in sex, have insomnia, and increased genital wetness: vaginal massage! The vulva is massaged with fragrant oils by a doctor or a trained midwife until the condition is brought to a "crisis." As they become available, electric vibrators are used for the same purpose. In Sweden, daily massages of the pelvic organs are available to women.

👎 **1893** There's relief for those nasty wet dreams. The U.S. Patent Office okays a water-cooled device that puts an end to sticky sheets. A container of water mounted on the wall is connected to a harness that fits over the penis. During sleep, the growing male member opens levers that allow cold water to rush forth and cool those overheated jets PDQ. The real wet threat occurs when the cooler springs a leak.

👎 **1897** Michael McCormick receives a patent on a surgical appliance that prevents "involuntary nocturnal seminal emissions," off-color thoughts, and self-abuse. A plate worn on a belt covers the abdomen and contains a spiked aperture into which the male member is inserted. If the penis remains flaccid, there's no problem. If

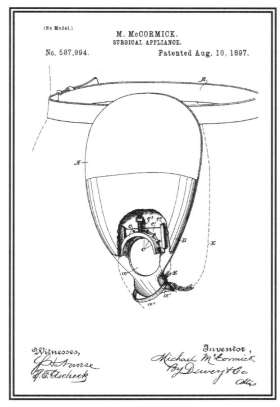

Metal spikes prevent "involuntary nocturnal seminal emissions."

you start to get an erection, the resulting pain gets your mind off sex quickly.

👍 **c. 1900** Artist Charles Dana Gibson puts pen to paper for *Life* magazine and creates a fantasy woman whom every man longs for and every real woman wants to be. The Gibson Girl is the first all-American girl. Her hair is pouffed, her face is lovely, her neck silken, her waist teeny-tiny. She wears a high-collared shirtwaist blouse with leg-of-mutton sleeves and a divided skirt that makes it possible for her to ride a bicycle around town. She's athletic for

I Vant to Bite Your Neck

👍**c. 1910** Neck nuzzling becomes easier with the plunging V-neckline. Tumbling softly off the shoulders, bodices dip down to show off well-tended tender skin. Prudish folks don't care for the look. Neither do doctors, who warn that increased exposure leads to goiters and thick necks.

the times, aloof but charming, gorgeous, liberated, acceptably flirtatious, and confident. Gibson makes a small fortune from his creation.

👍**c. 1910** The bee-stung mouth—those deliciously red lips that pout and pucker so sensually—is the rage. Lips are full but small, always as if pronouncing "P" words and always ready to be kissed. Red lips stay in fashion during World War I, when women work in factories. After the war, the lack of men creates a new class of bachelor girls who have a limited but disposable income. Lipstick is a cheap route to easy sex appeal. Now say "prune."

👍**1920s** How can you tell a peasant from an aristocrat if both are nude? The peasant's skin is tanned from working in the sun. That notion holds true throughout history until designer Coco Chanel makes tan lines for the leisure class chic. Chanel returns from a trip aboard the Duke of Westminster's yacht with a tan. If Coco has one, everyone wants one. Parasols and wide-brimmed bonnets are stored away with the hoop skirts as people pursue a year-long tan, the mark of a well-to-do person. Pale skin becomes the sign of a factory worker.

Rosalina, a pretty young lass,
Had a truly magnificent ass:
Not rounded and pink
As you possibly think—
It was grey, had long ears, and ate grass.

Count Palmiro Vicarion's Book of Limericks, *1955*

c. 1924 Skirts are raised to mid-calf, but this is only a sample of things to come. Flappers bob their hair, flatten their chests, and toss away the undergarments that caged them and their mothers, leaving them as liberated as their lifestyle. By 1928 hemlines land just below the knee, giving men their first good look at women's gams. Flesh-colored (white flesh, that is) silk stockings add to the look, though most men prefer black hose. After hundreds of years of being covered, it's a hip flapper who knows how to walk, sit, and stand with a new sensuality.

1932 The only part of the female body that hasn't been designated a fashionable erogenous zone is the back. That's taken care of with the backless dress. Tallulah Bankhead wears one in *Thunder Below,* and soon it's shoulder blades for everyone. Dresses aren't the only backless garments; bathing suits dip down now that they're actually being worn for swimming.

1940 Shown at the New York World's Fair in 1939 to great reviews, nylons go on sale this year to the general public. Women love them. They're "shrink proof, moth proof, non-allergic,

resists mildew, warm as wool." They make legs look great, too. At \$1.25 a pair, more than twice the price of silk stockings but rumored to "last a lifetime," the 72,000 pairs allotted to New York are sold out in eight hours. Nationwide, a reported 780,000 pairs sell on the first day. There's never a sales slump. Demand exceeds the supply a year later when America becomes involved in World War II and the military corners the nylon market. During the war, Macy's might not carry nylons but the black market does—for \$10 a pair. Women are reduced to wearing silk stockings or, during warmer weather, using leg makeup, which requires them to draw a seam up the back of the leg.

c. 1940 There are only two hip kinds of fashion for men. One is the zoot suit. Inspired by mobsters who need to hide guns, the oversize jacket has padded shoulders and wide lapels and hangs down to mid-thigh, covering double-pleated, high-waisted pants that balloon out at the thigh and then taper tightly at the ankle. Perfect for jitterbugging. It's topped off with a wide-brimmed hat, a key chain that hangs from the belt to below the knee, a wide satin tie, and cuff links the size of Rhode Island. Hepcats love the zoot. Soldiers, wearing the other acceptable fashion, don't, since most zoot-suiters haven't enlisted or been drafted. Preachers don't care for zoot suits, either, since they supposedly appeal to loose women. The government steps in and bans the manufacture of the suits because they're a waste of fabric during wartime.

☝ **1940s** U.S. soldiers are "over there," but U.S. women are over here. To remind the guys of what they're fighting for, pinup girls do their part to boost morale. Glossies line lockers, Quonset huts, the inside of helmets, and anywhere else one of our boys can ogle a beauty in a bathing suit, a negligee, or short shorts. Hollywood starlets like Ava Gardner, Lana Turner, Diana Dors, and Chili Williams say cheese the most. Rita Hayworth's likeness is said to have graced the atomic bomb dropped on Hiroshima. The most popular pinup is Betty Grable. Over two million photos of her are sent out to GIs, but a soldier's favorite pinup is the photo of his girl back home.

☝ **1946** Designer Louis Réard introduces the scanty two-piece bathing suit and dubs it the bikini. Four days prior to the fashion show, the

United States had tested an atomic bomb at the Bikini atoll in the Marshall Islands. Réard adopts the name for his explosive suit. Extremely daring for its time, none of Réard's regular runway models want to expose themselves to such scrutiny or scandal. Micheline Bernardini, a dancer from the Casino in Paris, helps him out and displays Réard's talents as well as her own.

👎 **1947** It's a fashion that's soft, ultrafeminine, and alluring. Not everybody wants to wear it at first, but it does catch on. The New Look, created by Christian Dior, is an old look. Hemlines are lowered to 12 inches off the floor, shoulders are softened and rounded, bosoms are padded, waists are narrowed. How chic! cry fashion mavens. Where are the legs? ask ex-GIs, who want to see the gams bared by wartime skirts, which were shortened to save material. Says one woman of the fashion, "It shows everything you want to hide and hides everything you want to show." Even the women of war-torn England, who are still scrimping on fabric, succumb to Parisian femininity.

☝ **1947** Disappointed at the state of women's apparel, Frederick N. Mellinger dreams of selling undergarments and clothing in the soft, sensual, clingy fabrics that he fantasized about while in a foxhole during World War II. He opens Frederick's of Hollywood, a mail-order business for women's clothing. Determined to make every female figure a feast for male eyes, Frederick's offers bras that lift, separate, and blow up to whatever size you'd like. Fannies are padded. Fannies are lifted. Feathers, lace, and ruffles adorn any piece of clothing that can rouse a male hormone. Spike heels, powder-puff slippers, and prosthetic nipples point the way to Frederick's success. In five years

Mellinger expands to include retail stores in Hollywood and then across the country, where his fashions sell at modest prices to ensure that all women can afford to look sexy.

👍 **1952** The setting: a college campus. The time: midnight. Someone yells, "To the girls' dorm!" and the panty raid begins. As many as three thousand college men rush the dorms in search of frilly female undergarments. Panties, slips, bras, and nylons are the sought-after trophies. The girls shriek, but most of them participate good-naturedly. They also counter with their own raids, demanding boxers and briefs. Psychiatrists compare the raids to Roman spring fertility festivals. Panty raids continue to be an annual ritual until the 1960s.

👍 **1952** Foot doctors hate them and warn women of problems to come. They dent floors and tear carpets. But men love to see women in them, and women love to see men watching them, so stiletto heels are the shoe du jour. Perching a body four or five inches over its normal height, stilettos shift a woman's weight, arching the back, emphasizing butt and hip movement, and contouring calves and feet. The high-heel fetish comes out of the closet

and into the street. What's not to like? Bunions, corns, hammer toes . . .

Every woman has her weapons on her.

Talmud

👍 **1960s** Another fetish tumbles out of the closet. Kinky boots become de rigueur. In regular leather or patent leather, kinky boots are knee-high or thigh-high boots with a stiletto heel, and are often buttoned or laced. Whips are sold separately.

👍 **c. 1964** Guys can't believe their eyes or their luck. Transparent blouses, some with necklines that plunge to the navel, become fashionable. While designers design them to be worn over the nude body, most women take cover under a nude-colored body stocking or a skin-tone bra.

👍 **1964** Rudi Gernreich designs a bathing suit with two straps attached to elongated trunks that V out between the breasts and over the shoulders, exposing perky rounded breasts or what have you. This design starts as a drawing of what bathing suits might look like in the future. But then it appears in a magazine and orders pour in. A few women wear the suits and are arrested for indecent exposure. They're banned in France. The Soviet Union takes one look and declares, "The decay of the money-bag society continues." English nudist colonies snub them, declaring that their members wouldn't be caught dead in one. But men know they exist and that seems to be good enough.

👍 **mid-1960s** Marlon Brando, James Dean, and Elvis do their part to popularize jeans but the youths of the sixties carry the fad to its sexual heights. To fit like a second skin, teens wear them into the bathtub, wet them, and wear them until dry. The finished result emphasizes every contour Mother Nature gave you. How do you zip them up? Lie on the bed or floor, suck in your gut, and pull hard. Women's rear ends have remained flat or rounded but always in one piece. Jeans lift and separate the cheeks, making watching walking away a pastime sport. Girls get to check out which side a guy dresses on. That bulge between the legs lends a definite quid pro quo to the unisex fashion.

👍 **1965>** The generation gap extends to fragrances for men. The hip male won't splash on his father's Aqua Velva or any aftershave that reeks of a traditional male scent, like leather, tobacco, or aged liquor. The trend in male colognes is toward a more floral, effeminate scent, even though the names imply otherwise: Hai Karate, Aztec, Canoe, Eau Sauvage. The "in" couple smells alike. Men also take over more of their ladies' dressing tables with their own cosmetics. Moisturizers, eye creams, lip guards, and hair preparations are part and parcel of male morning grooming.

👍 **1965** Mary Quant introduces the miniskirt, the new woman's flag of sexual freedom. Quant takes rising hemlines to new heights, showing off knees and attitude. Tongues click but not for long. The miniskirt is made acceptable when former first lady Jacqueline Kennedy wears one to lunch. The mini continues to evolve, riding higher on the thigh each year until the micro-mini takes over. Bending is done at the wearer's own risk. Feminists applaud the fashion for its

freedom, but change their tone as the miniskirt becomes too much of a favorite with men.

👍 **1970s** You can't tell the boys from the girls. Women don pants for comfort and freedom of movement. Men are into lace-ruffled shirt-fronts. Jackets for men and women are body-shaped with wide, floppy collars, and crushed velvet is a favorite fabric of both sexes. Hairstyles are unisex. Women wear their hair long or short. So do men. The older generation doesn't understand how the younger generation tell each other apart. They do. And in the era of free love, they make the most of the difference.

To be loved, be lovable.

Ovid

1970 Top of the thigh-high short shorts appear in Europe and become a hit in America early in 1971. *Women's Wear Daily* calls them hot pants, and they take off faster than the miniskirt. Hot pants are more practical than miniskirts because they let you sit, bend, and walk upstairs without letting the world know what color your underwear is. Acceptable as everyday fashion from the workplace to black-tie parties, they're most often worn to singles bars. Hot pants are designed for men to wear, too, but women aren't turned on and soon the entire hot pants fad fades from the scene and becomes the uniform of prostitutes.

1973 There's something for women to look at on the beach. Those muscle-bound hard bodies are wearing Speedo's Lycra bikinis, which stick to a man's body like a woman's wet T-shirt. They even make watching Olympic swim competitions more fun. Athletes opt for wearing suits two or three times smaller for hydrodynamics. Women cheer them on all the more.

1974 The string bikini hits the beaches of the world. Three minuscule pieces of fabric that barely cover a woman's erogenous zones are held together by delicate fabric strings. Tan-

talizing enough? No way. The strings are tied at the hips and the back of the bra, and with just one little tug . . . well, guys get the picture. While only the most able-bodied wear them, most mouths gape at how little costs so much ($45).

1974 Like most crazes, streaking starts on college campuses. You take off your clothes and dash out in public and then disappear just as quickly. Men have a corner on streaking, but a few women join in the fun. Some say it's pure exhibitionism. Others feel it's one more slap in Puritanism's face. The fad begins at the start of the year. By graduation anyone who's still streaking has definitely flunked out.

1975> S&M, bondage, domination, and fetishes come flying out from behind closed doors with the punk look. Faces are pale; hair is spiked; vinyl, leather, and rubber are the fabrics of choice; chains and studs adorn clothing; dog collars encircle necks; and safety pins are stuck through ears, noses, or any desired body parts. The Marquis de Sade would feel right at home.

1980s The era of free love comes to a screeching halt with the advent of the herpes II virus. Referred to as a cold sore in the wrong place, there's no known cure for the painful sores that last for three weeks and recur every few months for life or go dormant forever. Besides slowing down a person's sex life, herpes can cause legal problems. Many a partner who contracts herpes sues the lover who didn't mention his or her affliction and carelessly passed it on.

<1990 Those who wondered what could be skimpier than a string bikini get their answer: it's called a thong and referred to as ass floss. The bra is borrowed from the string bikini, but the bottom is reengineered. Introduced in Brazil

THE BUTTOCKS

(As legally described by Saint Johns County, Florida, to decide if a bathing suit is too skimpy)

"The area at the rear of the human body (sometimes referred to as the gluteus maximus) that lies between two imaginary straight lines running parallel to the ground when a person is standing, the first or top such line being one-half inch below the top of the vertical cleavage of the nates (i.e., the prominence formed by the muscles running from the back of the hip to the back of the leg) and the second or bottom such line being one-half inch above the lowest point of the curvature of the fleshy protuberance (sometimes referred to as the gluteal fold), and between two imaginary straight lines, one on each side of the body (the "outside lines"), which outside lines are perpendicular to the ground and to the horizontal lines described above and which perpendicular outside lines pass through the outermost point(s) at which each nate meets the outer side of each leg. Notwithstanding the above, buttocks shall not include the leg, the hamstring muscle below the gluteal fold, the tensor fasciae latae muscle or any of the above described portion of the human body that is between either (i) the left inside perpendicular line and the left outside perpendicular line or (ii) the right inside perpendicular line and the right outside perpendicular line. For the purposes of the previous sentence, the left inside perpendicular line shall be an imaginary straight line on the left side of the anus (i) that is perpendicular to the ground and to the horizontal lines described above and (ii) that is one third of the distance from the anus to the left outside line, and the right inside perpendicular line shall be an imaginary straight line on the right side of the anus (i) that is perpendicular to the ground and to the horizontal lines described above and (ii) that is one third of the distance from the anus to the right outside line. (The above description can generally be described as covering one third of the buttocks centered over the cleavage for the length of the cleavage.)"

years ago, the thong (also worn by men) consists of a small front piece that covers the genital area, then narrows down to a thin strap that slides between the cheeks and connects with the waistband. Only youthful Aphrodites and Adonises need apply; on anyone else the thong can turn into a cellulite sideshow. Men are split on its sexiness. It leaves nothing to the imagination. No mental undressing is possible. Law enforcement officials feel the same way. More than one beach bans thongs because the gluteus is just too maximus.

Chapter Twelve
WORD ORIGINS

A.D.

c. 160 The Greek physician Galen adopts the word "gonorrhea" as a name for a venereal disease. But he misapplies the word to denote its discharge symptom. The word "gonorrhea" literally means "a flow of seed."

1040 The term "peeping Tom" has its origin in the tale of Lady Godiva's ride through the streets of Coventry. The lady's husband, Leofric, Lord of Coventry, is heavy-handed in imposing taxes on the townspeople. To her plea for financial leniency, Leofric offers this challenge: ride through the streets naked and he'll rescind the taxes. Godiva asks the townspeople to shutter their windows and stay inside so she can modestly fulfill her mission. The request is honored by all except Tom the tailor who can't resist sneaking a peek. Legend says he is instantly struck blind.

c. 1100 In Old English and Old Norse a "whore" is a woman who sells herself. While most whores trade their services for cash, some whores are just loose women. By the end of the sixteenth century whores work in "whore-houses." Neither term is considered vulgar until the Victorian age. Luckily, a seventeenth-century term is available to clean up the image. "Whore" is replaced by "prostitute."

c. 1230 The root of the word "cunt" is uncertain. It could be from the Latin *cunnus,* the Greek *konnos,* or the Germanic *kunton.* It refers to a woman's external genitalia, and until the seventeenth century, it's a standard term. Then there's a complete flip-flop. "Cunt" becomes the most vulgar taboo word in the English language. When it is written, it is as c**t, c——t, or just c——. To print it in a book immediately brands that book obscene. Grose's *Dictionary of the Vulgar Tongue* (1811) reluctantly lists the word because it's frequently used, but calls it "a nasty name for a nasty thing."

<1250 A man who clumsily reaches for and feels a woman's breasts or genitals, whether she's a willing participant or not, is said to "grope" her.

<1300 By the fourteenth century a woman who has her "maidenhead" (an intact hymen) is called a "virgin." While only women have

**Willing or not, this woman
is being "groped."**

maidenheads, the word "virgin" is applied to chaste men as well. How does a woman lose her maidenhead? Through "fornication," though "fornicators" (c. 1377) are generally unmarried men and women, or adulterers. Once lost, the double standard begins: a randy man is acceptable but a woman with the same tendencies is a "slut" (c. 1450).

Also: Men use the word "piece" to denote a woman as a sexual object. Around 1861 American males use "piece of calico"—a material used in women's dresses—for the same reason and gradually it's shortened, once again, to "piece." Twentieth-century men are more direct. A "piece of ass" can refer to the vagina or copulation.

c. 1303 A person's buttocks are a "tail," a more polite word than the vulgar "arse." After about four hundred years the meaning expands to include having sex, the woman being the tail a man is after.

c. 1325 The scrotum becomes "balls," probably because of its rounded shape. By 1744 they're called "bollocks." American GIs in World War II find out that you can "have someone by the balls"—that is, you can be in a position of power. "To ball," meaning to have sex, is of African-American origin and becomes slang in the mid-twentieth century. Although men say this certain type of woman has been around forever, the term "ball-breaker," describing a woman who destroys the self-confidence of a man, doesn't gain popularity until the 1970s.

c. 1400 The word "cock," meaning "penis," comes into use in this century but is not considered vulgar until the nineteenth century. At the end of the 1800s the word is expanded. A "cock-sucker" is a person who performs fellatio, but the word is also used as an abusive term. A "cock tease" is a woman who gives a guy the come-on but never follows through.

Also: By the fifteenth century the word "brothel," once used to denote a worthless person, refers to a woman who sells sexual favo in a "brothel house."

"Tail"
is more
polite
than
"arse."

Eventually "house" is dropped and "brothel" acquires its current meaning.

c. 1425 Men finally get "testicles." Curiously, they don't have a "penis" until 1693, just a few years after women get a "vagina" (1682).

<1483 The act of sex is "copulation," taken from the Latin *copulare,* to join together. In earlier times the word meant any coupling or joining. By the end of the fifteenth century it pertains only to couple coupling.

1500s The French excel at sex. At least the English language reflects that belief. The word "French" is used alone or as an adjective to describe any act, lewd or kinky. "Frenching," "French job," and "French kiss" all pertain to oral sex, both fellatio and cunnilingus. In the nineteenth century a "French letter" is a condom, and a "French family" is a two-child family—the limited family size the result of using French letters. World War I vets return from France versed in the "French way," another euphemism for oral sex. In the mid-twentieth century "French ticklers" are French letters with nubby protuberances for added pleasure.

Also: About A.D. 1000 a heretical sect centered in Bulgaria angers the Catholic church not only because they worship differently but because children aren't allowed to be conceived by the congregation. However, sex is allowed. The church believes they practice anal sex as contraception. They are called Bulgars, and the word erodes to bugger. By the sixteenth century "buggery" describes an act of anal intercourse and includes bestiality.

1503 "Fuck" is first recorded in northern England as a verb and overtakes terms like "jape," "sarde," and "swive." By 1598 a "fucker" is a person who fucks or someone who isn't likable. Although "fuck" is slang, it's accepted for a couple of hundred years until it starts showing up as "f**k" and then fades from print altogether. But people still use it. In the 1700s it becomes a four-letter noun, as in, "She's a good fuck." Soon it becomes totally unacceptable, second only to "cunt." The twentieth century sees its comeback, even its expansion. "Fucking the fist" (masturbation) and "fuck film" (porno movie) are sexual in meaning, but "fuck off," "fuck up," and "fuck you" are merely abusive. Though it's commonly used, allowed in print, and back in the dictionary, "fuck" still hasn't regained the acceptance it enjoyed in the sixteenth century.

<1520 If your sixteenth-century admirer asks you to go for a "ride," he's not talking about a trip in his carriage. This man wants to mount you, although it's fair game for a woman to get on top and ride the man.

1530 The plague that has been ravaging Europe is finally given a name: "syphilis." Girolamo Fracastoro coins the word in his poem, *Syphilis sive Morbus Gallicus.* Syphilis is a Greek shepherd who is struck with the disease after falling out of favor with the god Apollo.

c. 1580 "Pussy" denotes the female genitalia and is probably derived from the association of cats with women. It's a sex object term, as is "twat," which comes into use during the middle of the next century. The slang for "vagina" softens in the early 1700s with the introduction of "honey pot."

c. 1587 Get the "clap" and you have gonorrhea. The word comes from either *clapoir,*

French for "swelling," or *clapier,* French for "brothel." Syphilis is referred to as a pox. By the twentieth century the clap includes other venereal diseases. Likewise, a pox doctor is a physician who treats VD.

<1592 Ah, the penis and all its names. It's called a "prick" because of the word's meaning "to pierce." By this time, "prick" is standard English and is used as a term of endearment. The penis is also known as "meat." Although men have masturbated since day one, it isn't called "beating the meat" until the 1960s. Private pet names are usually variations on the owner's name, but "dick," a nickname for Richard, catches on about 1891, and two years later dick finally gets a "hard-on." Around the turn of the twentieth century the penis is called a "rod," though it has to earn that name with an erection. In the 1920s a dick is a "dong." Testicles get the nickname "rocks" after World War II, probably from the British slang "stones," and "getting your rocks off" means being satisfied sexually. By the 1970s the penis becomes a "shaft."

c. 1598 To have sex is "to knock." But beware. It causes a woman to get "knocked up," that is, pregnant. By the early eighteenth century the same kind of action is "to roger," taken from a man's name that is also used for penis. (Roger, a favorite name for male animals, quickly lends itself as an alternative for the word sex). "Flourishing" is the same as rogering, but is done with the clothes kept on. If the missionary position is used, it's "bread and butter." In the 1880s the rugged man "puts the boots to" his woman.

1600s Women's breasts are "tits," but it's not slang and has no negative connotation. The word "teat" is used; "tit" develops through a mispronunciation. Not until the twentieth century is the word considered vulgar.

Also: When the French create the "brassiere" it is a garment that is wrapped around the torso. Its literal translation is "bodice." Brassiere doesn't get its present-day definition until the early 1900s. Its shortened version—bra—comes along in 1935.

Also: "Clitoris" is most likely derived from the Greek *kleitoris,* which comes from a related word meaning "close." That would apply in two ways: the clitoris is hidden by the labia and, unlike the penis, has no urethral opening. The word is around for over three hundred years before its shortened slang—clit—gets tossed around.

Also: American colonists put their spin on the English "arse" with "ass," referring to both the buttocks and the anus.

c. 1636 A man who procures women for other men is a "pimp." However, he doesn't get a "pimpmobile," that big flashy car, until the 1970s.

<1647 Sexual intercourse is a "grind"—not in the sense of hard work, but from the grinding motion. That same hip rotation is what strippers use in their acts. Their erotic dance is referred to as a grind or "bump and grind" by the 1940s.

<1650 To have an orgasm is to "come." The word is expanded in the 1920s to refer to ejaculated semen and is also written as "cum." By the 1960s, semen is "cream." And if you come in your denims, you've "creamed your jeans."

1717 The word "condom" appears in a treatise on syphilis but stories differ as to its origin. One tale has the protector named after a Dr. Condom or Conton, a physician at the court of Charles II who, around 1660, invented the device to prevent the randy king from producing so many illegitimate offspring. Or, it could be named after a Colonel Condum of the Royal Guard. Most likely it's derived from two Latin words, *cunnus,* referring to the female pudenda, and *dum,* to limit function.

c. 1725 To "screw" means to have sex and it's most likely taken from the motion of putting a key, which is called a screw, into a lock. "Screw" gains popularity and stays in use because it's more proper to say than "fuck." When eighteenth-century gutter talkers enlarge their vocabulary, they add the verbs "pump" (c. 1730) and "hump" (c. 1785) to mean the same thing.

1756 Your eyes may look like limpid pools, your lips like cherries. But your gluteus maximus is a "moon," or moons—one for each cheek. Dropping your pants and bending over "to moon someone" isn't new, but it isn't described as such until the 1950s.

<1846 The quick exposing of the genitals, breasts, or undergarments is to "flash." The word "flasher" is a twentieth-century police term for a person who does this. The word spills over into mainstream use in the 1960s as flashers become more common.

1847 Little Red Riding Hood isn't the only one having problems with a "wolf." The word describes an aggressive male seducer of women—though briefly, around the time of World War I, it's a tag for homosexually aggressive men. By the 1930s it's hung on men who go after their friends' wives and girlfriends or any guy who builds up his ego by chasing a lot of women.

<1850 Victorian era or not, a man with large genitals is said to be "well hung."

c. 1860 A homosexual man with feminine mannerisms is a "poof." At the turn of the century, he's a "fairy" and the man who introduces him to the gay lifestyle is his "fairy godmother." By the 1920s there's a larger list of pejoratives from which to choose. "Fruitcake" is first attached to the insane then envelops homosexuals as well. Its shortened version, "fruit," is used, too. "Fluter" reflects the image of the penis as a flute and the fluter as one who plays it. A "pansy" denotes a weak, effeminate homosexual. And some are just "queer," as in odd or degenerate. A "queen" is one who plays the feminine role or is especially attractive to other homosexuals. By 1963 hiding one's gay tendencies is to "stay in the closet." Admitting it publicly is "coming out of the closet." In the late 1960s a person who tries to keep his sexual orientation a secret is a "closet queen." There is a reason for the secrecy. "Queer bashing," assaults on homosexuals, begins to rise.

c. 1861 Known for his sexual appetite, Civil War General Joseph Hooker of the Union Army

WORD OF MOUTH

Oral sex is nothing new. But the words to describe it are. Cunnilingus (he gives it to her) and fellatio (she gives it to him) are both late nineteenth-century creations. From the Latin for "vulva" *(cunnus)* and "lick" *(lingere)* comes cunnilingus. The Latin for suck *(fellare)* gives "fellatio" its head.

gives his name to prostitutes. When brothels are allowed in Washington, D.C., to amuse the soldiers, the women become known collectively as "Hooker's Division" and individually as "hookers." There is a shortage of food, clothing, and ammunition on both sides during the war, but lack of female companionship is never an issue. There are over 450 brothels in Washington alone. Troops refer to visiting them as "going down the line."

General Hooker lends his name to prostitutes.

1865 "Gamahuche" is slang for oral sex, either fellatio or cunnilingus, and comes from the French slang *gamahucher,* to denote the same acts. By 1916 "go down on" is the euphemism of choice, since you have to physically move down to perform either act. By 1928 it's just called "sucking." "Blow jobs"—or "BJs"—don't enter the language until the 1950s. It's a toss-up whether the term is taken from a comparison between ejaculating and the spouting of a whale, or from blowing, musicians' jargon for playing an instrument.

1869 "Homosexuality" and "heterosexuality" are coined by Karl Maria Benkert. Until now there was no one word to describe a same-sex attraction. "Inversion" is used, as is "contrary sexual feeling," or the practice is classified as sodomy, bestiality, or pederasty. It takes a decade for both terms to take hold.

1870 The word "lesbianism," meaning female homosexuality, is taken from the Greek island Lesbos where Sappho wrote her poetry. In 1890 female homosexuals are called lesbians.

Also: A man wearing women's clothes is said to be "in drag." Women's long dresses *drag*

ILIA-LY SPEAKING

Acousticophilia: arousal by sounds

Acrophilia: arousal by heights

Acrotomophilia: arousal by the thought of having sex with an amputee

Agalmatophilia: arousal by a statue or mannequin

Agoraphilia: arousal by being in public places or outdoors

Agrexophilia: arousal when others can hear one's lovemaking

Algophilia: arousal gained by pain, such as being bitten

Amaurophilia: arousal by sex with a blindfolded person

Choreophilia: arousal by dancing

Claustrophilia: arousal by being confined to small spaces

Coprophilia: arousal by feces

Gerontophilia: attraction to significantly older people

Nasophilia: arousal by sight, touching, licking, or sucking partner's nose

Pediophilia: sexual attraction to dolls

Podophilia: arousal by feet

Rhabdophilia: arousal by flagellation

Sitophilia: use of food for sexual purposes

Somnophilia: arousal by having sex with a sleeping person

Urophilia: arousal from sex acts involving urine

Xenophilia: arousal by strangers

Word Origins

on the ground and are comparatively heavier than traditional male clothing. The action and the feeling of being weighed down give rise to the euphemism. A "drag queen" is a male homosexual transvestite and doesn't get crowned until the early 1940s.

1887 French psychologist Alfred Binet coins the word "fetishism" to denote a degenerative disease. The fascination with objects like high heels, corsets, fur, gloves, silk, leather, and velvet, which lead to sexual excitement and can border on obsession, is mostly a male domain.

Also: A few years ago, a man's girlfriend or wife was his "tart," calling to mind something sweet. By 1887 the word is applied to prostitutes and women with loose morals.

69

1888 The French word "soixante-neuf" literally translates to "sixty-nine" and refers to the mutual act of oral sex—that is, cunnilingus and fellatio performed at the same time. The term is based on what the couple looks like when performing the act.

1893 Richard von Krafft-Ebing uses the word "masochists" for those who get their jollies from being dominated, whipped, and bullied. The author of domination novels, Leopold von Sacher-Masoch, unwittingly lends his name to psychiatric journals.

<1895 A woman of the late Victorian era is no better off than her present-day sister if she has a selfish lover who's faster than an egg timer. The phrase "wham, bam, thank you, ma'am," makes him sound courteous but it's still as frustrating.

Also: A man who is sexually potent, as in animal magnetism, and loves the ladies is a "stud." His son, a little less animalistic but still chasing the women in 1922, is a "cake-eater," "cake" meaning the female genitalia or a good-looking woman. His grandson, in 1968, who is

easy on the eyes and has a nice body is a "hunk." By the 1980s, everything old is new again. Great-grandson is a stud once more.

c. 1896 Having sex standing up is the most physically exhausting position and puts an inordinate amount of strain on the legs. That's why it's called a "knee-trembler."

<1900 If you still have your "cherry," you're a virgin. It's said that the fruit bears a resemblance to the hymen. The vagina is a "box" by 1942—that is, a container the penis can be put into. Hence, a deflowered woman may say, "I don't have my cherry but I still have the box it came in."

Also: If a "P.I." (pimp) procures your sex partner you may wind up with "Cupid's itch" (venereal disease). STDs (sexually transmitted diseases) in the 1920s are called "crud," although the word can also be used for dried-up semen on you or your clothes. After World War II venereal diseases, especially gonorrhea, give men "blue balls."

Also: If you're "wanking off," don't let your mother catch you. The term for masturbating seems to have spun off from "whang," a euphemism for penis, or "whack," meaning to hit or slap. In the mid-century, the act of self-gratification is called "jacking off" or "jerking off." And you still don't want your mother to catch you.

1905 The word "hormone," from a Greek word meaning "to arouse activity" or "to excite," is given to the body's chemical substances that surge through the bloodstream carrying specific commands to specific organs.

Also: The use of the words "fag" and "faggot" for a homosexual may have had their origin as a slang term used by English schoolboys to describe a boy servant. During World War I, cigarettes are called fags and are considered feminine compared to pipes and cigars. The word passes easily to effeminate men. By 1920 they're common slang.

1909 A person's sex drive now has a name, thanks to Sigmund Freud. "Libido" appears in an English translation of his *Selected Papers on Hysteria.*

<1910 If you have a "steady," you're dating one person and not seeing anyone else. By the mid-1940s "going steady" carries a special status, though it's not as serious a commitment as being engaged. Within a decade the practice is so common among teenagers that concerns are raised over whether exclusive dating forces young people into sexual relations.

Also: He kisses you. You kiss back. There's touching, caressing, fondling. You're "petting." And even though there are only two of you, it's still a "petting party." Around 1925, "petting" is replaced by "necking." Same thing, different word. But it's still "sexy," a word that's coined in 1925.

1910> "Lounge lizards" are men who hang around tea dances. These afternoon dances are popular with ladies, both married and single, who while away their hours and money with these men who flatter, romance, and brighten up their dreary lives, and often resort to blackmailing the women.

1914 Margaret Sanger, the woman most responsible for bringing contraceptive methods to America, realizes the importance of a catch-phrase when discussing family planning. Suggestions are tossed around including "voluntary motherhood," "conscious generation," and "population control." Sanger comes up with "birth-rate control." "Drop the 'rate,'" a friend tells her. "Birth control" is born.

Also: Oh, those loose women! But you can't call them that. Try "chippy" to describe a promiscuous woman, especially if she works at a dance hall or as a bartender. A prostitute is nothing more than a "broad," and the word is said with a lack of respect. Actress Theda Bara, playing a vampire in *A Fool There Was,* is the model for the word "vamp," which can be said of both a seductress and the act of seducing.

Also: Jazz develops in steamy New Orleans brothels, so it's no surprise that, for prostitutes, "jazz" equals sex and "to jazz" means to fuck.

<1915 The term "gold digger" is used to describe a lady who uses her charms to attract those gentlemen who have enough greenbacks to make them look good in any light. By 1925 there are so many of these women that the concept and the word are in common use.

Also: A "hickey" refers to any skin blemish, such as a pimple or that love bite on your neck. As the years roll by, the word is used to describe those little sucking marks exclusively.

Also: A prostitute picks up a "trick" or she can "turn a trick," the difference being that the former is a client, and the latter the act of sex. Or she calls her client a "john," a nineteenth-century colloquialism for a sweetheart that prostitutes appropriate and use to call out to potential clients.

c. 1918 You can "make it" or "make out" with someone, or you can be "on the make." No matter how you slice it, you've having sex, or at least looking for it.

<1920 Do you have a thing for women in high heels? Like to be flogged? Want more than one woman at a time? Wear women's lingerie? Friend, you're "kinky." The word is used to describe a person or any unusual sexual yearning or practice.

1920s The word "dyke" is used as a pejorative to describe a lesbian, "bulldyke" if she's especially masculine. In the 1940s, she's "butch." Lesbians seize the word "dyke" as their own and rid it of its negativity.

1921 The "flapper" is nothing like her mother. She sheds her petticoats, rolls her stockings below her knee, wears daring fashions that show more of her body than seems decent, crops her hair, and cops an attitude. Her morals are as loose for the day as her lipstick is bright. The word "flapper" isn't born in America. The British use it as early as 1893 to denote a very young prostitute. If she's a loose flapper, she's a "biscuit."

<1922 A sweetheart, a honey, or a beau is more aptly called a "boyfriend" or "girlfriend." Originally these words are applied only to a fiancé but become a standard reference to mean the person in your life. By 1970 that same person is your "main squeeze," an older term that was used around 1896 to indicate an important person, such as a boss.

Also: The female genitalia get a new moniker: "beaver" refers to the pubic area and probably has its origins from the furry animal. In the 1950s a "beaver shot" is a pornographic photo that shows a woman with her pubic hair revealed. Skin magazines in the 1960s have more freedom to include not only beaver shots but "split beavers," which reveal the vulva.

c. 1925 The Latin lovers of the silent movies affect the slang of the 1920s. A "sheba" (a good-looking girl) "falls for" (is infatuated with) her "sheikh" (her male love interest, especially if he's the dark, brooding type). He tells his friends he has a "heavy date," which means he's expecting to neck, if not make love. An older woman can have a heavy date with a younger man whom she supports or is generous with. But he's not her sheikh, he's a "Valentino."

Also: If she's old enough but you're entirely too old for her, then you're a "cradle snatcher." If you make love to a girl who's *too* young, you may wind up in prison. That's why in 1934 young girls are called "jailbait."

I'm too fucking busy, and vice versa.

Dorothy Parker

c. 1927 A "bimbo" is a loose woman, though earlier in the century the word describes a man, especially if he's large and dumb. "Bimbo" picks up momentum in the 1980s when it's applied to good-looking but empty-headed female celebrities and subsequently trickles down to the masses.

Also: In the 1970s hot pants are the fashion. In 1927 "hot pants" means you're sexually aroused. The term is also applied to a woman who likes sex.

<1928 Getting a little sex is called "nookie" or "poontang." Most likely the former comes from the word "nook," a dark little corner. The latter is drawn from the French *putain,* a prostitute. Neither term is endearing, since they are devoid of any emotion.

c. 1929 A person who is "ambisextrous" is one who has sex with either men or women. By 1940 the electrical term for alternating current and direct current, "AC/DC," is used for bisexuals. In the late 1960s, you're just "bi."

1930s The word "gay" is adopted by homosexuals as a positive term to define their lifestyle. The word was used to describe eighteenth-century libertines who lived a less than moral life and later was applied to prostitutes. The

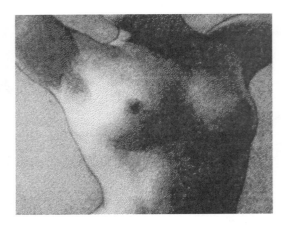

word becomes standard usage for homosexuality by the end of the 1960s.

c. 1932 The woman you have sex with is a "lay." Shortly, the word is expanded to include the sex act. The term is used by men at first, but during the sexual revolution of the 1960s, a man becomes a lay and is subject to the same scrutiny that gets him labeled a good lay or a bad one.

c. 1934 Breasts are "boobies," though they'll be figuratively shortened to "boobs" by 1949. In between time they're called "knockers" (c. 1941). In the mid-fifties people will call them "bazooms," a corruption of "bosom." Originally applied to male breasts, "bosom" is later used only for females and becomes the only acceptable word for breasts in the Victorian era.

Also: "Smile, darling, and give 'em a little 'cheesecake.'" A glamour girl's sensuality is transmitted by a sultry look, a sexy pose, or a bit of skin. Women have to wait until the 1950s to get "beefcake," the male equivalent.

c. 1935 Masculine aggression is reflected in the term "bang" (to have sex), taken from the

knocking action of the word. An unemotional term, it lends itself to "gang bang," the act of several men having sex with one woman at a given time, which enters the language twenty years later.

Also: Little did Alexander Graham Bell realize when he invented the telephone that he would add a new dimension to prostitution. The "call girl" uses the telephone to arrange her trysts, ensuring a classier clientele and placing her a cut above the streetwalker. "Call girl" may have spun off from "call house," an older euphemism for a brothel.

1940s Large breasts become more shapely when packed into an uplift bra. Men draw a comparison between women and cars and refer to breasts as "headlights." If you pack those headlights into a tight cardigan you're a "sweater girl," like some Hollywood starlets. And if you're single, it won't be long before you have a "heartthrob"—that is, a sweetheart of your very own.

Also: Three types of women are known to entertain GIs during World War II. The "B-girl" hangs out or works in bars and mingles with customers, getting them to spend money on drinks. She gets a commission on the drinks, but more often she's an amateur hooker looking to make money on the side. A "V-girl" is a patriotic wench who sleeps with soldiers gratis to boost their morale. The *V* stands for victory, but GIs are warned that it's also the first letter in "VD." The third lady entertains soldiers only in their dreams. The "pinup girl" is a scantily clothed, voluptuous starlet whose photograph is posted wherever a soldier can tack it up.

c. 1945 Hard-hat blue-collar workers have been doing it for years. But now the act of whistling to show approval of a woman's physical attributes is referred to as a "wolf whistle."

1951 Sexual slang shows the influence of baseball on American male minds. This year, when on a date, men can get to "first base," "second base," or "third base." More say they hit a "home run" than really do. In reality, most probably just "strike out."

Also: The term "girlie magazine" now denotes a magazine that features provocative pictures of women.

1956 Elizabeth Taylor, Marilyn Monroe, Jane Russell, or any one of the bevy of beauties who sensuously grace the silver screen is described as a "cinebabe."

1959 The word "pheromone" is created from the Greek "pherein," meaning "to carry," and "horman," to excite. Unlike hormones, which regulate development within a body, pheromones cause an attraction or repulsion in another member of the same species and are found in most living things including insects, birds, animals, and humans.

Also: Licking the anus of one's partner during foreplay is called "rimming." In its broadest definition, it can include sodomy.

c. 1962 The Catholic church condones one type of birth control: rhythm. Taking the risk of having sex when you're supposedly not fertile is called "Vatican roulette." The term is taken from Russian roulette, with the penis as the gun, the sperm as bullets, and the odds about the same.

c. 1963 The 1960s usher in the age of free love. Commitments aren't a necessary prelude to having sex. Borrowing an old theatrical

phrase, a "one-night stand" describes a partner for that night. Should the liaison occur more than once, there's still no emotional attachment.

c. 1967 A female fan who makes herself sexually available to members of a rock band earns the title "groupie," a pejorative coined by the musicians.

c. 1970 There are no dues and only one requirement for membership in the "mile-high club": you must have sexual intercourse while flying in an airplane.

c. 1971 Passion is heating up. You're in a full embrace but also fully clothed. All the motions of sex are there but there's no penetration. It's called "dry-fucking."

1981 Turnabout is fair play. Older men dating younger women is no big news. When an older woman starts being seen on the arm of a younger man, her escort is identified as a "toy boy." Toy boy is the equivalent of a female bimbo.

1998 The *New York Times* includes a feature on "arm candy." An escort engaged for one night with no relationship or acquaintance necessary prior to or after an event, arm candy is usually a female, often a model, whose stunning good looks and great body make her date the object of envy. No cash is exchanged. The quid pro quo is that the arm candy is able to flaunt her stuff at an event she wouldn't otherwise be admitted to. The trick is to keep your arm candy quiet. Once the other men find out that she's only a one-night escort, the pretense of having a beautiful woman on your arm whom you may be sleeping with is destroyed.

INDEX

abortion, 5, 28, 29, 31, 35, 54, 72, 74, 170, 171, 180, 188
abstinence, 2, 31, 39, 61, 62, 69, 132, 181
AC/DC (use of term), 239
actors and actresses, 80, 83, 85–96, 98, 104–14, 121, 138, 140–43, 145
adultery, 27, 30–36, 38–40, 43–49, 51, 60, 72–76, 81, 98, 101, 171, 172, 174–76, 209
advertising, 115–30
   of cosmetics, 120–21, 123–24, 126–29
   and fashion, 116–18, 120–30
   of food and drink, 118, 119, 121, 125, 128–30
   nudity in, 120, 122, 124, 126, 128, 130
   of prostitutes, 115–19
   of sexual aids, 117–20
   of tobacco products, 120, 123–25
AIDS, 17, 57, 76, 110
alcohol, 53
ambisextrous (use of term), 239
anal sex, 2, 4, 31, 35, 39, 41, 59, 75
anaphrodisiacs, 210–12, 214
anatomy, 7, 8, 63
anthropologists, 71–72
aphrodisiacs, 63, 74, 151–55, 157, 158, 173, 176, 210–11, 215
aquariums, 137
arm candy (use of term), 241
armpits, 215
art, 138, 153, 156–57, 167, 175, 177–78, 190–95, 197–99, 201–2, 204, 214
artificial insemination, 9
aspirin, 11
ass (use of term), 232
automobiles, 55, 125, 162

baccanalian rituals, 30
baldness, 64, 98, 112
balls, tinkling, 5
balls (use of term), 230
bang (use of term), 240
baseball slang, 241

baths, public, 42, 57, 134, 154, 174–75
bazooms (use of term), 240
beaver shots, 163, 239
bedrooms, introduction of, 6
beefcake (use of term), 240
bestiality, 35, 41, 50, 72, 75, 234
betrothal, 39
B-girl (use of term), 240
bi (use of term), 239
bidet, invention of, 8–9
bigamy, 28, 48
bimbo (use of term), 239
birth control, 1–19, 31, 34, 39, 50–51, 54, 63, 64, 66–68, 70–72, 74, 76, 118, 121, 160–61, 180, 183, 188, 211, 237, 241
biscuit (use of term), 238
bisexuality, 44, 69, 96, 150
blow jobs (use of term), 234
blue balls (use of term), 237
body fluids, 8
boobs (use of term), 240
bordellos, 43, 217
box (use of term), 236
boyfriend (use of term), 238
bra (use of term), 232
breasts, 81, 82, 93–96, 117–19, 143–45, 149, 152, 156, 161–64, 168, 187, 214–16, 219, 220, 225, 232, 240
broad (use of term), 238
bromides, 67
brothels, 3, 9, 25–26, 41–42, 46, 53–54, 65, 134, 136, 137, 158–59, 166, 217, 230, 232, 240
buggery, 39, 175, 231
bulldyke, butch (use of terms), 238
bundling, 158
burlesque, 140, 143
buttocks, 228, 232

cake-eater (use of term), 236
call girl (use of term), 240
castration, 35, 38, 46, 47, 53, 209
celibacy, 23, 25, 31, 33, 36–39, 45, 46, 48, 50, 56, 66–67

censorship, 177–80, 182–84, 186–88, 192, 194–98, 204, 206–7
cervical caps, 2–4, 10
chastity, 22–23, 28, 31–34, 45, 50, 66–68, 134, 170, 171, 174, 181
chastity belts, 213
cheesecake (use of term), 240
cherry (use of term), 236
child abuse, 187
childbearing, 61, 62, 153
children, sexuality of, 70
chippy (use of term), 237–38
church, see religion
circumcision, 30, 208
clap (use of term), 231–32
clitoris, 57, 59, 70, 73, 219–20, 232
clothing, see fashion; underwear
cock (use of term), 230
cock rings, 7
coitus interruptus, 4, 10, 35, 68, 171
coitus reservatus, 10, 26, 68
cold baths, 210
cold lead plates, 211
come (use of term), 232
coming-of-age rituals, 10
communal living, 10, 158–59
communication, nonverbal, 16
communism, 56
conception, studies of, 9, 64
concubines, 36, 39, 54, 80, 134, 170, 171, 174, 175, 210
condoms, 2, 7–10, 12–14, 17, 18, 117–18, 127, 130, 183, 232–33
continence, 67–68, 102
contraceptives, see birth control
copulation (use of term), 231
corruption, political, 181
cosmetics, 120–21, 123–24, 126–29, 158, 161, 165, 169, 208–11, 216, 226
courtly love, 39–40, 62–63, 81, 192
cradle snatcher (use of term), 239
cream (use of term), 232
crud (use of term), 236–37
cuckolding, 40

cum (use of term), 232
cunnilingus, 61
cunt (use of term), 229
Cupid's itch (use of term), 236

dancing, 50, 78–79, 85–88, 92, 108,
    131–33, 135, 137–45, 149, 173,
    175–76, 178, 182, 184, 203, 219,
    223, 232
death and afterlife, 209
death and burial, 173
death in the saddle, 84, 102
debauchery, 174
devil, 41
diaphragms, 10, 11, 161, 183
dildos, 2, 74
divorce, 22, 27, 29–31, 34–37, 43,
    45, 51, 54, 57, 62, 69, 81, 86, 88,
    97, 98, 106, 160, 170
douching, 4, 8, 9
drag (use of term), 234–35
dreams, 35, 40, 41, 60, 61, 65,
    69–70, 73, 174, 218, 221
drugs, 209, 211
dry-fucking (use of term), 241
dyke (use of term), 238

effeminacy, 49
egg, human, 9
ejaculation, 26, 35, 73–75, 102
elder sex, 68, 74
elopement, 35
emperors, 29, 30, 36, 42–43, 80,
    84, 85, 97–99, 135, 191
entertainment, 131–50
    drive-in movies, 162
    nudity in, 142, 144–47
    sexually explicit, 146–47, 167
    see also specific media
erections, 7, 12, 13, 17
escorts, 136, 142
eugenics, 55–56, 68, 159
eunuchs, 29, 37, 44, 74, 100, 209
excrement, 211, 212

fag (use of term), 237
Fallopian tubes, 7
family values, 21–23, 54, 56, 186
fashion, 82, 85, 88, 90, 104–5,
    116–18, 120–30, 160, 164, 168,
    173, 175, 183, 213–27

fellatio, 35, 61
fertility, 2, 11, 12
festivals, 30, 79, 132, 135, 136,
    143–44, 152, 153, 225
fetishes, 68–70, 74, 95, 225, 235
fingers, uses for, 6
flagellation, 9, 65
flapper (use of term), 238
flasher (use of term), 233
flight attendants, 125
flourishing (use of term), 232
food and beverages, 1, 6, 118, 119,
    121, 125, 128–30, 157, 214
footbinding, 211–12
foreplay, 59–60, 62, 71, 75
fornication, 31, 34, 35, 41, 48, 230
free love, 56–57, 75, 227, 241
French (use of term), 231
fuck (use of term), 206, 231
fumigation, 5

gamahuche (use of term), 234
gang bang (use of term), 240
gay (use of term), 239–40
geishas, 137
genitals, washing of, 7
gigolos, 142
girlfriend (use of term), 238
gladiators, 133–34
gods and goddesses, 1, 3, 22,
    24–25, 29, 41, 59, 79, 170
going steady (use of term), 237
gold digger (use of term), 238
gonorrhea, 229, 231–32; see also
    sexually transmitted diseases
grind (use of term), 232
groping (use of term), 229
groupie (use of term), 241
group sex, 75, 164

harems, 37, 44, 81, 98, 131, 171,
    209
harness, 14
heartthrob (use of term), 240
hedonism, 32, 44, 47, 109
hermaphrodites, 43, 59, 192
heterosexuality (coining of term),
    234
hickey (use of term), 238
history, 20–58
home videos, 148

homosexuality, 23, 26–28, 31–32,
    35, 39, 40, 43, 44, 47–49, 54, 55,
    57, 59, 66, 68, 69, 72, 73, 106–7,
    109, 110, 146, 175, 178–79, 181,
    184–88, 193, 203, 233, 234, 237,
    239–40
honey pot (use of term), 231
hookers (use of term), 233–34
hormones, 12–13, 19, 237
hotels and motels, 158, 162, 164
hot pants (uses of term), 239
hump (use of term), 233
hunk (use of term), 236
hymen, 69, 229

illegitimate children, 44–45, 86
impotence, 19, 153, 155
incest, 34, 39, 42, 104
intercourse
    frequency of, 71, 72
    positions for, 11, 20, 35, 41, 57,
        59–64, 71, 74, 75, 173
    words for, 232, 233, 240
interfemoral sex, 35
Internet, 114, 167–68, 188
intrauterine devices, 12, 14
inversion (use of term), 234

jailbait (use of term), 239
jazz (use of term), 238
jerking off (use of term), 237
jewelry, 151, 209, 220
john (use of term), 238

Kegel exercises, 13
kinesics, 16
kinky (use of term), 238
kissing, 32, 35, 59, 61, 74, 139,
    150, 153, 215, 237
knee-trembler (use of term), 236
knocked up (use of term), 232
knockers (use of term), 240

laws, 170–88
    marriage, see marriage
    pornography, 180, 196, 202, 204
    on prostitution, 52–53, 134, 171,
        172, 175, 177, 180, 182
    religious, 23, 34–42, 45–48,
        172–75, 184
lay (use of term), 240

lesbians, 2, 4–5, 35, 49, 59, 150, 165, 190, 234, 238
libido (use of term), 237
licentiousness, 40, 47–48, 55, 81, 102–4, 132, 171, 173, 174
literature, 190–207
lounge lizards (use of term), 237
lovelorn columns, 161
love table, 18, 19
lubrication, 12

magazines, 114, 164–67, 187, 221, 239, 241
magic and mysticism, 5
maidenhead (defined), 229
main squeeze (use of term), 238
make it, make out, on the make (use of terms), 238
male supremacy, 21, 23, 27, 36, 41, 43, 50, 51, 54, 173
marriage
    attacks on, 66, 68
    laws, 21–23, 26–40, 43–54, 56, 60, 62, 152, 153, 156, 170–71, 177, 188
    manuals, 62–63, 70–75
    monogamy, 20, 36, 37, 48, 53, 54, 72
    polygamy, 23, 27–28, 34–37, 42–43, 45, 48, 51, 52, 70, 159, 171, 179
    studies of, 72–73, 76
masochism, 65, 68, 74, 236
masturbation, 11, 26, 35, 41, 57, 58, 64–68, 70–76, 165, 170–72, 178, 188, 213, 219, 237
mate-swapping, 75, 164
mattresses, 6
mechanical aids, 6–8, 12–14, 16–17, 75, 128, 151–69, 218, 221
media
    censorship of, 177–80, 182–84, 186–88, 194–98, 206–7
    pornography in, 58
medicine
    anatomy books, 7
    artificial insemination, 9
    drugs, 209, 211
    fertility cycle studied in, 11
    opinions of, 61

sex manuals, 59–76, 155
    for venereal disease, 6, 13, 45
men, 97–114
    actors, 98, 104–14, 145
    handsome, 97, 99, 100, 102, 105–13, 121–22, 130, 208
    height of, 119–20
    manly, 99, 101, 107–11, 123
    as rulers, 97–104; *see also* emperors
    shaving by, 219
menopause, 74
menstruation, 4, 5, 10, 11, 20, 21, 25, 30, 34, 37, 59, 60–62, 68–69, 71, 73, 172
mile-high club (use of term), 241
mime, 132, 134, 173
mirrors, 5
mistresses, 30, 64, 79–87, 97–103, 106, 111, 188, 214
mooning (use of term), 233
movies, *see* actors and actresses; censorship
movie slang, 239, 241
murder, 43, 86–87
music, 47, 104, 110, 111, 132, 134–41, 144, 147, 149, 150, 205–7

necking (use of term), 237
necrophilia, 209
nightclubs, 147–48
nipples, 62, 95, 143, 145
nookie (use of term), 239
nude calendars, 161
nude centerfolds, 163, 166, 168
nymphomania, 65, 68, 80

obscenity, 46, 57–58, 66–68, 146–47, 165–67, 180, 182, 184, 188, 189–207
olfactory responses, 17
Onanism, 64–65, 171
one-night stand (use of term), 241
oral sex, 9, 31, 35, 41, 54, 58, 59, 61, 66, 71, 74–76, 96, 147, 234, 236
orgasms, 13, 19, 26, 59–60, 62, 68, 70–76, 114, 221
orgies, 134, 153
ovaries, 8

overpopulation, 50–51
ovulation, 11

pederasty, 26, 44, 98, 171, 172, 234
peeping Tom (origin of term), 229
penis, 73, 165
    mechanical aids for, 6–8, 12–14, 16–17, 128, 218, 221
    names for, 231, 232, 237
    size and shape of, 4, 61, 63, 64, 74, 75, 155, 233
    surgery for, 10, 13, 50, 168, 217
penis envy, 70
performance anxiety, 164
perfume, *see* cosmetics
perversions, 66, 68, 70, 96, 238
pessaries, 68
petting (use of term), 237
phallic symbols, 3, 70, 132
phallic worship, 23, 157
pheromones, 17, 168–69, 241
-philia word endings, 235
phone sex, 58, 167
photography, 13, 96, 160, 207, 239
phrenology, 67
piece (use of term), 230
pilgrims and puritans, 176–77
pimps, 48, 54, 232
placenta, 7
Playboy, 75, 95, 96, 109, 144–45, 150, 163, 165, 166, 187
poontang (use of term), 239
popes, 33, 44–45, 47, 53, 57, 99–100, 188
pornography, 57–58, 146–48, 165–68, 180, 184, 186–88, 189–207
potency, 5, 12, 62
pottery, lewd scenes on, 190–92
pregnancy
    causes of, 5, 21
    fear of, 71
    of nuns, 45
    prevention of, *see* birth control
    sex for pleasure vs., 8
premarital sex, 36, 48, 54, 57, 72, 74, 188
prick (use of term), 232
priests, 33, 37–39, 45, 46, 49, 132, 135, 136

procreation, 22, 23, 25, 30–34, 36, 39, 41, 46, 48, 49, 68, 172, 173
prostate gland, 13
prostitutes, 2–4, 22, 25–28, 33, 41, 43, 45–49, 51–54, 61, 62, 67, 68, 70, 72, 74, 75, 77–82, 107, 111, 114, 115–19, 133–39, 141, 154, 166, 170–72, 175, 177, 179, 180, 182, 210, 220, 234, 236, 238, 240
pump (use of term), 233
purification, 32, 34, 39
pussy (use of term), 231

rape, 41, 43, 49, 61, 133, 170, 213
religion, 11, 22–23, 25, 26, 31–55, 153, 172–75, 183, 184, 189, 241
repression, 52–53, 65, 217
reproductive system, anatomy, 7, 8
resorts, 144, 164, 166
respectability, 52
rhythm method, 3, 11
ribs, number of, 7
ride (use of term), 231
rimming (use of term), 241
roger (use of term), 232
rulers
    men as, 97–104; see also emperors
    rights of, 37, 51, 77
    sperm of, 2
    women as, 43, 77, 79–85, 101, 104, 137, 215

sadism, 49, 65, 68, 74, 100, 132, 197, 217
safe sex, 76, 168
screw (use of term), 233
semen, 4, 14, 26, 40, 41, 58, 59, 62–64, 170, 172
sex clubs, 158
sex crimes, 55, 57–58, 68, 170
sex education, 161, 184
sex manuals, 59–76, 155
sexual harassment, 185
sexually transmitted diseases, 6–9, 11–13, 17, 42, 45, 46, 52–53, 55, 57, 70, 71, 74, 76, 100–102, 111, 178, 181, 217, 220, 227, 229, 231–32, 236–37
sexual revolution, 15–16, 74–76, 92, 111

sexual therapy, 75–76
sexy (coining of term), 237
singles, as adjective, 164
sixty-nine (use of term), 236
slaves, 2–3, 51, 53, 158, 182
sneezing, for birth control, 4
sodomy, 31, 44, 48, 49, 55, 57, 100, 175, 185, 187, 234, 241
Spanish fly, 49, 210
sperm, 2, 4, 8, 9, 26
sterility, 154
sterilization, 181–82
streaking, 227
striptease, 76, 86, 124–25, 138, 140, 143, 148
stud (use of term), 236
suppositories, 5
swimwear, 164, 168, 223–25, 227–28

tableaux vivants, 138, 139, 141
tail (use of term), 230
tarts (use of term), 236
tea-houses, 136
television talk shows, 146
tenderloin districts, 139
tenderness, 76
testicles, 8, 9, 73, 231
theater, 48, 132, 133, 137–41, 145–47, 172, 173, 177, 182, 190, 191, 194–95, 202–3
thighs, 214
tits (use of term), 232
toy boy (use of term), 241
transsexual operations, 163
transvestites, 39, 47, 49, 74, 184
trick (use of term), 238
tubal ligation, 11
twat (use of term), 231

underwear, 90, 108, 112, 120, 122–23, 125–29, 161–63, 167, 168, 169, 178, 215–19, 223–25

vagina, 7, 61, 63, 73, 231
Valentine's Day, 157
vamp (use of term), 238
vasectomies, 11, 16
Vatican roulette (use of term), 241
vaudeville, 139
vegetarianism, 68

venereal diseases, see sexually transmitted diseases
V-girl (use of term), 240
vibrators, 12, 16
Victorian era, 52–53, 66–69, 104, 138, 160, 177–78, 182, 217–20, 236
virgin (defined), 229–30
virginity, 3, 23–24, 27, 30, 37, 41, 43, 47, 49, 61, 72, 75, 76, 135, 217, 236
virtual sex, 19, 167–68
vitamin E, 12
voyeurism, 68

wanking off (use of term), 237
water beds, 16
well hung (use of term), 233
wham, bam, thank you, ma'am, 236
whore (defined), 229
witchcraft, 41, 50, 174, 175
wolf (use of term), 233
wolf whistle (use of term), 240–41
women, 77–96
    actresses, 80, 83, 85–96, 121, 138, 140–43, 145
    Amazons, 90
    beauty of, 77–95, 118–22, 125, 135, 142, 186, 208, 212
    eroticism of, 65–66, 70, 75
    fertility of, 11, 12
    frigidity of, 70, 71, 73
    and gynecology, 61
    horseback riding by, 179, 214
    hysteria of, 2, 66, 221
    inferiority of, 23, 27, 32, 33, 36–41, 43, 45, 48, 53, 54, 62–63, 70
    pinups, 90, 92, 95, 119, 120, 162–63, 221–22, 224, 240
    as property, 23, 53, 133
    rights of, 27–30, 34, 36, 38–39, 44, 50, 51, 53, 56, 57, 61, 62, 73–75, 79–81, 95, 186–87
    as rulers, 43, 77, 79–85, 101, 104, 137, 215
    as seductresses, 77–95, 124–27
    teachers, 78, 82–83
    veiled, 23, 36, 39, 115
words, 229–41

youth rebellion, 55, 56

ABOUT THE AUTHOR

Cheryl Rilly's curiosity about the history of sex and how it affects people today prompted her to write this book. She found that history does have answers. And she's not so pleased to tell you that our forefathers and ancestors were just as messed up as we are. As with most history, everything old is new again. But if the history of sex causes angst with the realization that in 75,000 years we're still not sure what we're doing, it also puts things into lighthearted perspective. One thing remains constant: that men are men (most of the time) and women are women (most of the time), and their mutual attraction will never fade no matter what kind of roadblocks are thrown in their way.

Ms. Rilly has written for numerous comedians, was the writer and editor of Airlines, a comedy information service for radio talent, and is the author of four comedy booklets for broadcast personalities. She is also a freelance writer whose articles have appeared in national magazines and the cartoonist of *Backyard,* a comic strip seen in *Texas Gardener* magazine.

You can reach the *Great Moments in Sex* Web site at www.greatmomentsin.com.